UNCOVERING CLIL

Content and Language Integrated Learning in bilingual and multilingual education

Peeter Mehisto

David Marsh

María Jesús Frigols

Macmillan Education
Between Towns Road, Oxford OX4 3PP
A division of Macmillan Publishers Limited
Companies and representatives throughout the world

ISBN 978-0-230-02719-0

Text © Peeter Mehisto, David Marsh and María Jesús
Frigols 2008
Design and illustration © Macmillan Publishers Limited
2008

First published 2008

Designed by Anthony Godber
Illustrated by Kathy Baxendale and Tõnis Kärema
Cover design by Andrew Oliver
Cover photograph by Corbis/Darnell Gulin

The publishers would like to thank Alan Pulverness
and Borja Uruñuela for their thoughtful insights and
recommendations.

The authors and publishers would like to thank the
following for permission to reproduce their photographs:
Plainpictures/Photography.com

The authors and publishers are grateful for permission to
reprint the following copyright material:
Science Across the World for an extract from Domestic
Waste a programme from the Association for Science
Education (UK) published on www.scienceacross.org
copyright © ASE 2006; HSE for the three tables 'Rates
of fatal and of over-3-day injury in Europe per 100,000
workers or employees 2003', 'Rates of fatal injury in Great
Britain, Germany, France, Italy, Spain and EU average
1999-2003' and 'Rates of over-3-day injury in Great Britain,
Germany, France, Italy, Spain and EU average 1999-
2003' published on www.hse.gov.uk © Crown copyright;
Thomson Learning Global Rights Group for an extract
from Dual Language Instruction: A Handbook for Enriched
Education 1st edition by Cloud, Hamayan and Genesee
2000. Reprinted with permission of Heinle/ELT, a division
of Thomson Learning www.thomsonrights.com.
Fax 800 730-2215; Copyright Clearance Centre for
the figure 'Story Map' from Classroom Strategies for
Interactive learning 2nd edition by Doug Buehl published
by the International Reading Association Inc copyright
© 2001; Pearson Education for a table from A Taxonomy
for Learning, Teaching and Assessing: A Revision Of
Bloom's Taxonomy Of Educational Objectives by Lorin W.
Anderson, David R. Krathwohl et al, published by Allyn
and Bacon, Boston, MA. Copyright © 2001 by Pearson
Education. Adapted by permission of the publisher;
The BBC for details about 'World Class' published on
www.bbc.co.uk/worldclass copyright © www.BBC.co.uk;

eTwinning School Partnerships in Europe for details
published on www.etwinning.net; HMSO for details about
Global Gateway published on www.globalgateway.org.
uk © Crown copyright 1995-2007; iEarn (International
Education and Resource Network) for details published
on www.iearn.org; Gemin-i.org for details about Rafi.ki
published on www.rafi.ki; FACTWorld The Forum for
Across the Curriculum Teaching for details published on
www.factworld.info; ePals Inc for details published on
www.epals.com; Plan for details published on www.plan-
international.org; SOS-Kinderdorf International for details
published on www.sos-childrensvillages.org;
Apple Inc for details about 'Connecting World Regions,
Geospatially' published on http://edcommunity.apple.
com/ali/story.php?itemID=786; The GLOBE Programme,
Warwickshire Wildlife Trust for a small extract about
GLOBE along with the 'goals of GLOBE' published on
www.globe.gov copyright © The GLOBE Programme;
Checklist adapted from the Immersion Teaching Strategies
Observation Checklist by Tara Fortune and is reprinted
with permission from the Centre for Advanced Research
on Language Acquisition (CARLA) at the University of
Minnesota. The original copy of this CARLA publication
can be found at www.carla.umn.edu/immersion/acie/vol4/
Nov2000.pdf

Printed and bound in Thailand

2014 2013 2012 2011

9 8 7 6 5 4 3

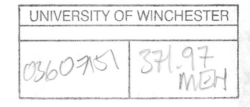

Contents

Acknowledgements

No book is an island! We are deeply grateful to a wide range of individuals from across the world who have contributed at different stages to the production of this book. This input, in the form of ideas, materials and feedback, has been a key source of inspiration.

Various organizations have also played a role in supporting the process. The Estonian Language Immersion Centre has shared many of its learning materials. Valuable contributions have also been made by the Continuing Education Centre of the University of Jyväskylä (Finland), the Toronto School Board (Canada) and the Complejo Educativo de Cheste (Spain).

No individual is an island! From the inception (Valencia, 2005) to the logistics (Helsinki, 2006) through to the finalization of drafts, the authors have received continuous insight and specialist support from a range of experts including Kai Võlli and members of the CLIL Consortium, Hugo Baetens Beardsmore, Do Coyle, Gisella Langé, Anne Maljers and Dieter Wolff.

Peeter Mehisto   **David Marsh**   **María Jesús Frigols**

Foreword

The airline industry and education may differ in terms of the length of their respective histories, but they are now showing clear similarities in how they adapt to the expectations of life in the knowledge society.

From the old times of pioneering flights across major oceans, the history of the airline industry has been marked by adaptability, dynamism and innovation.

The speed at which the industry can adapt to challenge is a key prerequisite for success.

In the airline industry, as in education, new necessities derive from broadening perspectives in a dynamic, increasingly integrated and convergent world. Using the new technologies, materials and tools in construction, maintenance, piloting and customer services has taken us forwards from the very beginning.

Innovation has always been the leading edge for achieving advancement. Sometimes this emerges slowly and has a subtle impact, and at other times it appears swiftly and challenges older operating approaches.

Aviation, training, education and other facets of our new societies are examining the ways in which innovation can lead to the integration of the best possible operating principles and outcomes. This is as relevant for the airline industry as it is for education.

In Air Nostrum, the concept of integration is core to our success. We have a dedicated programme to encourage and train employees to develop both technical and communicative skills, and CLIL has been used in our training courses for some years to aid this development.

The authors of this book first came up with the idea of a CLIL handbook whilst working on a film concept for the European Commission, on location at an Air Nostrum hangar. Now we are pleased to be associated with this book on CLIL methodologies and hope that you, the reader, will find this a useful tool in examining how integration and innovation can be developed in your work with the citizens of today and tomorrow.

Emilio Serratosa
Chairman, Air Nostrum

Introduction

This book is for the reader who wants a practical insight into how the learning of both content and a second language can be combined into a single educational experience.

It is for those who want to further their understanding of on-the-ground practice of Content and Language Integrated Learning (CLIL). They may be working with younger children at primary level or with older age groups in secondary or vocational schools. The reader may also be a parent, an administrator or a researcher interested in education.

We live in a time of innovation, and new ways of living and working. This often involves changing the way we do things. Across our societies we can see integration replacing fragmentation. This process is creating fusion between sectors that may have been quite separate in the past.

CLIL is one example of this process. It invites convergence between the learning of content and language. It enables educators to move away from fragmentation, whereby we handle subjects as separate areas.

We have known for a long time that teaching languages and other subjects separate from one another, in a vacuum, does not produce optimal outcomes. Both language and content teachers have already made important strides in revitalizing their teaching for this modern age within and even across their subjects. CLIL provides the opportunity to go a step further. It creates fusion between content and language across subjects and encourages independent and co-operative learning, while building common purpose and forums for lifelong development. This provides significant added value for language learning.

Fusion can be found throughout the world. The information and communication sectors are integrating technologies in direct response to social demand. Phones now provide photographic, navigational and a wide range of media features, alongside Internet access. Yet, they also remain true to the original purpose for which they were created.

Entertainment is following the same trend. *Cirque du Soleil* has emerged as a new fusion far removed from the traditional concept of a circus. It has synthesized circus styles from around the world, integrating acrobatics, dance and theatre; as well as new technologies; into one single scripted theme. Fusion has become a fact of life. The fusion in CLIL has emerged to help young people build integrated knowledge and skills for this increasingly integrated world.

The eight chapters in this book, *Uncovering CLIL*, quickly move from the initial *why do CLIL* and guide the reader towards the *how to do CLIL*.

Approaching CLIL describes the rise of CLIL in modern education and offers some practical models. **Getting ready for CLIL** takes the reader closer to the core features of CLIL methodology. This is then followed by **Starting CLIL in the classroom**, which translates CLIL methodology into practice at the primary, secondary and vocational levels. **Putting CLIL in motion** examines how to provide language support in content learning, and content support in language learning. **Opening windows for personal achievement** describes how teachers and students can take greater control of the learning process and improve outcomes. **Making CLIL come alive** is about connectivity – connecting learners, and learning, to the wider world. **Cruising with CLIL** sums it all up: It takes the reader back to the bigger picture of CLIL, and describes how that bigger picture can positively influence classroom practice. The final chapter, **More tools**, provides additional materials for implementing CLIL.

About the series

Macmillan Books for Teachers

Welcome to Macmillan Books for Teachers. The titles are written by acknowledged and innovative leaders in each field to help you develop your teaching repertoire, practical skill and theoretical knowledge.

Suited to newer and experienced teachers, the series combines the best of classic teaching methodology with recent cutting-edge developments. Insights from academic research are combined with hands-on experience to create books which focus on real-world teaching solutions.

We hope you will find the ideas in them a source of inspiration in your own teaching and enjoyment in your professional learning.

Adrian Underhill

Titles in the series

500 Activities for the Primary Classroom
Carol Read

700 Classroom Activities
David Seymour & Maria Popova

An A-Z of ELT
Scott Thornbury

Blended Learning
Barney Barrett & Pete Sharma

Beyond the Sentence
Scott Thornbury

Children Learning English
Jayne Moon

Discover English
Rod Bolitho & Brian Tomlinson

Learning Teaching
Jim Scrivener

Sound Foundations
Adrian Underhill

Teaching Practice
Roger Gower, Diane Phillips & Steve Walters

Teaching Reading Skills
Christine Nuttall

Uncovering Grammar
Scott Thornbury

1 Approaching CLIL

This book explains content and language integrated learning (CLIL). It uncovers the pieces of the puzzle that make up the essence of CLIL.

In short, CLIL is a dual-focused educational approach in which an additional language is used for the learning and teaching of both content and language. For example, CLIL has involved Malaysian children learning maths and science in English. CLIL has been used for Norwegian students to do drama in German, Italian students to learn science in French, Japanese students to learn geography in English and Australians to learn maths in Chinese. The combinations of languages and subjects are almost limitless.

Pre-CLIL

The term CLIL (content and language integrated learning) was coined in 1994 in Europe. However, CLIL practice has a much longer history. The first known CLIL-type programme dates back some 5000 years to what is now modern-day Iraq. The Akkadians, who conquered the Sumerians, wanted to learn the local language. To this end, Sumerian was used as a medium of instruction to teach several subjects to the Akkadians, including theology, botany and zoology. If Sumerian instructors were true to the basic principles of CLIL, they supported the learning of Sumerian, as well as the learning of the content in theology, botany and zoology.

Another example from history of the use of a second language to teach content is the widespread use of Latin. For centuries, Latin was used as a language of instruction in European universities and became the primary language of law, medicine, theology, science and philosophy. Yet, despite having strong similarities with CLIL, the use of Latin cannot be considered, in the purest sense, an example of CLIL. Latin in academia left little room for the development of local languages. CLIL, by contrast, seeks to support second-language learning while also favouring first-language development.

In Europe, in more recent centuries, many people have understood the value of multilingualism. However, bilingual or multilingual education seemed, above all, a privilege belonging to the wealthy. The well-to-do hired governesses or tutors who spoke to their children in a foreign tongue with the express purpose of having them become fluent in another language. Some people sent their children abroad to study in private schools.

In other cases, geographic, demographic and economic realities have given rise to multilingual programmes. In 1965, a group of English-speaking parents living in the majority French-speaking Canadian province of Quebec had become worried that their children would be at a disadvantage later on in life if they did not achieve fluency in French. These English-speaking parents believed that standard second-language teaching would not lead to fluency in French, thus making it more difficult later on in life for their children to compete in the local job market. The parents encouraged the local authorities to establish a language-immersion programme that would enable English-speaking children to study all of their subjects entirely in French.

Teachers in this immersion programme initially faced major challenges. Appropriate teaching and learning strategies had not been agreed upon. They were developed by trial and error. Teachers began by focusing on helping students to understand the second language and to develop oral communication skills. A more balanced approach that included all four language skills (listening, speaking, reading and writing) was introduced once the students' aural (listening) and oral (speaking) skills had developed sufficiently to allow for basic communication. As students progressed through school, some subjects were also taught in English. In general, the programme was highly successful. The use of immersion teaching began to spread throughout Canada and much of the rest of the world.

In the 1970s, with the expansion of language-immersion programmes, bilingual education became more easily accessible to children coming from a diversity of backgrounds. Similarly, work done on Languages Across the Curriculum in the 1970s (UK) helped raise awareness of the need for all teachers to help students improve their language skills, whether it be their first or second language. An increased understanding that content and language needed to be taught and learnt hand in hand was developing. At the same time, it was becoming apparent that standard second-language teaching alone was not achieving adequate results on a widespread scale.

The rise of CLIL

By the mid-1990s globalization was placing greater linguistic demands on mainstream education, from the primary level through to institutions of higher education. In Europe today, there is a desire to improve language-learning opportunities for all young people in order to increase European cohesion and competitiveness. In Asia, thanks in no small part to the exponential growth of China's economy, interest in improving lingua franca languages such as Mandarin Chinese and English is on the rise. These languages are of essential importance for the economies and societies of several Asian countries.

Globalization has made the world interconnected in ways not seen before. New technologies are facilitating the exchange of information and knowledge. This, in turn, is driving the integration of the world economy and change in all spheres of our lives. The world is rapidly becoming a very mixed global village. Mobility, both physical and virtual, is becoming an ever-increasing reality and this is having an impact on languages. The reality of life in a mixed global society is having an impact on how we teach and what we teach – and this concerns language education, as much as any other form of subject learning.

In an integrated world, integrated learning is increasingly viewed as a modern form of educational delivery designed to even better equip the learner with knowledge and skills suitable for the global age. Moreover, the mindset of Generation Y (generally recognized as born anywhere between 1982 and 2001) is particularly focused on immediacy as in 'learn as you use, use as you learn' – not 'learn now, use later'. Those born into the Cyber Generation (born after 2001) will be even more influenced by their own early, personal, hands-on experience with integrated technologies. These are the generations now in classrooms across the world, and CLIL is one innovative methodology that has emerged to cater to this new age.

CLIL foundation pieces

The CLIL strategy, above all, involves using a language that is not a student's native language as a medium of instruction and learning for primary, secondary and/or vocational-level subjects such as maths, science, art or business. However, CLIL also calls on content teachers to teach some language. In particular, content teachers need to support the learning of those parts of language knowledge that students are missing and that may be preventing them mastering the content.

Language teachers in CLIL programmes play a unique role. In addition to teaching the standard curriculum, they work to support content teachers by helping students to gain the language needed to manipulate content from other subjects. In so doing they also help to reinforce the acquisition of content.

Thus, CLIL is a tool for the teaching and learning of content and language. The essence of CLIL is integration. This integration has a dual focus:

1) Language learning is included in content classes (eg, maths, history, geography, computer programming, science, civics, etc). This means repackaging information in a manner that facilitates understanding. Charts, diagrams, drawings, hands-on experiments and the drawing out of key concepts and terminology are all common CLIL strategies.
2) Content from subjects is used in language-learning classes. The language teacher, working together with teachers of other subjects, incorporates the vocabulary, terminology and texts from those other subjects into his or her classes. Students learn the language and discourse patterns they need to understand and use the content.

It is a student's desire to understand and use the content that motivates him or her to learn the language. Even in language classes, students are likely to learn more if they are not simply learning language for language's sake, but using language to accomplish concrete tasks and learn new content. The language teacher takes more time to help students improve the quality of their language than the content teacher. However, finding ways in the CLIL context to inject content into language classes will also help improve language learning. Thus, in CLIL, content goals are supported by language goals.

In addition to a focus on content and language, there is a third element that comes into play. The development of learning skills supports the achievement of content language goals. Learning skills goals constitute the third driver in the CLIL triad.

The three goals of content, language and learning skills need to fit into a larger context. Parents are most interested in having their children learn the CLIL language, continue to develop their first language and learn as much of the content as children who are not in CLIL programmes. Therefore, the ultimate goal of CLIL initiatives is to create conditions that support the achievement of the following:

- grade-appropriate levels of academic achievement in subjects taught through the CLIL language;
- grade-appropriate functional proficiency in listening, speaking, reading and writing in the CLIL language;
- age-appropriate levels of first-language competence in listening, speaking, reading and writing;
- an understanding and appreciation of the cultures associated with the CLIL language and the student's first language;
- the cognitive and social skills and habits required for success in an ever-changing world.

The CLIL method can give young people the skills required to continue to study or work in the CLIL language. However, language maintenance and learning is a lifelong process requiring continued use and ongoing investment.

The many faces of CLIL

CLIL is an umbrella term covering a dozen or more educational approaches (eg, immersion, bilingual education, multilingual education, language showers and enriched language programmes). What is new about CLIL is that it synthesizes and provides a flexible way of applying the knowledge learnt from these various approaches. The flexibility of the approach is, above all, evident in the amount of time devoted to teaching or learning through the second language. CLIL allows for low- to high-intensity exposure to teaching/learning through a second language. The approach can also be used for short-term high-intensity exposure (see figure opposite).

THE MANY FACES OF CLIL

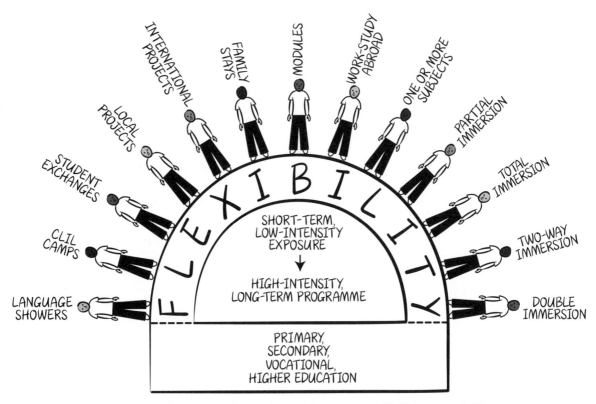

Here are four examples of the varying types of CLIL-style activities:

1 Language showers

Description

Language showers are primarily intended for students aged between four and ten years old, who receive between 30 minutes and one hour of exposure per day. This includes the use of games, songs, many visuals, realia, handling of objects and movement. Teachers usually speak almost entirely in the CLIL language. Routines are developed and considerable repetition is used so students know what to expect. This creates a sense of security, lowers anxiety and boosts learning.

Goals

Language showers aim to help students to:
· be aware of the existence of different languages;
· be prepared for language learning (positive attitude, familiarity with sounds and structures).

Suggested activities

Teachers focus on routine activities with which the students become comfortable. They set the stage by telling students what to expect and then switch to the CLIL language, for example:

- to manage breaks or lunchtime. Instructions are given in the CLIL language, vocabulary for foods is learnt and students answer questions about what they are eating. The teacher says: *Mmm, apples. Shelly has an apple. Who else has an apple? What is that, Paul? Yes, very good. That's right, it's an apple. What colour is the apple, red or green? Is it red like Igor's shirt or green like Chantal's skirt?* Simultaneously pointing to Igor's red shirt and Chantal's green skirt facilitates comprehension.

- to help students get dressed for breaks or for going home. Articles of clothing can be put on in various sequences while the students repeat the new words. Considerable gesturing/pointing is used to help students associate the object with its name in the CLIL language. The teacher may say: *What shall we put on first? Our gloves? Our hats? Our coats? Our boots? What colour is Shameem's hat? What colour is Penny's scarf? Today, let's put on our gloves first. Now let's put on our coats and try to button them. Is that difficult?* (said with a grimacing face) *Is that easy?* (said with a smiling face). Students answer with one word or in short phrases using the CLIL language.

- singing songs that include considerable movement and that help teach vocabulary (eg, the Shimmy Shimmy Shake or the Hokey Cokey: *I put my left hand in, my left hand out, my left hand in and I shake it all about …*). Using actions together with new vocabulary helps students to learn and more easily recall vocabulary. Also, words in songs are more easily retained than, for example, through lists and speaking.

2 One-week CLIL camp

Description

Camps can consist of groups ranging from fifteen to sixty students or more, coming from one school or from an entire school district. Students come together at a purpose-designed location, often an outdoor learning centre, during the school year, or holidays, for several days.

Some school districts may organize weekend camps and others five-day camps during the school week. Five days is long enough to have a profound impact and short enough for students to give it a try. Students are given a certain degree of choice in picking activities. The students are sub-divided into four teams of fifteen. Each group decides on its own name, motto and logo. The primary non-negotiable ground rule is that all participants use the CLIL language throughout the stay. Students are asked to develop strategies that will help ensure the use of the CLIL language. Students may agree on a system of tokens and fines. Students themselves charge other students one token each time they hear someone speaking a language other than the camp language. In this way, students often begin to assume all responsibility for keeping everyone on track with CLIL language use. In this example, the team with the greatest number of tokens wins a prize at the end of the camp stay.

Goals

CLIL camps aim for students to:

- experience success in living in a second-language environment;
- have fun and associate the CLIL language with an enjoyable experience;
- motivate students to continue second-language study;
- inspire students to continue learning the CLIL language.

Suggested activities

a) Hiking and orienteering: brainstorming what participants already know about hiking and orienteering (vocabulary, safety issues, tips, etc), learning key vocabulary and phrases, pre-activity instructions from a facilitator and a language teacher indoors, testing learning outdoors, various hiking and orienteering activities, having some students photograph or film the activities, making presentations about the activities using the photos or films, discussing and celebrating the experience.

b) A final talent show: a general meeting to discuss the nature of the event, daily times set aside for preparation of presentations, roleplays or scenes, building up the event during dinner speeches and the big event itself.

c) Student teaching: students sign up to teach workshops for their fellow students. Preparatory meetings are held with teachers to plan and to provide language support. After the session, short debriefing sessions are held where the students discuss the experience and celebrate success. One of our colleague's students ran a belly-dancing workshop. She wrote the required expressions on a piece of paper and stuck it to the wall. The students learnt to isolate three different kinds of stomach muscles – the diaphragm, the pelvic muscles and the obliques. The students learnt to control each set of muscles separately and then contract them, in a rolling motion, one after the other. It was hard work but they really had fun with it. Students ended up incorporating belly-dancing as one of the steps in a relay race, and into the final talent show. One student gave an origami workshop, another did a *t'ai chi* workshop, and yet another showed slides and talked about a trip to South America. One of the most popular workshops was about how to set up your own blog. Providing language support required some serious advanced planning from staff.

NB: Camps work for all age ranges from the early years of school to the end of secondary school. With very young children the emphasis is more on instructor-led activities. Far more games and competitions are used. For example:

- a walkabout in the natural environment to learn about various plants, insects and animals;
- a scavenger hunt to find and possibly photograph various plants, stones, live insects, etc;

- planning, building and celebrating the creation of birdhouses, sandcastles, etc;
- doing competitive and non-competitive sports.

Instructors would reinforce vocabulary throughout the week. Many objects such as a table or an oak tree would have labels attached to them indicating ⌐table⌐ or ⌐oak tree⌐. Also, students would be asked to pick their group names from the various species of trees or insects that are found in the area. Students might work with an instructor to stage a play about life in the forest.

3 International projects

Description

Special projects need to lead to concrete accomplishments and enable students to connect with new ideas, sources and/or people. Schools can either join existing projects or create a project of their own. A worldwide network such as Science Across the World* is easy and inexpensive to join. This Internet-based network allows classes of students from schools in several countries to study and discuss a host of science topics such as acid rain, biodiversity, food, diet, health, genetics, the environment and energy. Students exchange ideas and findings with peers abroad and students work as a class to try to reach a consensus about what they have learnt. The network provides some worksheets and teacher's guides.

Another option is to start a project of one's own. An example from a primary school including children from kindergarten right through to year six involves having a school adopt a village in Africa. This is done in co-operation with a major aid agency that has considerable experience in Africa. It can become a school-wide project that also includes parents and members of the local community.

Goals

International projects aim to:

- help students assume greater responsibility for their learning;
- motivate students;
- provide a framework for synthesizing learning from several subjects;
- create opportunities for contact and communication with other speakers of the CLIL language;
- develop skills in communication, information and communication technologies (ICT), teamwork and problem-solving;
- develop reasoning, enquiry, critical and creative thinking and evaluation skills.

Suggested activities

1) Science Across the World
- Introduction – students begin to consider what sort of and how much waste they create.
- Accessing prior knowledge and skills – teachers help students to articulate their prior knowledge of waste using a framework (ecosystems, percentages, categories of materials, measuring mass, reading thermometers, interpreting

* http://www.scienceacross.org

diagrams and tables, precautions to take when measuring waste).
- Pre-teaching language – draw out vocabulary and discourse patterns by reading a short introductory text or by working through instructions with the class.
- How much waste do you create? – students survey the solid domestic waste produced in their own home in the course of a week and categorize the waste.
- What happens to collected waste? – students investigate the ways that the local community deals with waste.
- Collating and exchanging information – the class collates information and exchanges it with schools in other countries.
- What happens to waste in other countries? – the class considers the information received from schools in other countries and discusses similarities and differences, problems and solutions and how countries can learn from one another.
- Information section – information about waste production and treatment across the world is summarized and presented.
- Planning, implementing and evaluating – developing an improved waste-management plan for the school and applying it.
- Celebrating success.

2) Adopting an African village
   Students:
- learn about international development agencies and programmes (eg, sponsoring a child, adopting a village);
- learn about Africa and the country in question (eg, write reports, produce an art show, run group projects on climate and/or lifestyle);
- determine costs and develop a plan for fundraising;
- organize a community fair (plan, advertise, manage the funds, run the activities);
- develop a display for the school foyer;
- begin corresponding with children in the village;
- summarize accomplishments and celebrate achievements with parents and the community.

 ## 4 Total early immersion

Description

Total early immersion programmes begin in kindergarten or during the first year of school. Total immersion programmes are only total immersion at the outset. As students progress through the programme from year to year, more and more of the curriculum is delivered through the medium of the first language. Often, after a few years of study, half of the curriculum is delivered through the immersion language and half through the students' first language. Many schools will offer the option of studying a third language.

The teacher usually speaks only the immersion language. Certainly a few months into the programme, it is considered good practice to speak only the immersion language with the students. Many schools apply the approach of one teacher/one language. This means that teachers teach in one language only. Students learn to address one set of teachers in the immersion language, and the other set of teachers in the students' first language.

Teachers in immersion programmes try to create a climate favourable for language learning. Much stress is placed on communication skills. Teachers use a great deal of repetition and gestures. Language is presented both systematically in a logical step-by-step manner and unsystematically according to what language students want to learn so they can express what is important to them. Young children generally acquire the second language quickly. By the end of the first year, they understand most of what their teachers say and are capable of responding well in the immersion language.

Although immersion programmes are successful in helping students achieve functional proficiency in the immersion language, there are concerns associated with them. As the programmes, generally speaking, place greater emphasis on fluency than on accuracy of language, certain errors can become ingrained. There is also a tendency to plateau: Language development reaches a certain level or plateau and then slows down greatly or stops. There are strategies to counter these concerns (see page 170).

Goals

Total early immersion programmes aim to support students in achieving:
· functional fluency in a second language;
· development of their mother tongue on an equal level with that of students not studying through immersion;
· curriculum expectations in all subjects that is on an equal level with that of students not studying through immersion;
· an appreciation of their own culture(s) and the culture(s) related to the immersion language.

Suggested activities

Initially, teachers use lots of routine activities such as a morning circle where students can speak about what they did the night before, or over the weekend. As students search for words, the teacher provides them.

During the first year, students learn content that is typical in the first year of any programme, such as the seasons or the five senses. With the five senses one could begin with the teacher modelling the following text: *I love the smell of roses. I smell roses with my nose. I love the smell of roses. Do you love the smell of roses? I love the smell of roses.* Once the students have assimilated and are able to use this model, it can be expanded: *I love the smell of ...* (student's own words). Students are likely to answer using the CLIL language for the first half of the sentence and their primary language for the end of the sentence. The teacher then recasts the sentence with the new word(s) in the CLIL language and then the student repeats the full sentence. Activities with the five senses could include:

· Students matching parts of the body to the senses (eg, *nose = smell*).

- The teacher introducing (in writing and orally) words that describe tastes, such as *sweet, sour* and *bitter*. Students name foods that match these tastes. These are listed on the board.
- Working in pairs, a blindfolded student tries to guess various foods such as honey, lemon or cinnamon, which have been placed in small jars. The student who is observing marks the results on an observation sheet. Students switch roles. (NB: To maintain the smell of a product, first line the jars with petroleum jelly.)
- The teacher presents (in writing and orally) words associated with touch such as *soft, rough* and *prickly*. Students brainstorm objects that are *soft, smooth*, etc.
- Students are given a handout with labelled pictures of objects such as a snowman or fire. Students write on each of these pictures: the word *hot* in red or the word *cold* in blue.
- Students are given a page divided into little squares containing words such as *pickle, honey, pine tree, rabbit* and so forth. They can be asked questions orally or be given them on paper or card, such as: *How many are soft? How many are rough?* Students answer the questions. If responding in writing, they can also cut out the squares and place them next to their answers.
- Students cut out pictures from magazines and place them on a table under headings such as *soft, rough, sticky, smooth* and *prickly*.
- Several students place their heads under a table that has been covered with a thick, dark blanket. Other students observe how the pupils of the students who were in the dark change when they come back into the light. Observations are written on the board and in students' notebooks.

NB: Double-immersion and two-way immersion programmes follow the same principles and use the same sort of activities as described above, but differ in the following ways:

In double-immersion programmes, for example in the United States, native speakers of Spanish sit in the same class as native speakers of English. About half of all instruction takes place in Spanish and half in English. Due to the high status enjoyed by English, some schools have had to find new strategies to help students value and improve their Spanish. One strategy has been to deliver 75 per cent of instruction through Spanish and 25 per cent through English.

There are double-immersion programmes in Canada that offer part of the day in Hebrew and part of the day in French. Students also have some hours of English-language instruction. Many students speak yet another language at home, such as Russian.

Students in both of the above programmes are, in general, learning the languages involved and acquiring subject content at age-appropriate levels on an equal level with students who study through one language.

Bumps in the road to good practice in CLIL

CLIL enthusiasts never seem to get tired of telling the willing listener about the benefits of CLIL. A considerable body of educational research attests to student success in CLIL initiatives. However, for the reader interested in starting up CLIL, it is wise to have some sense of the problems others have faced with CLIL programmes, and to learn how those problems were addressed. CLIL creates long-term expectations. Students and parents who have tasted the benefits of CLIL usually want to see programmes continued and often expanded. Thus, a useful first step is to analyse one's own long-term capacity and that of one's colleagues against some of the challenges others have faced with CLIL.

Some common potential barriers on the road to successful CLIL practice, coupled with strategies for addressing and possibly avoiding them, are listed below.

1. Grasping the concept and grappling with misconceptions

For many adults, CLIL is counterintuitive. It is hard for an English speaker to conceive of learning another language like German, or for a Spanish speaker to conceive of learning Mandarin Chinese, let alone science or some other subject in those foreign languages. In their early lives, these adults may have found language learning difficult. A major obstacle to CLIL is the attitude of the cynical Susans and doubting Thomases both inside and outside the education profession. After all, these people have usually come through an educational background where all subjects in the curriculum were neatly separated, and this personal experience influences their perception of how learning should be organized.

Common sense seems to say that students studying in a second language cannot possibly learn the same amount of content as students studying in their first language. Some people are even convinced that CLIL students will fall behind their peers academically and that their native-language skills will suffer.

In fact, CLIL students perform as well as or even outperform non-CLIL students in terms of learning content. Far from interfering with content acquisition, CLIL can actually facilitate it. Academic results reflecting testing in a wide variety of subjects show that students generally achieve the same or better results when studying in a second language. Unexpectedly, students in CLIL programmes often even outperform their peers in regular programmes on first-language reading, writing and listening tests. This is partly because CLIL students develop meta-linguistic awareness. This means that they are better able to compare languages and be more precise in their word choice and in passing on the content of their message. They learn to check whether their message was accurately received by the listener. They also learn to draw out meaning from context. They become more skilled at using languages in general.

Another big misconception surrounding CLIL is that it is suitable only for the brightest, most academically inclined students. There are several nations from Luxembourg to Singapore that have multilingualism as a nationally established aim and where students undergo their education in several languages.

We are also seeing a wide spectrum of learners benefiting from CLIL in a variety of very different countries. The results are excellent. Research shows that average C-grade students do well in CLIL programmes. They still have a C-grade average, but they learn to speak another language and gain many socio-cultural skills that will enrich their professional and personal lives.

CLIL is a just-in-time approach as opposed to a just-in-case approach. CLIL students are not learning a language simply for the sake of language learning and future use, but are putting just-learnt language to immediate use while learning and manipulating content that is relevant to their lives. For certain students, learning content in a CLIL class can be more motivating than in regular programming. They like the hands-on and participatory nature of the CLIL classroom, finding learning through CLIL to be fun and challenging. In fact, CLIL appears to suit a broad range of preferred learning styles found within any classroom.

However, giving people the facts about CLIL is only part of the solution. People need to be engaged in an open and frank dialogue, which allows those attending school staff meetings and home and school meetings to express their concerns. Concerns are best addressed directly during those meetings. Responding to each concern with research facts of the kind listed above is an important practice. Inviting parents whose children have been in CLIL for years to these meetings is also very helpful, even if their children go to another school. Hearing from and questioning higher education experts who have studied CLIL student performance can also help create a sense of confidence, as will being able to speak to local government education experts. These experts can refer to relevant research and give evidence-based insight into CLIL's potential. Furthermore, visits to schools with successful CLIL programmes are particularly effective at convincing those who doubt CLIL's viability to reconsider their position.

2. The shortage of CLIL teachers

This is a typical, universal problem when educational innovation outpaces teacher education provision. As a programme expands from primary into middle school or secondary school, an increasing number of teachers are required. Teacher training institutions in many countries do not yet specifically prepare teachers for CLIL. The number of individuals who speak a given CLIL language and have subject-area qualifications is limited. Moreover, even if they have the prerequisite skills, not all teachers are prepared to focus on content and language goals.

A multi-faceted approach is required to address this issue. There are often a few people in a school who speak the CLIL language. The first step is to do an audit of the staff's language skills. Some people may never have considered the CLIL option or may be too critical in assessing their own language skills. They might simply require a language refresher course. It is also helpful to encourage university students who speak the CLIL language to do their teaching practice at your school. This can be facilitated by developing ties with local or regional universities.

Thinking in the long term, some teachers who already have relatively good skills in the CLIL language may consider doing a teacher exchange. This could allow a native speaker of the CLIL language to come to your school and for your colleague to go abroad and develop his or her language skills. It is also important to involve local authorities and universities so that they understand future staffing needs and so that they can support you. National organizations that represent teachers or head teachers/principals can lobby for increased training or for policies and funding that support CLIL programme implementation.

Networking is important. Teachers who speak the CLIL language are likely to know other bilingual people in the profession. Because CLIL programmes require considerable teamwork, and because they constitute a professional challenge, CLIL schools can become magnets for like-minded teachers who want to try something new.

The staffing issue is not only tied to finding suitable teachers, but to keeping them. Teachers need training and support for programme implementation. These issues are addressed under the following points.

3. Greater workload for teachers; shortage of materials

Teaching in CLIL requires more preparation time and greater co-operation among teachers. It takes a conscious effort to set content, language and learning skills goals for every lesson and to develop activities that involve a maximum number of students at a given time. Since off-the-shelf CLIL materials are in short supply, teachers often spend considerable time developing and/or adapting existing learning resources. It also takes time to arrange contact and communication with speakers of the CLIL language. Moreover, as well as all of the above, student interests need to be assessed and taken into account, and, with younger learners, co-operation with parents increased.

Some people are not prepared to invest the time required for preparation and follow-up. As teachers become adept at co-operating in the delivery of CLIL programming, they actually find that this co-operation can relieve stress, save time and bring considerable personal and professional rewards. After all, there is no need to reinvent the wheel when reciprocal relationships have been established and experience can be readily shared. Moreover, co-operation among teachers will contribute to improved student learning. However, at the outset, the task of working in a coordinated manner can be overwhelming. School leaders have a particular role to play here, by setting aside time for and embedding co-operation into the school ethos.

With CLIL modules or programmes that begin in late primary, secondary or vocational schools, finding appropriate materials is a particular challenge. The language input needs to be simple enough and presented in a reader-friendly manner so as to facilitate comprehension, while at the same time being sufficiently content-rich and cognitively challenging to capture students' interest. This book provides ideas on how to adapt materials intended for native speakers, and includes sample materials.

4. School administrators understanding the implications of CLIL programming

CLIL programmes that admit students based on marks or testing often take the high achievers. If a programme is made up of the school's strongest students it is likely to be viewed as elitist and cause resentment. Since research clearly shows that CLIL is suitable for students of varying levels of ability, it is suggested that entry to the programme be granted on a first come, first served basis. In some countries demand outstrips availability and a lottery system is used. Students and/or parents are also made aware of the long-term nature of committing to CLIL.

Head teachers or other administrators may not speak the CLIL language and may not feel equipped to support teachers. Consequently, it is important for administrators to become versed in CLIL methodology. It would also be advisable for the administrators to learn, at least, the basics of the CLIL language.

From a management perspective, there are several strategic implications associated with implementing CLIL programmes that are worthy of consideration. New programmes are initially likely to receive additional attention and resources, which can lead to jealousy and tension within a school. Large budgets for CLIL may do more harm than good, as they create resentment. The CLIL programme and the standard programme are deserving of equal attention. Official visitors to the school need to visit both CLIL and standard classes. Achievements of students and teachers in both programmes need to be highlighted. All languages used to teach in a school are deserving of high status.

Since CLIL teachers usually have a heavier workload at the start of the programme than regular teachers, head teachers need to find ways to support them. For example, head teachers can timetable preparation periods so that several CLIL teachers are free at the same time. A head teacher can on occasion take students from three or four classes and show them a film and lead a follow-up discussion, thus freeing up three or four CLIL and non-CLIL teachers for a lengthy planning session. Moreover, it is important to ensure that CLIL teachers have space to meet.

Sometimes schools with CLIL programmes face a two-schools-in-one phenomenon, where the CLIL teachers and the regular programme teachers form two separate teams that are not in the habit of co-operating. Cross-curricular projects based on themes such as the environment or Independence Day can foster co-operation. When CLIL teachers and non-CLIL teachers co-operate, not only do they help avoid the two-schools-in-one phenomenon, but they are better placed to enrich their own professional lives and to build a better learning environment for students. Above all, it is important for school managers to model, support and manage co-operation.

View from the field ①

A bumpy start

After learning about CLIL, our English department wanted to pilot a CLIL programme. We explained the concept to the entire staff and tried to identify interested teachers.

The reactions from the staff were varied. Some of them were very interested, others referred to it as 'science-fiction' and there were even people who laughed out loud! Taking into account that in our school, part of the programme is taught in Valencian and part in Spanish, some people's negative reactions were surprising.

Nevertheless, we decided to forge ahead. We had four teachers whose English was good enough to teach through English, and who wanted to participate. One taught heating and cooling, one maths, one technology and another Spanish. We paired each teacher with an English teacher who was to help with language. Teachers prepared and delivered a sample lesson. The sample lessons went well. However, in the long term the results and feelings about the experience differed greatly.

The cooling and heating teacher was eager to carry out his CLIL lesson. He taught a group of seventeen to eighteen year olds about removable energies using a computer presentation. Most of the students could follow the lesson, which was taught entirely in English, and were satisfied with the experience. The teacher wanted to continue to teach in English. In fact, his idea was to start the next year with a whole group whose subjects would all be taught in English. There were several problems with this idea. It was difficult to find enough qualified teachers who were willing to take this on. There was also a shortage of teaching materials and there were some certification issues. The teacher in question was not certified to teach senior students. As for the shortage of teaching materials, this teacher felt he could do rough translations from Spanish. My English department colleagues and I felt that rough translations would not be of sufficient quality. We felt that the written materials for CLIL classes had to be accurate and use high-quality language. The teacher was tempted to drop out of the CLIL working group, but in the end, he decided to stay. He has become one of the most active members of the team and his students are doing well.

Things did not go so well with the Spanish teacher, who was to teach theatre arts in English. Upon further reflection, my English department colleagues and I realized that we could only properly prepare the materials for one course for the upcoming year. We picked technology. The Spanish teacher was very disappointed and dropped out of the CLIL team.

The technology course was taught in English by our technology teacher and a maths teacher. The maths teacher felt comfortable teaching technology despite the fact that it was not his area of expertise. Both teachers are very satisfied with the experience and want to continue. They feel that student results are good. Teaching materials continue to be a concern. The teachers would like to translate materials. However, they do not fully grasp the challenges of producing quality translations.

In general, one could say that the certification issue has been the single greatest problem. Initially, we did not fully understand what the regulations permitted us to do or not to do. Moreover, our region is officially bilingual and we needed to be careful not to interfere with the teaching and learning of the two official languages – Valencian and Spanish.

Finally, I would like to add that it seems that the English teachers have had to take on a lot of responsibility. We have helped to prepare materials and have coordinated the programme implementation with other staff. Someone needs to take the lead!

In conclusion, it has been a lot of hard work, but we still feel that it has been worth doing it. The teachers in the CLIL team feel it has been professionally rewarding. The multidisciplinary team that was created has become a model for others in the school. There is no shortage of CLIL students as they all seem convinced that CLIL will give them an edge in the labour market.

Olga Paricio Font, secondary school teacher, Castellón, Spain

2 Getting ready for CLIL

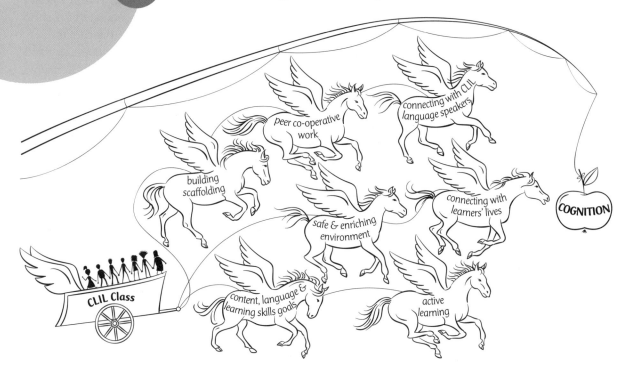

This chapter introduces the core features of CLIL methodology. Many of the features are not just specific to CLIL, but are part of basic best practice in education. Even so, all need to be taken into account during the planning and delivery of CLIL lessons. It is precisely the integration of many of these features into the average lesson, and all of these features into one's teaching repertoire, which presents a challenge to teachers. It also assumes that a significant effort be made in terms of planning and coordination with colleagues.

Orientating towards CLIL

Hollywood comes closest to portraying excellence in teaching when the character of John Keating, played by Robin Williams in *Dead Poets Society*, gets his students to stand on their desks so they can see the world from a new angle. Shifting perspectives is helpful in stimulating creative and critical thinking. If this film had been a showpiece for CLIL methodology, the standing-on-the-desk assignment would have included specific content and language goals. The students would have been given a greater opportunity to speak and write about what they observed, to share observations with one another, to explore how different perspectives affect their own lives and communities and to learn how to help people develop a common perspective. The students would have summed up what they learnt and how the learning took place, and would have decided what to do with their new-found knowledge.

To help structure this type of discussion and analysis, CLIL students would have been provided with words and phrases in the target language. Some of this language may have been posted on the board or on the walls. Students having trouble finding the appropriate vocabulary to express themselves would have immediately received it orally from the teacher. The teacher may also have added it to the board. Of course, watching the CLIL class would not have made for gripping cinema or filled seats at the local multiplex. However, the viewer would have seen students actively engaged in a deep and enriching educational experience.

More recently, films have shown a more multifaceted view of education. The French film *Être et Avoir* portrays a teacher in a one-class school navigating his pupils towards becoming independent learners who can work respectfully in co-operation with others. The German film *Rhythm Is It! You Can Change Your Life in a Dance Class* documents how by creating an enriching learning environment, students can be empowered to overcome peer pressure and gain the confidence to take charge of their own learning and lives. Each of these films focuses on creating meaningful connections between the learners' lives and the content being taught in school. These young people actively co-construct their understanding and learning. This is the essence of CLIL.

We do not learn to play football or the piano without kicking a ball, without placing our fingers on the keyboard. New football or piano skills are acquired by working and practising with others. Independent work is also part of the learning process, but co-operation takes us even further. Learning a language is no different. It also requires personal enagagement with the learning process, as well as extended opportunites for students to use the language.

It is widely acknowledged that young children usually acquire their first (or second, or third) language effortlessly and rapidly. One overwhelming feature of CLIL is to partially replicate the conditions to which infants are exposed when learning their first language. CLIL sets out to expand the student's learning capacity by tuning into the natural way the child learnt his or her first language. A young child's environment is full of resources that the child learns to use as tools. Children learn to use language, and use language to learn.

Thus, the natural ways a child learns his or her first language can be used to learn other languages. A CLIL environment can unleash a child's language-learning potential by providing rich *input*, and opportunities for rich *intake* and *output*. However, not all *input* becomes *intake*. And if there is limited *intake*, then there will be equally limited opportunities for *output*. Learning will be hindered.

In Nicaragua, deaf children were isolated, in large part, from one another until a government education reform in 1979. Schools for the deaf were created where these children were drilled in lip-reading and speech. The results were dismal. Yet, each child found his or her own way to communicate through signing. The students began to create their own sign language. As very young children joined the schools, they instinctively systematized the signing. Their signing was more fluid and concise. They introduced grammar to the signing. A new language was born.

The deaf children in Nicarauga were not prepared to wait until they learnt to lip-read. They wanted to communicate in the here and now about what was important to them, and found a way to do just that. CLIL students also want to enjoy the benefits of learning right away. Thus, CLIL seeks to provide 'just-in-time' language so that students can immediately enjoy the payoff of actively working with their peers. The payoff is being able to use newly presented content and language to create something meaningful in the here and now.

What is and isn't unique about CLIL?

Although CLIL does involve a new approach and a certain degree of change, it can easily fit into the parameters established by the national or regional curriculum. Moreover, CLIL cannot be separated from standard good practice in education. CLIL is a valued-added, as opposed to a subtractive, approach that seeks to enrich the learning environment.

Not again!

Q: Is someone expecting me to throw out what has worked well for me, and my students?

A: Absolutely not!

The CLIL approach encourages teachers to keep using their favourite strategies and to apply standard best practice in education. However, it does require an understanding of those strategies that are essential for CLIL, such as having a three-way focus on content, language and learning skills. Thus, CLIL is more likely to require a modification, as opposed to a major change, in daily classroom practice. Most strategies that are essential for CLIL can also be considered good practice in education. It is the need to take simultaneously into account standard good practice in education and teaching/learning strategies unique to CLIL that can be difficult for teachers.

When changing the language of instruction, some content (eg, maths, science, art) teachers find it difficult to support language learning. Some language teachers find it equally difficult to imagine content teachers, not trained in languages, being able to support good practice in language learning. Language teachers sometimes find it difficult to support the learning of maths, science or other content subjects in their language classes. Co-operation and skills exchange among language and content teachers thus becomes an important strategy for implementing CLIL. This requires the time and the will to agree collectively on common teaching strategies and student learning activities.

Stepping outside one's comfort zone into partly uncharted territory is an essential step in the CLIL journey. Interdisciplinary fusion is part of this journey. This book provides a host of strategies for addressing these challenges. Essential elements of good practice in CLIL and in education in general are listed on page 29. Fused together, these strategies support the successful delivery of CLIL lessons.

View from the field ② 2

I had to change my methods of instruction …

I had wanted for some years to teach music or musical topics in English. Students were interested. Some parents asked for CLIL, but my headmaster and some colleagues weren't convinced. Since we already strongly supported the learning of foreign languages by having all our students take internationally recognized foreign language exams, they didn't think CLIL would make a substantial additional contribution.

I explained that CLIL teaching and learning was more than marketing or gimmickry – that it provided students and the school with an experience that really opened doors and inspired students.

Then I got a chance to get started. I felt I had sufficient language skills, lots of experience teaching, and my students were eager to begin. But my first few lessons didn't go so well. The students were happy, the learning goals were achieved, but I knew that something was not quite right – and it was about me. I found myself talking far more than I usually would have done in German – more monologue, less interaction. Why was I talking so much? Was it the stress of starting something so different? When I teach in German I know that I can wing it – get on and off the train of thought so to speak – but not in English so maybe this made me less versatile, less myself. I had given so much attention to the language, I had forgotten to think through the activities and the methodologies. That was when I realized that changing the language of instruction means changing to some extent the methods of instruction.

Erwin Nigg, music teacher, Switzerland

A positive foundation for language learning

We faced a long-standing problem with English language teaching in our school. We had good teachers, materials and even equipment, but the learning outcomes remained dismal. English was a foreign language, something scary.

Then, one of our regional language experts suggested that we run 20 hours of activity-based 'language showers' before starting our regular English language classes. A group of teachers volunteered, even though some of them were very worried about their language skills. We formed a team and decided to use a blend of Thai and English for a module on water. We combined language and content objectives, but for the children it was a 'project', not language or subject learning. And to reinforce why we were doing it in English, we ran a very simple project with a school in Sweden, exchanging information through email. Our main objective was to build self-confidence, groupwork skills and show how English was a tool for entering the wider world. Once they got started with the activities they stopped worrying about the language, concentrating instead on content and process. The result? Well, we will do it again. We think we succeeded in laying a positive foundation for English language learning, and we also really enjoyed this project-based teacher teamwork. We all seemed to become winners, learners and teachers alike.

Punnee Buato, English supervisor, Thailand

Reminder: students aren't native speakers

We really forget too often that our CLIL students are learning in a second language. Fluency is something we almost take for granted with our students who have a good/very good/excellent ability to speak the target language (English in my case). Many times, you are almost 'charmed' by their accents and slight errors, so much so, that you forget that it is your job to help them as much as possible with the language. When you grade the writing, however, you are sometimes overwhelmed by the errors you see. Deciphering their text can be an arduous task. You always have to consider the objective of the assignment when grading these pieces of work and you must force yourself to reconsider the cultural context in which you find yourself as an educator (and as an administrator). My staff and I have to regularly remind ourselves not to treat our CLIL students as we would native speakers.

Andrew Frezludeen, teacher and CLIL programme manager, Qatar

Core features of CLIL methodology

Multiple focus

- supporting language learning in content classes
- supporting content learning in language classes
- integrating several subjects
- organizing learning through cross-curricular themes and projects
- supporting reflection on the learning process

Safe and enriching learning environment

- using routine activities and discourse
- displaying language and content throughout the classroom
- building student confidence to experiment with language and content
- using classroom learning centres
- guiding access to authentic learning materials and environments
- increasing student language awareness

Authenticity

- letting the students ask for the language help they need
- maximizing the accommodation of student interests
- making a regular connection between learning and the students' lives
- connecting with other speakers of the CLIL language
- using current materials from the media and other sources

Active learning

- students communicating more than the teacher
- students help set content, language and learning skills outcomes
- students evaluate progress in achieving learning outcomes
- favouring peer co-operative work
- negotiating the meaning of language and content with students
- teachers acting as facilitators

Scaffolding

- building on a student's existing knowledge, skills, attitudes, interests and experience
- repackaging information in user-friendly ways
- responding to different learning styles
- fostering creative and critical thinking
- challenging students to take another step forward and not just coast in comfort

Co-operation

- planning courses/lessons/themes in co-operation with CLIL and non-CLIL teachers
- involving parents in learning about CLIL and how to support students
- involving the local community, authorities and employers

What drives the 30 core features?

Thinking drives the teaching/learning process. The more powerful the thinking, the greater the learning. CLIL is no exception: good CLIL practice is driven by cognition.

Thinking (cognition) is the mental faculty of knowing, which includes:

- perceiving;
- recognizing;
- judging;
- reasoning;
- conceiving;
- imagining.

Analysing facts and figures as well as differing perspectives and understandings, imagining where one wants to be, articulating and conceiving plans, assessing or judging progress in meeting planned outcomes and thinking about the learning process are all helpful techniques in supporting cognitive development and learning.

CLIL supports the holistic development of learners. Its ultimate goal is to guide students towards becoming capable and motivated, bilingual or multilingual independent learners who:

- gain needed content and language knowledge and skills;
- actively seek and successfully make use of opportunities for communication with other speakers of the CLIL language.

In CLIL, the primary focus is on substance (content) as opposed to form. Parroting language patterns and memorizing vocabulary or facts in any subject area are unlikely to contribute to their long-term application. In order to acquire new knowledge and skills, people usually need not only to access new information, but also to connect that information with their own existing knowledge, skills and attitudes.

Moreover, as meaning-making is both a personal and a social process (community), new knowledge and skills develop through personal as well as co-operative reflection/analysis (cognition) and through a communicative process (communication). Long-term retention also usually requires that we experience the application of new knowledge and the use of related skills in a meaningful context. Finally, discussion and reflection, and the drawing of conclusions related to the experience associated with the application of new knowledge and skills, helps to cement learning.

In its most reduced state, the following principles can be said to drive the CLIL model:

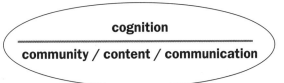

These principles can serve as a reference point for lesson planning. The following are examples of how these four principles, which contribute to successful outcomes, can be found in a CLIL lesson.

Cognition
- content, language and learning skills outcomes are articulated in co-operation with students
- learning builds on a student's existing knowledge, skills, attitudes, interests and experience
- students analyse achievement of learning outcomes independently, with other students and with the teacher, and work to set new outcomes
- students synthesize, evaluate and apply knowledge and skills acquired in several subjects

Community
- students feel that being members of a learning community is enriching
- students have the self-confidence and skills to work within a group and the local community, balancing personal interests with those of others
- teachers, students (and parents, employers, etc) are partners in education
- students can define their role within the classroom, the local and the global context

Content
- content is clearly linked to the community within and outside the classroom
- students apply new content and develop related skills through experiential activities
- content is substantive without being overwhelming
- content from various subjects is integrated
- cultural content is integrated into all subjects

Communication
- students actively use the right to participate in activities and communication, in the classroom and in the community
- desk placement, displays on classroom walls and other available resources support learning and communication
- students and teachers co-construct and negotiate meaning
- language/communication skills are developed in all subjects

How does CLIL work for students?

'I am ... a cucumber,' said one of our colleague's English-speaking students in French to a farmer in a small market square in France. The student was on an exchange programme. 'Well, you're the first talking cucumber I've met in 20 years of farming,' quipped the farmer, huskily. Seeing the blank look on the youngster's face, the farmer asked slowly in French, 'So, you want a cucumber?' And the student answered, 'Yes, I want a cucumber, please.' The student must have done an instant replay of the scene in his head as he repeated out loud in French '*am* a cucumber' and, suddenly laughing, went on to say 'no, no *want* a cucumber'. The farmer laughed too. A small dialogue ensued about the exchange programme and despite, or rather thanks to, the mistake, the student and the farmer had a meaningful dialogue. The English-speaking student was clearly happy to have been able to make use of his French.

CLIL classes work to create life experiences and at the same time to tap into the innate language learning ability we all had as young children and adolescents. In CLIL classes, communication and learning take place in a student's second★ (or third, or even fourth) language. In a systematic manner, teachers begin to provide students with second-language discourse patterns and vocabulary, while also teaching content and guiding students towards accomplishing concrete tasks. Although the building blocks of language are provided systematically, teachers also respond to a student's immediate linguistic needs as they arise. When a student wants to say something that is important to him or her, but lacks the needed word or expression, it is given to him or her right away. Within a few months of starting the programme, students are usually able to use the CLIL language for almost all classroom communication.

The language learning, which is certainly not considered incidental by parents or teachers, in many ways is incidental to the students. They are above all interested in the subject content, not the vocabulary and mechanics of the CLIL language. For students, language is a means to an end. Yet the teacher always needs to be aware of language. Just like the French farmer who realized he had to adjust his speed of delivery and simplify his use of language, so CLIL teachers adjust their language. Initially, teachers often speak slowly and use plenty of repetition, demonstrations, visuals and realia. Later, teachers speak at a more natural pace and encourage peer co-operative and independent learning. They work to create a climate that fosters continuous language growth. However, paradoxically, more language is learnt when the focus on direct language teaching is reduced and the content teaching is increased. By guiding students through experiments or activities that relate directly to their lives and communities, and by focusing on the learning of content while providing language support, language learning is actually maximized.

★ For the purposes of simplicity, we will refer to the CLIL language as the second language.

What about me? What do I do for a 60-minute lesson?

A typical lesson plan could include the following:
- holding a warm-up discussion or playing a game that somehow connects with the topic (five minutes)
- discussing language, content and learning skills outcomes with students (three to five minutes)
- finding out what the students already know, guiding them in organizing that information and helping them articulate what else they want to learn about the topic (eight to ten minutes)
- having students individually read a short text looking for specific information (five minutes)
- doing peer co-operative work to compare results from the reading, and using information to create something new such as a plan or a list of recommendations (fifteen minutes)
- asking two or three questions of the entire class that encourage students to think critically/constructively about how they could improve the end result of their groupwork (content and language) (five minutes)
- presenting one group's outcome and having other groups contest or add to the information presented, and agreeing on one class outcome (ten minutes)
- reviewing the lesson's learning outcomes, deciding the extent to which outcomes were achieved and deciding on the next steps (three to five minutes)

The learning materials used in CLIL classes are often from current sources such as newspaper articles, books, brochures, web pages or blogs. Students are supported in using these materials. The texts are adapted by cutting information into manageable chunks and adding synonyms or a glossary. Often visual or textual organizers are provided so students can see or read a summary of what they will be working through.

We have mostly looked at the *why* of CLIL. The rest of this book is all about the *what, when, where* and *how* of CLIL.

③ Starting CLIL in the Classroom

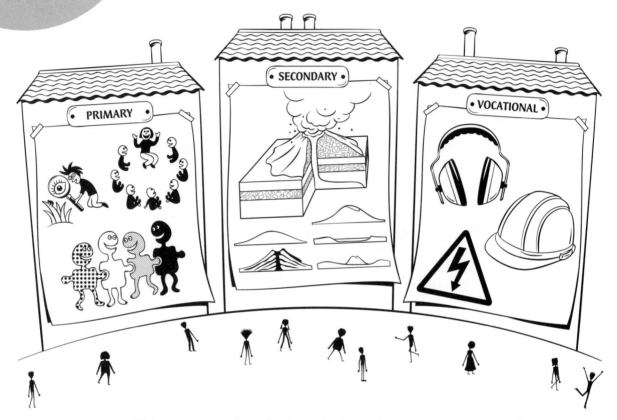

This chapter translates CLIL methodology into classroom practice. It proposes activities for the first week in a CLIL classroom at the primary, secondary and vocational levels. The lessons are based on the core features of the CLIL method and the guiding principles of CLIL described in Chapter 2. This chapter includes the textual materials for use in class, an analysis of the logic behind the proposed activities and some views from the field.

How does the CLIL methodology translate into classroom practice?

A week in the life of a primary school CLIL teacher – getting started

The following is an overview of activities teachers can use in year one during the first week of school at the start of a CLIL programme. Many of these ideas originally come from CLIL educators Olga Little and Lynda Boynton.

It is assumed that the majority of students entering school have very little or no prior knowledge of the CLIL language. Although the activities described below would fill the entire school day for a week in a high-intensity CLIL programme, they can also be used over a number of weeks for a low-intensity programme.

Although students are encouraged to use the CLIL language from the outset of the first lesson, they will often answer questions in their first language. This is natural and should not be discouraged. The teacher can recast the student's answer in the CLIL language. Also, providing praise to students for even attempting to respond in the CLIL language will encourage them to start using the language.

The length of the activities delivered during CLIL lessons may need to be modified. At the start of a CLIL programme, students learning in a second language may become tired more quickly than students studying in their first language. Their attention span may be limited, as CLIL students need not only to concentrate on the content, but on understanding the language as well.

Yes, but!

Q: What about immigrant children who do not speak the national or regional language? Should they avoid CLIL?

A: CLIL actually helps to level the playing field as all children usually begin CLIL classes without any prior knowledge of the new target language.

View from the field **3**

Taking risks should be rewarded

Learners need to be rewarded not only for being right, but for being close to right, as they work towards the 'standard'. Learners must be able to take risks and to make mistakes as they attempt new language structures. We must expect and accept approximations.

Yves Desrochers, CLIL teacher

Week one learning outcomes for students

Language	Content	Learning skills
• answer questions or instructions given in the CLIL language about the date, days of the week, the month at hand, the weather, colours, numbers from one to ten, clothing and about how they came to school and how their parents went to work (responses will often be in their mother tongue and include some words in the CLIL language) • respond to questions or instructions by matching pictures with printed words • greet one another in the CLIL language • create their own book	• identify key areas of the school, such as the nurse's and head teacher's offices, the toilets and the gymnasium through mix-and-match exercises • students conduct themselves politely • use a calendar for the month at hand and use concepts such as *yesterday*, *today* and *tomorrow* • students create their own books about colour and their new school	• students can predict expectations based on classroom routines

First contact

You are at the door of the classroom and greet each arriving student in the CLIL language. You use a simple one- or two-word greeting such as *hello* or *good morning*. You are wearing a name tag.

Setting the stage: the morning circle

There is a rug or a carpeted area that is large enough to allow the entire class to sit on the floor in a circle or in a series of semi-circles. Each student is asked to look for his or her name tag. There are several books on the carpet. These are picture books that might also contain a small amount of text. These books will help hold the interest of the students as their classmates arrive. The books help reinforce the image of school as an interesting place.

Names and first phrases (morning circle continued)

When everyone has arrived and the day has officially begun, you introduce yourself. Pointing to yourself you say: *My name is xxx.* Then, pointing to a student, you say: *What is your name?* You will need to repeat *My name is xxx.* and *What is your name?* several times. This question is asked of each student. As comfort levels rise, you encourage each student to answer the question using the full sentence being modelled: *My name is xxx.* After it is clear that the students understand how to answer, you encourage them to look at the next student in the circle and ask the question in unison. After receiving the answer, the students will also be encouraged to say hello to each student and repeat his or her name.

The WHY

The carpet helps create a sense of security. It brings students together in a family-like, familiar setting and reinforces a sense of group.

It also has a calming effect, which can be used when children need help refocusing on learning.

Calendar (morning circle continued)

Prior to class, a calendar with empty squares is prepared. Ideally, this is laminated. Number cards (1–31) are prepared, as are cards with the names of the days of the week and the names of each month. There are also cards with ordinal numbers (1st to 31st). These are posted on the wall in an orderly fashion in separate groups next to each other.

The students are asked to place the days of the week on the calendar. You point to each day of the week and have students repeat the name several times. The students also place the number for the first day of school on the calendar.

Students are asked to repeat the names of the days of the week several times. At the same time, the teacher points to the printed word. The teacher continues:

Today is Monday. (pointing to the day)

Yesterday was Sunday. (pointing to the day)

Tomorrow is Tuesday. (pointing to the day)

Today is the first of September 2008.

Yesterday was the 31st of August 2008.

Tomorrow is the 2nd of September 2008.

Today is Monday, the first of September 2008.

Yesterday was Sunday, the 31st of August 2008.

Tomorrow is Tuesday, the 2nd of September 2008.

> **Four in one**
> **COGNITION**
> • thinking skills
> **CONTENT**
> • dates, concept of time
> **COMMUNICATION**
> • new words and phrases
> • listening, speaking, reading
> **COMMUNITY**
> • building self-confidence in morning 'school family' circle

You ask questions related to the calendar and initially answer them yourself. Pointing to the calendar can help learners to understand the concepts of *yesterday*, *today* and *tomorrow*. Then the entire class is asked the same question one by one:

What day is it today?
What day was it yesterday?
What day is it tomorrow?
What is the date today?
What was the date yesterday?
What is the date tomorrow?

This becomes the morning routine on every single day for the rest of the school year. Students will gain a sense of security from being able to count on how their day starts. This routine also provides students with an opportunity to feel successful. As students' comfort levels rise, they should be able to ask the questions and run the activity themselves. Students can also learn to answer questions in pairs and groups. This will help them adjust to working in groups and pairs.

As the week progresses, it is helpful to write on the calendar something special that happened yesterday such as a big storm, receiving the nurse in class, visiting the head teacher's office or the name of a book read.

The weather (morning circle continued)

You either cut pictures out of magazines, print pictures from the Internet or make drawings to describe various kinds of weather. Phrases such as *It's windy. It's cold. It's hot.* are written separately in block letters on paper or cardboard. You determine whether any students already know how to say something about the weather in the CLIL language. If some students know some of the expressions about the weather, have them help you describe the various types of weather. It is helpful to make gestures or sounds or to modulate one's voice as one would when one says it is cold. Students repeat after you. Once students have grasped the basic concept, you show sentences describing the weather and have students place the sentences under the appropriate picture. After practising this with the students, you remove two of the sentences from under the pictures and ask students to put them back in the right place. You then remove three sentences, and so forth. By the end of the week, the students will probably be capable of placing the appropriate sentences with the appropriate picture.

As the week progresses, students repeat the various sentences associated with the weather together with movements that mime, for example, rainfall or the sun shining. Later on, students can take on the role of the cold wind, the hot sun or warm weather. Within a day or two it will be possible to integrate the weather topic into the routine centred on the calendar, using the following sample questions:

What was the weather like yesterday?
What is the weather like today?
What was the weather like on Sunday?

Yes, but!

Q: Isn't this too difficult? Children haven't even acquired some of these concepts in their mother tongue. How can they be expected to learn them in a second language?

A: Primary education is activity-based and it makes little difference what language the activity takes place in. The concepts are less dependent on the language than on the manner of presentation and the activities organized to support learning.

Weather and clothing

You draw or trace the outline of a bear on a piece of plastic or cut one out of cardboard and laminate it. The bear should be the same size as the students. This becomes the Weather Bear. You may choose to create two bears – one female and one male – and name them both. Pieces of clothing are drawn that are appropriate for various types of weather (eg, summer hat, winter hat, scarf, jacket, winter coat, raincoat, winter boots, rubber boots, shorts, trousers). You talk about all these types of clothing. Students repeat the vocabulary after you. On the first day, you ask the students to dress the bear or bears based on the weather. The following prompts, which would include lots of gestures and pointing, are proposed:

Should the bear put on a winter coat today?
No.
Should the bear put on a jacket today?
Yes.
Who will put the jacket on the bear?

You can also ask the students about their own clothing. Initially, students could be asked to touch their shirts, trousers or shoes. As they gain an understanding of the vocabulary and the confidence to speak, the students can be asked to name the clothing they are wearing.

Students also need to start seeing how the vocabulary associated with clothing is written. As the week proceeds, you associate cards bearing the names of the clothing with the visual images. Mix-and-match exercises are done with the whole class where students try to match the words with visual images.

Breaks

Children need a break from using the second language. Unstructured break time where pupils can run around and speak freely is an excellent way of letting off some steam.

Reading

Reading a book right after the break helps the students to calm down. Reading is done on the carpeted area. Pattern books with large print and pictures are ideal. Pattern books are built up on a simple pattern: *My mother has a green hat. My father has a brown hat. I have a blue hat. I like hats.* Pattern books are also easy to create. Students find teacher-made pattern books as interesting as glossy, professionally produced books. A sample created by Estonian teachers follows.

The students sit on the rug or carpet in front of you. You show them the cover of the book while speaking about it and pointing to the things you are talking about. The book is open facing the students, so they can see it. You read the text out loud, show the pictures and talk about them. You can also ask questions. The students will probably answer the questions in their mother tongue. You can model the answer in the CLIL language. Some students will give you back the sentence or a word or two of what you have just modelled. By giving those children particular praise other students will be motivated to do the same.

> **COMMUNITY**
> • building the confidence to speak

School tour

Take the children on a school tour. Toilets are labelled with the word | toilets | , and other rooms and areas are also labelled in the CLIL language and the students' first language(s). Students are asked to repeat the names of the various rooms and areas. When visiting the dining hall, the nurse's office or the head teacher's office, it is important to introduce people. This is a good opportunity for these people to show that they value the CLIL language by, at least, saying hello in the CLIL language.

It is wise to include some concrete activities such as washing hands before going into the dining hall or measuring one's height in the nurse's office. These are all opportunities for language learning.

As you progress through the week, the school can be toured a few more times. These tours would include some new information and provide an opportunity to review and reinforce previous learning. Students can be asked to identify and name various rooms and people. However, during the first weeks, you will do most of the speaking, being careful to repeat new language, using gestures, visuals, realia and context.

Returning to the classroom after a tour, students can help the teacher label pictures of various areas in the school. The words to identify various rooms and people are on large cards. One at a time, students can place the vocabulary cards next to the images identifying people and rooms in the school. As the week progresses, the learners can do mix-and-match exercises to identify rooms or people with the printed names for people or rooms. Students can copy words. They can also begin to create their own book entitled *My school*. This would include their own drawings of the classroom, three or four other rooms and a picture of two or three people. The rooms and people would be identified in writing (*My classroom, The office, Mrs Diamond*, etc).

Art

During the first day, the students should simply be allowed to paint or draw. The focus would be more on how the class prepares to draw, where the drawing is done, how materials are shared and used, safety and how clean-up is done. As the week progresses, these procedures will continue to be reinforced, but the art lesson will need to be more closely associated with subject content goals.

Lunch

Getting ready for lunch involves developing routines and there are once again opportunities for learning language and content. This is also the case with returning from lunch. After lunch is a good time to begin to introduce some language to do with food in order to learn what students ate for lunch and the foods they like. Learning about hand washing and other important habits is also an opportunity for language teaching. Learning is likely to increase exponentially if content and language learning are embedded in action.

Linking to student interests

Developing
- routines
- language
- self-reliance

Playtime

Watching children play can help to reveal their interests and how they like to spend their time. It will also help reveal their mood and comfort level. Moreover, playtime is an excellent opportunity to connect with the children and to teach vocabulary associated with what they are doing. If students are cutting out something, it is possible to point to the scissors and say *scissors*; if they are playing with blocks to say *block* or to speak about colours. Students should be encouraged to repeat these words. During the first week, playtime can be used as a way of giving the students a break. During the following weeks, it is important to look for ways of linking playtime with the curriculum.

Language arts

Although students are learning the second language throughout the school day, some fifteen minutes a day should be devoted expressly to teaching language. Students are likely to be most interested in vocabulary that relates directly to them – about their bodies, clothing, families, etc. Students should also begin writing right away. On the first day, it might involve printing their own name. As the week progresses, the students are asked to copy some of the new words learnt and draw pictures associated with the words. Although the students may not yet know the alphabet, they begin to use words by recognizing entire words and matching them with pictures and through copying exercises.

You can begin to introduce the alphabet during the second week and continue to do so throughout the first few months. All the while, students are still being exposed to written words and sentences. Many students will be able to recognize complete words and reproduce them before they have learnt the entire alphabet. By the third month in CLIL, students should already be doing some independent writing.

A daily message is another routine activity that can be done every day. Starting from the second day, working through the message takes place at the end of the morning circle.

These messages are posted on the wall one after another. Some sample messages follow and these are followed by suggestions about how to use them.

Day one
Good morning. This is year one. Today is the first school day. I am pleased to meet you. Today is a good day, the first school day.

Day two
Good morning. Yesterday was the first day of school. Today is the second school day. I liked yesterday. What about you?

Day three
Good morning. Today is a beautiful sunny day. The sun makes me happy. I like the sun. Today is the third school day. Today we are going to the gym.

Day four
Good morning. Today it is raining. If it is raining at playtime, we will not go outside. Rain does not make me happy. Rain makes me sad. Do you like rain?

Day five
Good morning. Today is the fifth day of school. We have an art lesson after lunch. I like art. I love art. We have a lot to do today. I like it when we have a lot to do. Do you like it too?

Day six
Good morning. Today is the sixth day of school. I am happy to see you all at school again. Today we are going to the gym. After lunch, we have an art lesson. I have a new book for you. I hope you like the new book.

The messages get progressively longer. There is considerable repetition and variations on related themes. Lots of pictures and gestures are used. Students can use the morning message to:

- count the number of words;
- count letters in words;
- count how many times a certain letter has been used;
- count how many times a word has been used during the week;
- guess which word is missing from the daily message (eg, *yesterday, morning, raining*);
- try to add a word such as *happy* that has been given to the students on a card to the daily message;
- use the language from the message to print;
- answer questions about their own likes and dislikes.

> **COGNITION**
> - developing thinking skills

Maths

Maths skills were used when speaking about the calendar (see page 37). In fact, there are opportunities all day long to integrate maths. There are so many new words being learnt and often it is possible to count the number of days, red shirts, windows, doors and so forth. It is also possible to group and categorize objects. Some maths exercises are listed below.

1) Ask students to match numbers and the corresponding words or reorganize blocks or other objects into groups of five, two, seven and so forth.

2) Ask students to place all their shoes in a pile in the middle of a circle. Help the students to categorize the shoes. Shoe size, type, function and colour are all options for categorizing. Organize the shoes into new piles. There are plenty of opportunities for counting. The various types of shoes can be marked on a large graph. The graph is then covered up and students are each given an empty graph that they are asked to colour in.

3) Introduce various modes of transportation (*on foot*, *by bus*, *by train*, *by car*, *by bike*) by using visuals (pictures and cards with the printed words). Students repeat these after you. Ask students to indicate how they got to school and how mum or dad gets to work. Various methods of transport are depicted on sticky notes. Each child goes and picks one or several sticky notes that depict how he or she got to school. These are placed on a ready-made chart with the words *on foot*, etc. On another day a chart can be filled in to show how mum and dad get to work. Students can print the means of transport and illustrate them. The charts can be used for counting and for learning expressions and concepts such as *the least* and *the most*.

> Linking content to students' lives

4) Students can be given free time to play with objects that are used to teach maths such as blocks, stars, building blocks or numbered cards.

5) Every day an outline of a big foot is added to the wall of the classroom to count the first 100 days of school. Other subjects can be integrated into this tradition. For example, the students can write on the foot one fact they learnt that day or give a very short overview of an important event such as a class party, someone's birthday, something funny that happened, the tooth fairy's visit and so forth.

Class rules and language use

These can be built on from day to day. Some teachers prefer to have someone else come into the classroom to introduce some simple rules to the students in the first language. Other teachers prefer to wait for natural situations that arise and then introduce each rule as it is needed, such as *We listen to others when they are speaking.* or *One person speaks at a time.* Some schools have a teacher use a puppet to present the rules. Only the puppet speaks the students' first

> **COMMUNITY**
> - creating a safe environment
> - balancing personal interests with those of others

language, the teacher does not. In situations when a child is distressed, it may be appropriate to use his or her first language.

The world around us

Colours are a good place to start. Teach one colour per day and the names of objects of that colour. Hold up the colour you are teaching. Have several common objects that are the colour you are teaching. For example:

The banana is yellow.
The book is yellow.
The shirt is yellow.
The pencil is yellow.

The new words are printed on the board and students are asked to draw the objects and print the words. Start getting students to identify the same colour somewhere in the room: *Yes, very good Natasha. The door is yellow.* Keep giving them more language. By the end of the week, each student can have made his or her own book about colour. Each page would consist of a drawing with text at the bottom, such as *The shirt is red.* or *My shirt is red.* The title page would have the student's name on it. The book is a good example of how art and language are integrated.

Ending the day

Bring the learners back into the circle. Review a few of the things you did during the day, making certain that the students feel successful. Tell them how you feel. Ask them how they feel, modelling three possible answers with a happy face, a sad face or a so-so neutral face. Say goodbye to them on an individual basis using their names.

Core CLIL features focused on during week one in primary school

The following chart shows all the core features of CLIL. Those features that were applied during the above activities are highlighted.

Multiple focus	Safe and enriching environment	Authenticity
• language learning in non-language classes • content learning in language classes • integrating several subjects • cross-curricular themes/projects • reflection on the learning process using routine activities	• using routine activities • displaying language and content • building student confidence • using learning centres • accessing authentic materials/environments • student awareness of and growth in language	• students indicating language needs • accommodating student interests • connecting learning and the students' lives • connecting with speakers of the CLIL language • using current materials
Active learning	**Scaffolding**	**Co-operation**
• students communicating more than the teacher • students help set learning outcomes • students evaluate progress in meeting learning outcomes • favouring peer co-operative work • negotiating meaning • teachers acting as facilitators	• building on a student's existing knowledge, skills, attitudes, interests and experience • repackaging information in user-friendly ways • responding to different learning styles • fostering creative and critical thinking • challenging students to take another step forward	• planning lessons in co-operation with CLIL and non-CLIL teachers • involving parents • involving the local community and authorities

Guiding principles focused on during week one

COGNITION
- content, language and learning skills outcomes are articulated in co-operation with students
- learning builds on a student's existing knowledge, skills, attitudes, interests and experience
- students analyse achievement of learning outcomes independently, with other students and with the teacher, and work to set new outcomes
- students can synthesize, evaluate and apply knowledge and skills acquired in several subjects

Community	**Content**	**Communication**
<ul><li>students feel that being members of a learning community is enriching</li><li>students have the self-confidence and skills to work within a group and the local community, balancing personal interests with those of others</li><li>parents, teachers and students are partners in education</li><li>students can define their role within the classroom, the local context and the global context</li></ul>	<ul><li>content is clearly linked to the community within and outside the classroom</li><li>students apply new content and develop related skills through experiential activities</li><li>content is substantive without being overwhelming</li><li>content from various subjects is integrated</li><li>cultural content is integrated into all subjects</li></ul>	<ul><li>students actively use the right to participate in activities and communication, in the classroom and in the community</li><li>desk placement, displays on classroom walls and other available resources support learning and communication</li><li>students and teachers co-construct and negotiate meaning</li><li>language/communication skills are developed in all subjects</li></ul>

A week in the life of a secondary school CLIL teacher – getting started

With secondary school CLIL programmes, students usually self-select, that is to say, they make the decision to join the CLIL programme themselves. They are likely to have a strong basis in the CLIL language, but could not be considered fluent. These students have usually had good grades in second-language classes. Students who have participated in a CLIL project or a language camp, or who have travelled to an area where the CLIL language is spoken, will have a clearer sense of what to expect.

It is possible that many of the students coming together in a CLIL class will not know each other. Taking the first class to get to know one another and to give information to students about how the class will proceed and what the students can expect will help establish a positive work culture and lessen anxiety. Students are usually most concerned about whether their grades will suffer and whether they will be able to cope with learning in a second language.

We propose that the first CLIL class take place outside the classroom, perhaps in a theatre arts room, gymnasium or in another large space. The new milieu sets the tone for a new experience and provides the space for playing name games that require movement and for sitting in a circle. The aim of the first class is to have some fun, lower stress levels, get to know one another, provide information and to give students an opportunity to discuss some of their concerns regarding the CLIL class. It is

> **COGNITION**
> • discussion facilitates analysis
>
> **COMMUNITY**
> • building a sense of group
> • teachers operate as a team
> • students and teachers as partners
>
> **COMMUNICATION**
> • authenticity – discussing students' concerns

suggested that the getting-to-know-you exercises be conducted in the CLIL language and that the discussion be held in the students' mother tongue.

If there are other teachers in the CLIL team, it would be good if one or two of them could join in this first class. This will help demonstrate that you are operating as a team and that students will benefit from all your support. Moreover, this initial meeting will require up to two hours. If necessary, this first class could take place outside the framework of the normal school day. You could access extra time by extending the day or combining classes.

Getting to know one another

Several options are suggested:

Name game # 1: Students and teachers sit in a circle. Pick someone in the circle and have that student say his or her name. The second student sitting to the right of the first student who named him- or herself repeats the first student's name and says his or her name. The third student repeats the first and second students' names and says his or her own name. This continues until the last person in the circle repeats all the names in the group and his or her own name.

Name game # 2: A variation on this name game is having each person say his or her name, together with a word in the CLIL language that starts with the same sound as his or her name. For example: *zany Zelda, honey Hubert* or *Hubert honey, computer Cathy, Cathy computer* or *Cathy quadrangle.* This is a good way of repeating names, bringing in vocabulary and having fun.

Mixer activity #1: Find someone who …

Make up a handout containing, among others, the following:

Find someone …
who speaks another language at home;
who spends at least one hour a week in a chat room;
whose favourite football team is Real Madrid;
who wants to be a rock star;
who is taking acting lessons;
who has seen an extinct volcano first hand.

Ask students to skim the handout for unfamiliar words. Ask a few questions to make certain that they understand some of the more difficult expressions such as *seen an extinct volcano first hand.* Give them the following instructions:

1) *Walk around the room and ask questions to find someone who wants to be a rock star, who has seen an extinct volcano first hand, etc.*

2) *Write the name of the person who says yes to your question on the appropriate line.*

3) *You, the interviewer, can only write each interviewee's name on the handout once.*

4) *You have ten minutes.*

Have a few students model how they would ask the question and then have everyone begin. Only if need be, a competitive element can be added to see who can get the handout filled in first. If students are actively engaged you may wish to give them extra time to do the exercise.

Once the exercise has been completed, have students sit down in a circle and ask: *Did anybody find someone who wants to be a rock star?*, etc. The debrief can turn into a free-flowing, fun conversation. *Yuko, will you give us free tickets to your concerts when you are playing in town?*

Discussion (using the first language)

Let the students know your planned outcomes for the discussion:

- everyone has raised their concerns about the CLIL class(es);
- all questions have received a response;
- we have in place an agreement on how to proceed.

> **COGNITION**
> * joint goal-setting
> **COMMUNITY**
> * building a safe environment
> * defining roles
> **COMMUNICATION**
> * favouring active participation

Students should be asked if they agree with these outcomes and whether they would like to see anything additional happen during the session. Outcomes will have to be adapted accordingly.

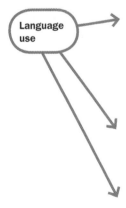

Language use

It would be best to have students ask questions that have been on their mind, as opposed to just lecturing to them. Students usually ask whether they will be able to cope with the second language, about grades, whether they can use their first language and what kind of help they can get. They may need some prompts to get them speaking, eg, *Is there anything about CLIL that makes you nervous?* Students need to know they will not fail a content test due to spelling. As long as they get their message across and as long as they are showing progress in improving their spelling and grammar, they will not be marked down for language.

Reach an agreement with your students that within, say, two months of starting the CLIL class, they will cease to use their first language during class. Explain the gradual nature of this process. You will keep reminding the students as you count down to the two-month deadline and will measure progress in meeting this target. Initially, when students use their mother tongue, you will mirror back the needed structures or vocabulary in the CLIL language. A student will be expected to repeat the modelled vocabulary or structures.

Suggestion

Invite a few students who started CLIL last year to this class to answer your new students' questions. This demonstrates your openness to the students' perspective and models the importance of looking at a question from several perspectives. The student will also act as living proof that CLIL works.

As you and your class progress towards the deadline, if a student switches to speaking in the mother tongue and you think he or she has the skills to get the point across in the CLIL language, you will ask some guiding questions and give some clues to help students to use circumlocution, eg, *You don't know how to say 'submarine' in the CLIL language, but how could you get your point across without using your mother tongue? You know the word for 'boat' and how to say 'under water', don't you?* As for you, the teacher, it is preferable if after the first class you always speak the CLIL language. Let the students know that this is what you intend to do.

Students will benefit from being told that while learning languages, a certain level of ambiguity is normal, that they are not likely to understand everything right away. Encouraging self-reliance will pay off for both the students and for you. Give them some coping strategies during this first discussion and explain that you will be returning to these over the next few weeks. For example, students can be supported in developing the habit of looking up words in dictionaries, inferring meaning, asking questions to clarify meaning and getting into the habit of using other coping strategies which are expounded upon in this book. If there are moments where you think several students have not grasped the essence of an important part of the content, a student can be asked to summarize the point in the students' first language. However, if this technique is overused, some students will become reliant on it and it may slow down their progress. Discussing this dynamic openly with students can be helpful. Within the previously agreed-upon timeframe (eg, two months), students should be able to restate the essence of a given point in the CLIL language.

To help students better understand the learning process and to help them manage their time and expectations, it is helpful to be straightforward about some of the challenges they will face. Students can expect that homework will take more time because of the extra challenge of learning in another language. As the return on the investment in language learning is not immediate, frustration can arise, especially around the middle of the first year in CLIL. However, well before the end of the first year in CLIL, most students should be fully back on track and feel there is little difference in studying in their first or second language. In fact, many students find that studying in a second language forces them to concentrate more on lessons and studying and helps them to avoid daydreaming.

The major concern students will have is whether CLIL will have a negative impact on their grades. They will want to know whether spelling and grammar mistakes will cost them a lot of marks in content classes. At this time, the mark breakdown for the term is usually shared with the students. They are told that in content classes language will not affect their final mark as long as they can make themselves understood and they continue to progress in improving the quality of their language.

Getting to the content

As an example of how to proceed, we will look at a one-week science unit on volcanoes for fourteen to sixteen year olds. Links will be drawn to other subjects. The amount of time taken for the various activities may vary considerably from the suggested duration, depending on their language level, and on whether students are used to doing groupwork and moving quickly from one activity to another.

Day 1

Activity 1: Warm-up/Setting the stage (3 minutes)

Watch a three-minute film on active volcanoes. These are easily found on the Internet by searching for *volcano video*, *volcano videos* or *volcano video clips*.

Activity 2: Free association (7 minutes)

After viewing the film clip, students write down on a separate sheet of paper three things that came to mind when watching the film. Each student passes his or her sheet to another student for language advice. Once corrections are made, the sheets are posted around the room. Students walk around and read what other students have written, identifying the number of people who had similar thoughts and the number of people who had very different thoughts.

> Connecting with students' feelings, interests and prior knowledge

You do a short debrief to have students share what they have learnt. Several students are likely to make a link to catastrophes and associated fears. This can lead into a presentation of the day's and week's learning outcomes, which will give students knowledge about volcanoes and how to draw lessons from the unit that can be applied to one's life.

Activity 3: Learning outcomes (5 minutes)

The following outcomes are discussed. Students are given an opportunity to modify them as long as prescribed curriculum requirements are taken into account.

Student outcomes for this class	Student outcomes for the week
Content • students articulate their existing knowledge about volcanoes • students identify three types of volcanoes and described their major characteristics Language • students construct descriptions logically • students correctly use the comparative • students use knowledge and vocabulary regarding volcanoes in different situations and with different registers of language	Content • students describe various types of volcanoes • students describe tectonic plates and their dynamics • students describe the cause of volcanic activity • students analyse the consequences of volcanic eruptions • students propose coping strategies for people faced with the possibility of a volcanic eruption, faced with an ongoing eruption and/or faced with the aftermath of an eruption Language • students correctly use the comparative Learning skills • students working in groups include all group members equally, listen to others and finish tasks on time • students define similarities and differences

Activity 4: Accessing existing knowledge (10 minutes)

Ask students to work in three groups to brainstorm what they know about volcanoes:

- volcano facts, including types of volcanoes;
- negative consequences of eruptions;
- positive consequences of eruptions.

> Anchoring into the student's knowledge

If you have the option of using computers, the results can be projected on a screen and revised or added to as need be. Groups of students can also write their thoughts directly on the board. Additions and revisions are made as required. Students deserve to be praised for the content. They can be encouraged to further develop their thinking by being asked if there are any points that came out in their brainstorming session that they are not sure are accurate. No judgement need be passed. These questions can be kept in mind and returned to during the week as you study volcanoes. Marking questions that may require further investigation can be identified as a critical-thinking technique that can be added to the students' learning skills repertoire. Some language errors can be corrected. As a first step, students can be asked if they would change anything in a word or phrase. If need be, you can suggest the correction.

Activities 5 & 6: Reading text about volcanoes and related assignments (20 minutes)

Students:

- read the text (see below) individually;
- fill in the empty boxes;
- create a Venn diagram to show similarities and differences between the three types of volcanoes (see illustration after the reading passage).

Date: _____   Name: _____

Volcanoes

Introduction

Even if volcanoes are located far from our home, they have played and continue to play a big role in our lives. About 80 per cent of our planet's sea floor and land mass was formed by the flow of molten rock. This molten rock has come from deep inside the Earth.

Volcano types

There are three <u>major types</u> of volcanoes:

- <u>shield</u> volcanoes (resemble a Roman soldier's shield lying on the ground)
- <u>cinder cones</u> (resemble an upside-down ice cream cone with the top cut off)
- <u>composite</u> or stratovolcanoes (resemble an upside-down layer cake made in a bowl)

Shield volcanoes

- relatively little explosive activity
- basaltic composition
- runny, low viscosity lava
- sides slope at 15 degrees or less
- relatively quiet eruptions with lava flows

Shield volcanoes are usually the largest volcanoes on Earth. Shield volcanoes are almost completely made up of solid basalt. Basalt can also be a type of lava or molten rock. During eruptions, it is very fluid. This is why these volcanoes are not steep. These volcanoes slope at fifteen degrees or less. After all, fluid material does not lend itself well to building steep slopes.

These volcanoes are not very explosive. Ninety per cent of the volcano is lava as opposed to <u>pyroclastic material</u> (ranges from blocks to ash blown or spewed out of the volcano). These volcanoes resemble fountains. Lava also erupts through the walls of the cone from vents along fractures. This lava can flow over many kilometres. This is why these volcanoes are dangerous for nearby communities. Usually people can evacuate in time. The Hawaiian islands are made up in large part of shield volcanoes.

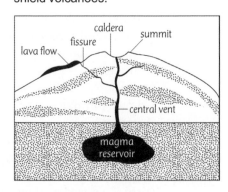

ANALYSIS

- **introduction connects to relevance of topic**
- **short, manageable blocks of text, including short sentences**
- **key concepts underlined**
- **explanation of terms in parentheses to ensure comprehension**
- **key information brought out in boxes**
- **labelled diagrams facilitate comprehension and address the needs of the visual learner**
- **above strategies support the acquisition of both language and content**

Cinder cones

- crater at summit
- steep with 30- to 40-degree slope
- •
- •
- •

Cinder cones start with an eruption. Particles and blobs of congealed lava are ejected from a single vent. Pressure blows the gas-charged lava violently into the air. The lava breaks up into small pieces or fragments called <u>pyroclastic</u> material. These pieces solidify and fall as cinders or rocks around the vent. They form a circular or oval cone. The cone has a steep, usually 30- to 40-degree slope. Most cinder cones generally have a bowl-shaped crater at the summit. They usually do not rise more than 300 m or so above the surrounding terrain. They rarely explode more than once. Cinder cones are numerous in eastern Russia and western North America, as well as throughout other volcanic terrains of the world.

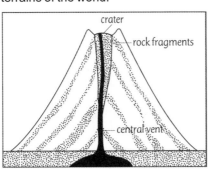

Composite or stratovolcanoes

- •
- •
- •
- •
- •

About 60 per cent of all volcanoes are composite or stratovolcanoes. The lava is viscous (thick) and traps gas that builds up to high levels. This build-up of gas causes explosive eruptions. The volcanoes measure 1 km to 10 km across. They are built up of alternating layers of lava and <u>pyroclastic</u> material. The lava consists of silica, andesite, dacite and occasionally, rhyolite. The pyroclastic material consists of volcanic bombs (lava that hardens into rock of varying shapes during flight), ash, dust, lapilli (walnut-sized rocks) and cinders. When active, these volcanoes are life threatening. They can spread gas and burning ash over tens of kilometres. People need to flee at the earliest sign of a possible eruption. Mount Fuji in Japan, Mount Vesuvius in Italy and Mount Saint Helens in the United States are examples of composite volcanoes.

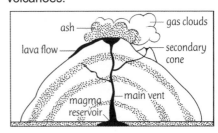

Activity 7: Reflection (10 minutes)

Have students work in three groups:

- group one students are experts in shield volcanoes;
- group two students are experts in cinder cone volcanoes;
- group three students are experts in composite volcanoes.

Each group writes the major characteristics of their volcano clearly, on ribbons of A3 paper. They place the traits that are unique to their type of volcano, those that are in common with one of the other types of volcanoes and those that are common to all three volcanoes into one large three-circle Venn diagram. Under your guidance, the results are reviewed and discussed. Particular attention is given to the use of the comparative. It would be helpful to have posted on the board a few model comparative sentences to which students' attention can be referred as need arises.

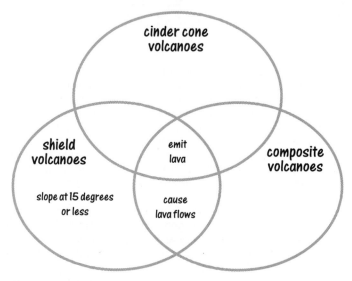

Activity 8: Achievement barometer (3 minutes)

You ask the students to stand. You say that it is time to evaluate whether today's outcomes have been achieved. As you repeat each outcome, the students will hold the palm of one hand on an approximate 180-degree angle high above their heads if they feel the outcome was achieved. If the outcome was more or less achieved, but work remains to be done, the students hold their hand at chest level. If they feel that the outcome was not achieved to any extent, they keep their hand very low. After measuring the achievement of each outcome, you and your students can interpret what each achievement barometer reading means and draw the necessary conclusions.

Day 2

Activity 1: Fortunately/Unfortunately (5 minutes)

Ask if one of the students is willing to be at the centre of a story you are about to tell. Also, ask the class to commit to not saying anything unkind or cruel. Ask them to suspend disbelief and to fantasize freely. Begin telling the following story.

While on a trip to Pompeii, in Italy, Eva (name of student in your class) *woke up one morning to an incredible rumbling. Unfortunately, Mount Vesuvius was about to erupt. Fortunately, Eva had her private helicopter parked in front of her hotel.*

Unfortunately, … (have the students continue the story)
Fortunately, … (have the students continue the story)
Unfortunately, … (have the students continue the story)

Activity 2: Reviewing/Accessing existing knowledge (7 minutes)

Have the statements shown in the box below written on the board or projected on a screen. Ask students to identify the statements that they are sure are false (answer key also follows). If a statement is completely false, cross it out. If a statement requires a small change such as stating that Pompeii is in Italy, not Spain, make the change.

> REVIEWING
> • volcanoes
> • comparatives

> DEVELOPING CRITICAL THINKING

Use plenty of follow-up questions: *Why do you think Mount Vesuvius is not a cinder volcano? What are cinder volcanoes like? How is Vesuvius different from the average shield volcano? Are cinder volcanoes usually taller than shield volcanoes? Why? How would you protect yourself from falling volcanic debris? How many of you have been to Italy? Can you describe the terrain you saw? Has anyone been to Pompeii? What did you feel as you walked through Pompeii? What impressed you?*

> CONNECTING TO PERSONAL EXPERIENCE

> POMPEII – 24 AUGUST, AD 97
>
> Pompeii is in Spain.
> Pompeii was flooded with molten lava.
> Pompeii was buried under ash.
> Some people tied pillows on their heads for protection from falling volcanic debris.
> Mount Vesuvius is a cinder volcano/a shield volcano/a composite volcano.
> When Mount Vesuvius erupted, it created a tsunami in the Mediterranean Sea.
> Pompeii is near Naples.
> Naples is south of Rome.
> Many people died.
> Two other towns were also buried.
> Many people fled.
> Italy is in north-eastern Europe.
> Pompeii was buried for centuries.
> A farmer rediscovered Pompeii when ploughing.

Answer key:

> POMPEII – 24 AUGUST, AD 97
>
> Pompeii is in Italy.
> Pompeii was buried under ash.
> Some people tied pillows on their heads for protection from falling volcanic debris.
> Mount Vesuvius is a composite volcano.
> Pompeii is near Naples.
> Naples is south of Rome.
> Many people died.
> Two other towns were also buried.
> Many people fled.
> Italy is in southern Europe.
> Pompeii was buried for centuries.
> A farmer rediscovered Pompeii when ploughing.

Activity 3: Learning outcomes (3 minutes)

The following outcomes are discussed. Students are given an opportunity to modify them as long as prescribed curriculum requirements are taken into account.

Student outcomes for this class

Content

- can articulate the living conditions and societal values in Pompeii in AD 79
- can identify facts and consequences of the eruption of composite volcanoes

Language

- can discuss living conditions, values, as well as facts and consequences of volcanic eruptions

Activity 4: Locating Italy and Pompeii (3 minutes)

Using Google Earth™, an atlas or a large map of Europe and/or Italy, have students locate Pompeii. Have them glean as much information from the map as possible: terrain, names of surrounding communities, distances, shape of bay, etc.

Activity 5: Reading an eyewitness report on the destruction of Pompeii (15 minutes)

Let the students know that they will be given an eyewitness report written by a young person who was near Pompeii on the fateful day in AD 79.

Ask the students to individually read the passage twice:

a) first, reading the text for general comprehension, underlining a maximum of five words that are preventing them from understanding the general gist of what is going on in the text. After completing the first reading students can look up any words in a dictionary that are really causing a problem.

To read out loud or not to read out loud
Q: Why not have students read the text out loud as a class?
A: This technique works best as a pronunciation exercise. The student reading out loud usually concentrates more on articulating the text than its content.

b) second, reading the text a second time looking for information on:
- what people in this area valued at that time;
- living conditions;
- facts about volcanic eruptions.

Working alone, these observations are printed on sticky notes or simply small squares of paper. Students need to know they will be sharing this information with others, so their writing has to be legible (large, neat, sufficiently dark, etc).

A few years after the event, Pliny wrote to a friend about it. He described the happenings of late August AD 79 when the eruption of Vesuvius obliterated (destroyed) Pompeii. It also killed his uncle and almost destroyed his family. At the time, Pliny was eighteen and living in the town of Misenum.

On 24 August, in the early afternoon, my mother drew my uncle's attention to (showed my uncle) a cloud of unusual size and appearance. My uncle was working at his books. He called for his shoes. He climbed up to a place that would give him the best view. It was not clear at that distance from which mountain the cloud was rising. The cloud was like an umbrella pine. It rose to a great height on a sort of trunk and then split off into branches. In places it looked white, elsewhere blotched and dirty, according to the amount of soil and ashes it carried with it.

My scholarly uncle saw at once that it was important enough for a closer inspection. He ordered a boat to be made ready, telling me I could come with him if I wished. I replied that I preferred to go on with my studies.

My uncle hurried to the place that everyone else was hastily leaving. He steered his course (direction, path) straight for the danger zone. Ashes were already falling, hotter and thicker as the ship drew near, followed by bits of pumice and blackened stones, charred and cracked by the flames: then suddenly they were in shallow water, and the shore was blocked by the debris from the mountain.

For a moment my uncle wondered whether to turn back. The helmsman (man who steers a ship) advised this, but he refused. The wind was in my uncle's favour, and he was able to bring his ship in. He embraced (hugged) his terrified friend, cheered and encouraged him. Thinking he could calm his friend's fears by showing his own composure, my uncle gave orders that he was to

be carried to a bath. After his bath he lay down and dined; he was quite cheerful, or at any rate he pretended he was.

Meanwhile on Mount Vesuvius fire and leaping flames blazed at several points. My uncle went to rest and certainly slept. He was a stout (big strong body, heavy) man and his breathing was rather loud and heavy. It could be heard by people coming and going outside his door. By this time the courtyard outside his room was full of ashes mixed with pumice stones, so that its level had risen. If he had stayed in the room any longer he would never have got out. He was wakened by members of the household.

They debated whether to stay indoors or take their chance in the open, for the buildings were now shaking with violent shocks, and seemed to be swaying to and fro (back and forth). Outside, there was the danger of falling pumice stones, even though these were light and porous. As a protection against falling objects, people put pillows on their heads tied down with cloths.

Elsewhere there was daylight by this time, but they were still in darkness, blacker and denser than any ordinary night. They lit torches and various kinds of lamps. My uncle decided to go down to the shore and investigate on the spot the possibility of any escape by sea, but he found the waves wild and dangerous.

Then the flames and smell of sulphur, which gave warning of the approaching fire, drove the others to take flight (to leave quickly). My uncle stood leaning on two slaves and then suddenly collapsed, I imagine because the dense fumes choked his breathing by blocking his windpipe. His throat was weak and narrow and often inflamed. When daylight returned on the 26th – two days after the last day he had been seen – my uncle's body was found intact and uninjured, still fully clothed and looking more like sleep than death.

Adapted from 'The Destruction of Pompeii, 79 AD', www.eyewitnesstohistory.com.

Activity 6: Analysing content of the letter in groups (17 minutes)

Have students form groups of four or five. Share the criteria about how groupwork will be evaluated (see Activity 7 below). Each group of students combines its sticky notes (values, living conditions, facts about eruptions) and works to come up with a common set of observations that it can agree on.

One group presents its observations about values. Other groups can add additional ideas or points, or express agreement or disagreement and explain their reasoning. Another group presents its conclusions about living conditions. Once again, other groups can add additional ideas or points, or express agreement or disagreement and explain their reasoning. Finally, a third group presents the facts that it has gleaned from the text about volcanic eruptions. Other students are invited to add additional ideas or points, or express agreement or disagreement and explain their reasoning.

Have students place their sticky notes in an organized fashion onto A4 sheets of paper, labelling each sheet according to the three categories (values, living conditions, facts about eruptions) and share the notes with each other electronically. Those who do not have computers at home should receive hard copies and the others should receive the document by email. It is likely that there will be students in your class who have scanners and can do this for the group.

Activity 7: Assessing groupwork (5 minutes)

Have students in each group individually rate on a five-point scale (5 = very much, 1 = almost not at all) the extent to which they:

- included all group members equally in their work (discussion and presentation);
- listened to each and every group member;
- used their time well.

Students share their results with each other, one point at a time. A few moments are allowed for discussion.

You can tie up the activity by asking students to what extent group members agreed in their assessment. One or two groups could be invited to draw conclusions about why they were successful or about what needs to change.

Activity 8: Assigning and discussing homework (3 minutes)

Students are given a simple A4-size map showing the contours of the continents and major islands. The map is entitled *Famous Volcanoes and Tectonic Plates*. The assignment is to mark and name five famous volcanoes and to draw lines on the map to show the major tectonic plates. On the back of the map students should state the cause of volcanoes in one or two sentences.

Students will benefit from a discussion about where and how to find this information. Key words in the discussion might include terms such as *table of contents*, *index*, *school library*, *textbook* and *Internet search engine*. Analysing the title and giving the students a key term such as *Ring of Fire* will help them locate the information they need on the Internet or in encyclopedias. It may also be helpful to the students to be told that the Earth has a crust. This is also a good moment to explain that bread also has a crust.

Activity 9: Assessing progress in meeting lesson outcomes (3 minutes)

The students can give feedback on whether they think the lesson's planned outcomes were met. Conclusions are drawn about how to continue to move forwards.

> **Link to language class**
>
> Mark Twain
>
> 'The buried city of Pompeii', Chapter 31 in *Innocents Abroad*

Day 3

Activity 1: Warm-up – inner and outer circle (5 minutes)

Begin by dividing the class in half by counting off the students using numbers (*one, two, one, two, one, two*, etc) or by following a pattern (*cinder volcano, composite volcano, cinder volcano, composite volcano*, etc). If there is an uneven number, join in the activity yourself. Two circles are formed – the outer circle facing inwards and the inner circle facing outwards. (If there is a lack of space in the classroom, the hallway is often suitable. One just creates a cigar-shaped 'circle' instead.) Students follow your instructions:

Tell the person in front of you what you did last night.

After 30 seconds, have the students in the inner or outer circle step one person to the right (it is important to have the students move on before they are all talked out on any one topic). Then ask the next question:

What would you do if you were on holiday on an island where a volcano was about to erupt? Continue in the same manner. Other possible questions include:

Imagine you are criminals. What would you try to do during the eruption?

Imagine you are a judge. What would you do with those criminals?

You work for the Emperor of Japan and you are the first to see a cinder volcano developing behind the Imperial Palace. What would you say or do?

What would you take with you from home if you had to evacuate on foot?

If you were the mayor of a town near the disaster area, how would you help?

Would you move back to the area after a volcanic eruption? Why? Why not?

How would you start a country-and-western song about a volcano?

Can you write the first two lines of a rap about volcanoes?

Activity 2: Outcomes (2 minutes)

Student outcomes for this class

Content
- describe the nature of tectonic plates
- name types of tectonic plates
- explain the cause of some volcanoes
- identify the consequences of volcanic eruptions

Language
- discuss tectonic plates and the consequences of volcanic eruptions with others

Learning skills
- improve groupwork skills

Activity 3: Reviewing homework (6 minutes)

We suggest reviewing the homework in a casual manner. You can begin by asking students where they found their information and what challenges they faced doing the homework. Try to get as much of the student-uncovered information about tectonic plates and volcanoes on the board as possible. Students can help. For example, two students can act as scribes with two checking for clarity and spelling.

Activity 4: Jigsaw for learning about tectonic plates and volcanoes (40 minutes)

As the name implies, the jigsaw helps students to put together different pieces of a picture to form a whole.

Step 1
Divide the text you want the students to work with into sub-topics. The sample text that follows the instructions has been divided into six sub-topics. With the jigsaw method, the number of sub-topics equals the number of students in each group (eg, five sub-topics = five members in each of the five groups). Since classes rarely consist of exactly 16, 25 or 36, students can buddy up to work in pairs.

Step 2
Divide your students into groups. For example, if there are 27 students in your class, have the students count off in fives. All six number ones form a group. All six number twos form a group. All five number threes form a group. All five number fours form a group, etc. In the two groups where there are six students, two students in each group form a pair that will later on move as one.

Classroom management

Initially there may be some resistance to this method, especially in highly competitive climates or in cases where the students are used to a teacher-centred approach. Also, the weaker students can get frustrated because they may find it difficult to teach others. The stronger students may not have the patience to listen to the weaker students. Circulating actively, asking probing questions, making suggestions and providing encouragement can go a long way in helping students to get used to the method. It is also wise to remind students of the learning skills outcome for the week which has to do with building teamwork skills. It is also helpful if you let them know what sort of behaviour you expect from them: *No making fun of others. Support each other.* Giving each group a mark can also contribute to creating a peer supportive culture.

Step 3

The students in each group work to understand the text that is common to the whole group. Their role is to create some simple form of visual material (a picture, a graphic organizer) and prepare to individually teach their text to another group who will not have a copy of the written text. After working through the text and developing some visual material the students create a few follow-up questions to make certain they got their point across. An alternative is for them to prepare a short test using copying paper or chart paper. Student-created tests can be very motivating. The group members can also practise teaching each other. The students will probably want to have your support in understanding the text or in saying certain things in the CLIL language.

Step 4

The students regroup. Each new group should have one person or a pair from the original group one, from group two, from group three, etc. Each student in the new group teaches his or her topic to the others. While teaching others, the students are not allowed to simply read the text. Afterwards, each student asks questions of the other students or administers and reviews a test on his or her topic.

Step 5

Students go back to their original group and answer at least two of the following questions:

What went well while teaching?

What would I do differently next time?

What did we do as a group that helped me to be successful at this task?

What should we as a group do differently next time?

Tectonic plates and volcanoes

There is a pattern to the way volcanoes are distributed over the Earth's surface. Most are located near the edge of tectonic plates. Tectonic plates are like huge thick pieces or slabs of hard-baked earth. These tectonic plates make up the Earth's surface. They form the Earth's crust. Thus, we can say that the Earth's crust is not in one piece. Scientists believe that tectonic plates are constantly moving. However, they move very slowly, about as slowly as our fingernails grow (one to ten centimetres a year).

In total, there are fifteen major tectonic plates (African Plate, Antarctic Plate, Arabian Plate, Australian Plate, Caribbean Plate, Cocos Plate, Eurasian Plate, Indian Plate, Juan de Fuca Plate, Nazca Plate, North American Plate, Pacific Plate, Philippine Plate, Scotia Plate and South American Plate). There are also about three dozen minor tectonic plates (a dozen = twelve). Various models identify slightly different numbers of plates. Scientists also speak of ancient tectonic plates that have fused with (become part of) existing plates.

Tectonic plates, which form the Earth's crust, are in constant movement. They pass each other, collide with each other, move under or on top of each other. The crust is only about 8 km (5 miles) thick under the oceans and 30 km (18 miles) thick under the continents. Some scientists believe the crust to be up to 100 km thick. The crust can also be divided into two – the oceanic crust and the continental crust. Below the crust is the Earth's mantle. The crust floats on the upper layer of the mantle, which is very hot and consists (is made up) of molten rock.

As tectonic plates collide (crash into each other) or move under or on top of each other, pressure builds. As one plate moves under another, it becomes so hot that it melts. This molten rock, or magma, releases gases. The gases push upwards and pressure builds. If the magma is thin, or highly liquid, it is easier for it and its gases to find a way to the surface of the Earth. They begin to leak from fissures or holes. When the magma is viscous or very thick, it has a harder time reaching the Earth's surface. As the magma and its gases build up, pressure increases greatly. Eventually, the pressure builds to such a point that it causes an explosion called a volcanic eruption. Magma that makes it to the Earth's surface is called lava.

The largest concentration of active volcanoes in the world partially circles the Pacific Ocean. This is often called the Ring of Fire. These volcanoes are located close to the edge of continents, along island chains or under the sea. Beneath the sea, these volcanoes have formed mountain chains. Volcanoes that are near the edge of plates are called plate-boundary volcanoes. Those volcanoes that are not located at the edge of a plate are called intra-plate volcanoes. New Zealand is an example of an intra-plate volcano hot spot.

It is thought that ten per cent of people live within the destructive reach of a volcano. Volcanic eruptions can be deadly for people, animals, plants and marine life; they can temporarily poison water and the air; and damage property. Major volcanic eruptions can affect the Earth's climate. In 1815, the stratovolcano Mount Tombora erupted in Indonesia and affected the climate over much of the world. Agriculture and food production suffered in many countries. In the northern hemisphere, the summer of 1816 was known as the year without a summer. However, volcanic eruptions can also have positive effects. For example, rich volcanic soil supports the growth of a wide range of crops. The slopes of some volcanoes are very steep. Steep slopes are quite inaccessible to people. This creates sanctuaries (protected areas) for rare plants and birds.

Activity 6: Assessing achievement of learning outcomes (3 minutes)

Return to the lesson outcomes and discuss the extent to which they were achieved. Discuss how effective they found the jigsaw method (likes, dislikes, what they learnt about teaching others, what they will do differently next time, etc).

Activity 7: Assigning homework (1 minute)

Students prepare for a ten-point quiz on this week's work. The quiz will require one-word or two-word answers.

Activity 8: Review (3 minutes)

We suggest orally working through a model quiz that is on the board. This could be a whole-class activity.

Sample review questions for summarizing the lesson

1 Stratovolcanoes are also called:
   a) cinder volcanoes
   b) composite volcanoes
   c) shield volcanoes
2 Viscous lava is ...
3 The town of Pompeii was destroyed when Vesuvius erupted in AD 79. What killed most of the people?
4 Describe life in Pompeii prior to the eruption. (5 facts)
5 ... volcanoes are generally more dangerous than ... volcanoes.
6 Describe tectonic plates.

Day 4

Activity 1: Analogies (8 minutes)

Start the class by squeezing a plastic ketchup bottle so that the tomato sauce squirts up out of the top of the bottle (if you feel uncomfortable doing this with a food product, you can simply ask students what will happen if you squeeze it). Begin a dialogue about the bottle:

What type of volcano resembles a squirting ketchup bottle?

In which ways is this analogy accurate?'

In which ways is it not accurate? (This will produce plenty of silly answers that allow students to have fun with language and will help review the topic at hand as well.)

Ask the students to split into groups of four to come up with an analogy for a type of volcano, the consequences of volcanic eruptions or about tectonic plates. They will need to use the comparative on at least two occasions to explain their analogy. Each group member needs to say something to explain the group's analogy. A sample comparative posted on the board will facilitate the students' work.

After a few minutes, each group presents its analogy. The analogies can be presented as a mystery and other students can try to guess what the analogy is about.

Activity 2: Outcomes (3 minutes)

Student outcomes for this class

Content
- use knowledge gained about tectonic plates and volcanoes
- construct accurate dialogues about volcanic activity

Language
- construct accurate dialogues about volcanic activity
- pronunciation does not interfere with comprehension

Learning skills
- reinforce groupwork skills
- develop a structure for a work plan

Activity 3: Quiz (10 minutes)

The following quiz can be drawn up with little effort and time. It is primarily aimed at motivating students to review classroom learning. We suggest having students mark it in class and that the mark be recorded by the teacher.

Date: _____   Name: _____

Volcanoes and tectonic plates quiz

1   What percentage of our planet's sea floor and land mass were formed by the flow of molten rock?
    a) 20%
    b) 50%
    c) 80%

2   Shield volcanoes are:
    a) not very explosive
    b) highly explosive
    c) moderately explosive

3   Mount Vesuvius is a:
    a) shield volcano
    b) composite volcano
    c) cinder cone volcano

4   When molten rock comes out of the earth it is called …

5   The Ring of Fire partially encircles the … Ocean.

6   Tectonic plates move …

7   Volcanoes that are near the edge of plates are called 'plate- …' volcanoes.

8   Pompeii was buried under … (two words)

9   Name one tectonic plate: The … Plate.

10 The slopes of volcanoes can provide … for rare birds.

Another option is to develop a quiz based on the following model:

Put yourself in the role of someone living next to either a shield, composite or cinder volcano. What dangers might you face and how would you deal with them? Give five dangers and five strategies.

Activity 4: Filming a scene (35 minutes)

The students plan and film one or several scenes, inspired by a TV programme. The scene must include something about volcanoes. Ask the students who among them owns video/digital cameras. Have the students form groups of five, ensuring that each group has at least one person with a camera. Should there not be enough video cameras in the class, ask if someone is willing to film another group. The other option is to simply have all the students present their scenes in class. The assignment is presented to the students both in writing and orally, as is the evaluation grid (see following page). Some of the vocabulary, such as *props*, will probably be unfamiliar. It needs to be discussed.

Classroom management

The students are most likely to want to start discussing the scenes right away. They may be overwhelmed by the work plan. It would be wise to ask the class as a whole what they think a work plan should include. Some clues are given in the evaluation grid. It will be helpful for students if you take their suggestions and create a framework for the plan.

Filming a scene for a TV show

1 List ten TV soap operas or sitcoms (situation comedy shows) that you like.

2 Pick one show from the list.

3 Read the evaluation criteria.

4 Write a five- to ten-minute segment for the show. The scenes take place before, during and/or after a volcanic eruption. Remember the evaluation criteria.

5 List the tasks involved in doing the work.

6 Develop a work plan. You will be given the majority of the remainder of this period and the majority of tomorrow's class to work on the project. Your CLIL language teacher will give you all of tomorrow's period to work on the project. He or she will answer any questions about language usage and pronunciation.

7 Film your scene.

8 Be prepared to show your film on Monday.

Evaluation grid
(to be assessed by science teacher, CLIL language teacher and students)

Items being assessed	Points
Work process	
work plan (assignments, schedule, quality control, props, etc) maximum one page	20
quality of groupwork (equal participation, listening to each other, efficient use of time)	10
Film content	
points for accurately including at least ten volcano facts	20
creativity (interest, props, etc)	20
Film language	
comprehension by viewer (clarity of pronunciation, accurate use of language)	20
inclusion of five comparatives	10
TOTAL	100

Activity 5: Assessing outcomes (5 minutes)

There is bound to be some tension at the end of this lesson as students will probably have developed a sense of the complicated nature of the filming project. Some time will need to be spent discussing the need to use time rationally and to do the best they can with limited resources. Expectations may need to be managed.

Day 5

Activity 1: Warm-up – sentence building (8 minutes)

Prior to class, write vocabulary associated with volcanoes on some 30 cards. Throw in the names of a pop singer, the name of the school nurse, the head teacher, etc. You might include words or groups of words such as *to dance, pyroclastic material, vent, crust, to explore, to leak, fissure, vent, crater, lava,* etc. Students form groups of four and each group gets five cards that they choose at random. Each group's assignment is to create the longest sentence possible using all five words.

Activity 2: Learning outcomes (2 minutes)

> **Student outcomes for this class**
>
> Content
>
> accurately use knowledge gained about tectonic plates and volcanoes
>
> Language
>
> construct accurate dialogues about volcanic activity
>
> Learning skills
>
> reinforce groupwork skills

Activity 3: Filming a scene (continued, 38 minutes)

The students can be asked if they have any concerns about the film project. They are likely to ask for more time, but this is when they need to face up to the reality of time constraints and make the most of the time allotted.

The students simply continue to work on the project. You circulate, help keep them on task and ask supportive questions.

Activity 4: Assessment of outcomes – achievement for the week (5 minutes)

Students can give a thumbs-up (yes), a wiggling hand (sort of) or a thumbs-down (no) sign after each outcome for the day and the week is reviewed. A few minutes can be taken to brainstorm a few suggestions for improving learning during the upcoming week. Students could vote on these to pick the one suggestion that you (individually, as a class) will take into account during the upcoming week.

This is also the moment to return to those points that came up during the first brainstorming session on the first day, where some points were raised that the students may not have been sure were accurate. These can be looked at again to see if the students can now decide on their accuracy.

Activity 5: The big circle (7 minutes)

It helps build a sense of community if you can sit in a circle at the end of the week. In the circle, each student can say one to three words about how he or she feels about the week. Many students will have trouble coming up with a feeling as opposed to giving a short analysis of the week. They will need support in speaking about feelings. Having some words on the board can help. A student can repeat something others have said, but usually will not do this. Some students are likely to use vocabulary from the week saying 'a cinder cone' or 'flowing lava'. If a student is having difficulty coming up with something, move on to another person. You can always try coming back to the person later. This exercise usually helps end the week on a high note.

More volcano ideas

SURVIVORS

interviewing those who fled Pompeii

REPORTS

- medical
- property damage
- government
- crime

SUPERHEROES

pretending to be a superman/woman and imagining how you would save Pompeii before Vesuvius erupts

CAREERS

exploring professions linked to earthquakes

SIX OR MORE HATS

looking at the aftermath of an eruption from different perspectives (eg, Debono's Six Hats: neutral & objective, emotional view, negative view, sunny & positive view, creative & new ideas perspective, organizer's view, or make up your own version)

MEGA METRES

In groups, students write the longest story about volcanoes they can on a roll of paper in 15 minutes (eg, toilet or adding-machine paper). Lettering is as high as the paper. Groups first take two minutes to plan. After celebrating the victors, the class debriefs group strategies that led to success

LANGUAGE

create idioms or proverbs about the Pompeii incident (eg, *vicious as Vesuvius, where there is a rumbling volcano, smart people are moving away*)

VISION

business plan for revitalizing a town buried by volcanic ash

SAFETY PLAN

Developing a safety plan for a community that lives in the shadow of a volcano. The first step could be deciding what such a plan should include.

YOUNG SCIENTIST

How many earthquakes have been recorded in the last seven days in the world/on your continent/in your country? What would be the consequences of a major eruption (seven on the VEI scale)?

CONNECTING TO MATHS

- using the Volcanic Explosivity Index (VEI) to predict when the next level-six and level-seven eruptions are likely to occur
- measuring the frequency of VEI level-four and level-five eruptions over the last 3000 years

CONNECTING ART AND SCIENCE

- students draw before, during and after eruption pictures
- studying Pompeii murals (content, style, preservation needs)
- building a model of a volcano and presenting it

Writing chains (provide the skeleton for a writing assignment)

Verb chain	Verb chain	Noun chain	Idea chain
build up	fall	destruction	ERUPTION
burn	feel	escape	
crack	give up	fissures	personal stories
crumble	panic	heat	ways of escape
drop	run (out)	lava fountain	obstacles
flow	scream	magma	mistakes
rumble	shudder	pressure	rebuilding of lives
shake	wake up	pyroclastic flows	
spew		vulcanologist	

Core CLIL features focused on during week one in secondary school

The following chart shows all the core features of CLIL. Those features that were applied during the above activities are highlighted.

Multiple focus	Safe and enriching environment	Authenticity
• language learning in non-language classes • content acquisition in language classes • integrating several subjects • cross-curricular themes/projects • reflection on the learning process	• using routine activities • displaying language and content • building student confidence • using learning centres • accessing authentic materials/environments • student awareness of and growth in language	• students indicating language needs • accommodating student interests • connecting learning and the students' lives • connecting with speakers of the CLIL language • using current materials
Active learning	Scaffolding	Co-operation
• students communicating more than the teacher • students help set learning outcomes • students evaluate progress in meeting learning outcomes • favouring peer co-operative work • negotiating meaning • teachers acting as facilitators	• building on a student's existing knowledge, skills, attitudes, interests and experience • repackaging information in user-friendly ways • responding to different learning styles • fostering creative and critical thinking • challenging students to take another step forward	• planning lessons in co-operation with CLIL and non-CLIL teachers • involving parents • involving the local community and authorities

Guiding principles focused on during week one

COGNITION
- content, language and learning skills outcomes are articulated in co-operation with students
- learning builds on a student's existing knowledge, skills, attitudes, interests and experience
- students analyse achievement of learning outcomes independently, with other students and with the teacher, and work to set new outcomes
- students can synthesize, evaluate and apply knowledge and skills acquired in several subjects

Community
- students feel that being members of a learning community is enriching
- students have the self-confidence and skills to work within a group and the local community, balancing personal interests with those of others
- parents, teachers and students are partners in education
- students can define their role within the classroom, the local and the global context

Content
- content is clearly linked to the community within and outside of the classroom
- students apply new content and develop related skills through experiential activities
- content is substantive without being overwhelming
- content from various subjects is integrated
- cultural content is integrated into all subjects

Communication
- students actively use the right to participate in activities and communication, in the classroom and in the community
- desk placement and displays on classroom walls and other available resources support learning and communication
- students and teachers co-construct and negotiate meaning
- language/communication skills are developed in all subjects

A week in the life of a vocational education CLIL teacher – getting started

We recommend the same framework for the first session with vocational students that is proposed on pages 47 to 50. However, some considerations that are often particular to CLIL vocational students follow.

Name game adaptations for vocational students

The *Find someone who ...* exercise (see page 47) can be adapted for vocational students by linking it to the subject (eg, *find someone who wants to be a mechanic, or someone who wants to invent a special cocktail or pastry*).

The Name Game # 2 exercise (see page 47) can be adapted by having students use words related to the field of study that start with the same sound as a word related to the branch they are studying. For example: *cook Carla* or *Carla cook*, *Bob bytes* or *bytes Bob*, *Ichiro insulin*, *agar Alex*, *engine Emily*, *electricity Ernesto*, *Boo Bacon* or *Ousmane outcrop*.

Vocational students tend to be more focused on the practical benefits to be gained from the programme. Brainstorming potential long-term benefits, watching and discussing related videos, receiving former students who use languages in the workplace and receiving an employer in class are all ways of helping students to gain a greater understanding of the benefits of CLIL. Language is a tool for professional advancement and the payoffs are manifold. Personal testimonies and specific examples are likely to best assist students in developing this understanding.

As fluency may seem too distant a goal for these students, it is wise also to explore during the first session how even a limited amount of language knowledge for special purposes can help open doors. Moreover, learning in a second language can actually facilitate comprehension because learners have to work harder at understanding and articulating the essence of what is being taught/learnt. This forces them to be more precise and organized in their communication.

In upper vocational streams, students are often older than secondary students, some are even mature adults. Their reason for choosing a vocational education programme is based on a personal decision to follow a certain career path. Some vocational students already have work experience. Moreover, many vocational CLIL programmes include a practicum or work placement where both the language and vocational content skills, as well as learning skills, are applied and further developed. These factors all help to create a favourable climate for CLIL.

Nonetheless, some students may consider themselves less able than those in more academically inclined streams. The students may not be fully confident in their ability to succeed and could be easily discouraged when they are faced with a difficult challenge. One of the main objectives of vocational teachers during the first weeks of a CLIL course is to instil self-confidence in the students and a hunger to learn language. This is best done by ensuring that students get to experience success and still feel intellectually challenged.

Empowering students to recognize and point out their learning needs will help you to keep them on the road to success. For example, encouraging students to know when and how to interrupt in order to ask for repetition and clarification supports students taking charge of their own learning. They will also benefit from hearing how you intend to provide them with ongoing feedback and support. Also, transparent evaluation criteria and marking schemes are of particular importance for vocational students. These help a student to understand the path that needs to be followed, the criteria that need to be met and how to measure progress.

Getting to the content

As an example of how to proceed we will look at how to prevent occupational risks, as taught in Spain. However, first we share a view from a highly experienced teacher who recently began teaching in a CLIL programme.

View from the field ④

Frankly, CLIL scares me

That's how I felt when I started with CLIL. I know I'm a good teacher. My students were successful. I felt my students and colleagues respected me. I have always actively participated in professional development programmes and been willing to try new things. Yet, when I was faced with starting CLIL and having to do a bit of a rethink, and to change several of my practices, it undermined my confidence. It made me feel anxious and incompetent, as if what I had done before was not good enough. No one actually said it, but that is what I felt.

Initially, I felt a little lost. I wasn't sure whether I'd found the right balance, whether I should do less or more groupwork, and so on. I was afraid we wouldn't cover the curriculum. I was upfront with the students about my nervousness and asked for lots of feedback. They really seemed to like the variety and trying new methods. I think we developed a more respectful and more relaxed relationship. They helped me to relax by letting me know what worked for them and what didn't. They really seemed to appreciate the effort I was going to.

For me, the principal made all the difference. He started citing me to others as an example of an experienced teacher who is taking some real risks, trying new things and moving out of my comfort zone. He said that is exactly what we want our students to do and having teachers model that behaviour was likely the best any of us could do. He built my confidence. It turned out that the head teacher considered the showing of weakness and fear, coupled with risk-taking, to be a strength.

Guillermo Narbona*

* Some names have been changed at the teacher's request.

Day 1

If it is possible to be in class prior to the start of the lesson you can welcome students individually. If you recall their names from the introductory session, it would be good to use them and if you have forgotten a name to have the student remind you. These first few minutes are an opportunity to begin to connect with students and make them feel at ease using the CLIL language for simple chitchat.

Activity 1: Warm-up/Setting the stage (10 minutes)

Students will arrive with their own understanding of how lessons should be conducted. Many may expect to be listening to lectures and taking notes. They may expect that school is, above all, about receiving and retaining information. They may be surprised by the warm-up exercise we suggest. You can tell them that business and sports coaches use this technique before a training session or a game to get groups into a frame of mind for action. At the same time, it may be worth saying that the following exercise is to remind us of people's names, to begin to use the CLIL language, to determine your goal for the class and to introduce the topic of accidents in the workplace.

Have each student take a sheet of paper. In the centre, the students print their names in large block letters. In the upper left-hand corner, they complete the sentence: *I like …* In the upper right-hand corner, they complete the sentence: *I learn best when …* In the lower left-hand corner: *We had an accident in our home when …* and in the lower right-hand corner: *In this class, I want to …* Students pin or tape the sheet of paper somewhere on their body. Let them know that you will be testing them (not for marks) to see who remembers what. Students are asked to get up and walk around and learn as much as they can about the others. They are welcome to ask follow-up questions. By participating in the activity you can demonstrate your interest in the students and help model the importance of making verbal contact with each person.

The WHY

This is a way of getting everyone speaking the CLIL language in a low-threat situation. It establishes a participatory dynamic from the outset. It reinforces the importance of learning and using classmates' names. It introduces the hazard prevention topic. It helps access existing knowledge. It helps students focus on their learning goals for the class. It opens the floor for discussing learning skills. It helps you to get to know your students.

After a few minutes, have the students sit in a circle or simply at their desks and go through a debrief. *Who can tell me the name of that person wearing the green dress? Who was the person who likes classical music? Can you show us who Fizza is? Who are some of your favourite composers or singers, Fizza? Can anyone remember what Marco wants to accomplish in this class? What accident occurred in Saleem's home? Why do you think this happened? How could it have been prevented? Did anyone learn something surprising, and if so, what?*

Activity 2: Learning outcomes (7 minutes)

Use the following graphic organizer to summarize the focus of this week's lessons. In addition to showing the organizer, speak about each section, ask some simple questions and ensure that students understand any new vocabulary. The visual representation helps students to understand what will be happening during the week. It indicates that there will be language support. This organizer can also be used to access some of the students' existing knowledge. The graphic organizer and the questions will contribute to building the students' sense of security – the belief that they can cope with this work.

What this unit is about.

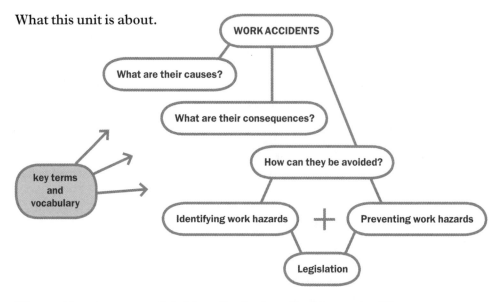

The week's outcomes are listed here for the benefit of the reader. These were covered with the students through the presentation of the graphic organizer. Presenting these written statements to the students as well would probably be overwhelming. However, these should be posted in the room.

Week one learning outcomes for students

Content
- can articulate the consequences of risks and accidents in workers' lives
- can articulate the effects of work accidents on society
- can articulate how prevention measures can minimize occupational risks and accidents
- can articulate occupational risks, prevention measures and elements of personal protection
- can describe the legislative framework aimed at creating a safe working environment

Language
- actively use the opportunity to communicate in the CLIL language, even if only partially
- can correctly use key vocabulary related to occupational hazards and their prevention

Learning skills
- know when and how to interrupt and to ask for repetition and clarification

Before discussing the day's outcomes in detail, ask the students to turn to the person next to them and say which part of this week's plan as indicated seems the easiest and which part seems the hardest. As you point to each part of the graphic organizer, ask people to raise their hands to indicate whether partners thought any given point of the upcoming week is going to be the hardest or the easiest. Legislation is usually the biggest concern. Let the students know you understand that and that much of the week will be spent helping them to master this aspect of the topic.

The following outcomes for the day are shown and discussed with the students.

Student outcomes for this class

Content
- can articulate existing knowledge about work accidents
- can identify work accident causes and consequences

Language
- actively use the opportunity to communicate in the CLIL language, even if only partially

Learning skills
- know when and how to interrupt and to ask for repetition and clarification

In future weeks, you can set language goals based on the needs that become apparent when students communicate. You work to remove obstacles to communication by teaching the missing pieces of language. You build scaffolding to ensure students have the language they need to understand and use content.

For example, if, as you are teaching biochemical typing, you notice that students do not know how to use adjectives to describe colour changes, an impromptu mini-lesson on how to use compound adjectives (*bluish purple, brownish green*) is in order. When presenting a new topic, you check for new vocabulary and expressions that students do not know and either teach the needed language or help students to explore/deduce meaning. You present instructions in writing and orally.

In future weeks as you plan lessons together with the other teachers, you can stress a lexical or grammatical point that is at the focus of the language lessons. In turn, the language teacher who is working to teach those lexical points can use material that reflects the vocabulary needed in content subjects.

Activity 3: Setting the stage – relevance (2 minutes)

Have each student individually estimate in writing:

a) the number of work-related deaths worldwide last year;

b) the number of work-related deaths in the European Union (or your region) last year;

c) the extent to which 18 to 24 year olds are more likely than older workers to have a non-fatal accident in the workplace.

Share the answers. They are a) 2 million b) 150 000 c) 50 per cent. ⋆

Activity 4: Accessing existing knowledge (15 minutes)

Ask students to give you the rules for brainstorming. At the very least, they usually include the following: no criticism of any ideas, all ideas recorded, wild and crazy ideas welcome. These rules are posted as they are agreed upon.

Have the students in three groups brainstorm the causes of workplace accidents. They list as many causes as they can in the left-hand column of the following handout, leaving the other columns blank.

WORKPLACE ACCIDENTS			
Causes			

one standard sheet of paper with space for about ten causes

⋆ http://osha.europa.eu/

Once the list of causes has been developed, have the students fill in the titles for the other three columns as follows:

WORKPLACE ACCIDENTS			
Causes	Negative consequences (worker, family, company, employer)	Positive consequences (if any)	Prevention measures

The students then work in the three groups to think through consequences and prevention measures using the above grid. One group shares its results. The other two groups get to add any additional ideas they have to the first group's work. If you have the option of using computers, the results can be projected on a screen and revised or added to as need be. If students have written their thoughts directly on the board, the same can be done on the board. Have students mark off any points they are not sure are true. These points in question are returned to on the fifth day to see if the students' doubts have disappeared.

Hold the horses! Stop the show!

Q: Where are the lectures? Surely, in vocational education, one needs to lecture?

A: We are not saying do not lecture. Lecturing can be very effective, especially if it is part of an interactive process where students are heavily involved in processing, commenting on or using the information being delivered. Lecturing can work well for students with an aural learning style. However, lecturing does not suit all students and can be easily overused or less effective than one would hope. For example, even very appropriate teacher-talk can deliver material at least 20 times faster than it can be learnt (Petty, 2006). Teacher output does not necessarily translate into student intake, let alone student output.

Vast amounts of educational research have been synthesized by researchers such as Marzano et al (2005) and Hattie et al as referred to by Petty (2006). They show that reduced teacher talk and increased student talk and active student participation can bring big returns. These researchers conclude that the use of advance organizers and graphic organizers, peer co-operative work, students teaching one another, active learning, challenging goals, peer assessment and interactive teaching, among other techniques, can contribute very significantly to learning.

The very nature of CLIL requires the application of many of those techniques. CLIL teachers often present material in highly organized small chunks, while providing language support. CLIL educators are always checking for student comprehension. The successful application of new learning is perhaps the best indicator of comprehension. When teaching in a student's first language, educators may feel less obligated to present material so carefully and to check so thoroughly for comprehension. This can give CLIL students an edge.

We can all benefit by expanding our repertoire of techniques that are known to be highly effective.

Activity 4: Reading and analysing charts/Writing and presenting summaries (27 minutes)

Have the students imagine that their boss is asking them to write a short summary of a table about workplace accidents. He or she is interested in comparing historical data from 2003. Look at Table 1 (see following page) together as a class. This will help build the students' confidence in their ability to do the assignment. Ask whether there are any conclusions that someone can draw from the table.

Look at the first column of Table 1 (indicating through gesture as well.) *It is entitled 'Rate of fatal injury'. What does 'fatal' mean? Find Great Britain and Portugal. What can you say about the rate of fatal injury in Portugal in comparison to the rate of fatal injury in Great Britain?* Writing the answers on the board will help students to use the sentences as models later on.

The students work in groups of four or five. As this is the first attempt to do this type of assignment, we suggest having each group only work on one table. (Later in the term, students can compare two tables.) Give the students the following handout. The handout supports students by summarizing the instructions and by providing a structure for the summary with some of the criteria for writing and presentation. It also provides some useful phrases. The phrases include a few visual clues. Work through this handout together, asking questions to ensure comprehension.

Guide for writing summaries of tables on workplace injuries

Process and presentation

1 writing a summary with your group

2 assessing your group's results by comparing with those of another group, looking for improvement ideas

3 each group member presents part of the work to the whole class

4 one clean copy given to teacher

Possible structure

- what the chart is about in general
- key facts
- key conclusions

Length

- two sentences for introduction
- five to seven sentences for key facts
- two sentences for conclusion

Helpful phrases

- the number of accidents per 100 000 workers
- the death rate per 100 000 workers
- the greatest number of/the smallest number of
- compared to the EU average
- data for 1964 showed that …
- has more than twice (2x) the number
- has more than three times the number
- considerably fewer
- below the EU average/above the EU average
- from 1999 to 2003
- in decline/on the rise
- in comparison to this year
- the number of accidents per year is on the rise/declining
- there is a downward/upward trend

Table 1 – Rates of fatal and of over-3-day injury[a] in Europe per 100,000 workers or employees, 2003

Country	Rate of fatal injury	Rate of over-3-day injury	Employed people covered
Great Britain [b]	1.1	1,614	workers
Sweden	1.2	1,252	workers
Denmark [b]	1.8	2,443	workers
Finland	1.9	2,847	employees
Netherlands [b]	2.0	1,188	employees
Germany	2.3	3,674	workers
Belgium	2.4	3,456	employees
EU Average	2.5	3,334	
Italy	2.8	3,267	workers
France	2.8	4,689	employees
Greece	3.0	2,090	employees
Ireland [b]	3.2	1,262	workers
Luxembourg	3.2	5,033	workers
Spain	3.7	6,520	employees
Austria	4.8	2,629	employees
Portugal	7.6	4,054	employees

Notes

a Eurostat excludes commuting accidents. Eurostat excluded transport industry accidents and road traffic accidents from rates of fatal injury but included them in rates of non-fatal over-3-day injury where the effect of their inclusion is relatively small. All rates of injury are based on nine branches of industry: agriculture (including hunting and forestry), manufacturing, utilities, construction, retail and wholesale distribution, hotels and restaurants, transport, financial services and real estate activities. Deaths are 'immediate' and exclude those that occur up to a year later.

b The over-3-day injury rate in these four member states are derived from the Labour Force Survey. Injury rates in other member states are based on claims made through insurance and/or other social security systems.

Table 2 – Rates of fatal injury in Great Britain, Germany, France, Italy, Spain and EU average, 1999–2003

Year	Great Britain	Germany	France	Italy	Spain	EU average
1999	1.4	2.4	3.4	3.4	5.0	2.9
2000	1.7	2.1	3.4	3.3	4.7	2.8
2001	1.5	2.0	3.2	3.1	4.4	2.7
2002	1.4	2.5	2.6	2.1	4.3	2.5
2003	1.1	2.3	2.8	2.8	3.7	2.5

Notes Rates of fatal injury are expressed per 100,000 employees in France, workers in Britain, workers in Italy, and insured workers in Germany.

Table 3 – Rates of over-3-day injury in Great Britain, Germany, France, Italy, Spain and EU average, 1999–2003

Year	Great Britain	Germany	France	Italy	Spain	EU average
1999	1,606	4,908	4,991	4,067	7,027	4,088
2000	1,607	4,757	5,030	4,049	7,052	4,016
2001	1,665	4,380	4,819	3,779	6,917	3,841
2002	1,632	4,082	4,887	3,387	6,728	3,529
2003	1,614	3,674	4,689	3,267	6,520	3,334

Notes Work-related road traffic accidents are excluded from rates of non-fatal injury for Great Britain but are included for the other member states.

Before the groups present their material, ask the students to help each other during the presentation by listening quietly, concentrating on what is being said, asking people who cannot be heard to speak up and thinking about what general conclusions can be drawn.

As a follow up, students can seek more current data. The more current statistics can be compared with the historical data presented in this chapter. Conclusions can be drawn about trends and measures needed. Drawing comparisons will help make the exercise more relevant.

Activity 5: Thumbometer (3 minutes)

This is a quick and simple way of getting feedback during or after any given activity, assignment or lesson. It is proposed by Paul Ginnis in *The Teacher's Toolkit*. Students stick out one arm with a clenched fist with the thumb pointing out. The thumb acts as a gauge. When it is pointing up, a student is saying that he or she is pleased with an activity or that he or she understands the topic at hand. As the thumb is turned downwards, it indicates lower levels of satisfaction or understanding. When the thumb is pointing straight down, there is a serious lack of satisfaction or a total lack of understanding.

To evaluate today's outcomes you repeat each outcome, preferably also showing the text. The students can gauge the extent to which each outcome has been achieved. You will need to verbalize what you think the average student is saying with their thumb and draw the necessary conclusions. If you get a thumbs-down for one outcome, it probably requires some discussion and joint decisions.

Day 2

Many employers in South Africa consider people coming from the northern province of Natal to often be excellent managers. They are inclusive of others and good listeners. When people from the northern Natal meet, they say *Sawu bona*. It means *I see you*. The other person responds *Sikhona*, which means *I am here*. In other words, I exist because you see me and acknowledge my existence (Senge et al, 1994).

As managers of a class, we often are so busy just before a class preparing our materials that we neglect to greet students individually. We sometimes do not even find the time to make rapid eye contact with each individual student at the start of the class. Students that feel welcome will be better prepared to learn. A positive classroom culture will have a positive impact on learning. Moreover, if informal talk before a class becomes part of the classroom culture, students will start showing up early and the number of latecomers will diminish.

Activity 1: Warm-up/Setting the stage (10 minutes)

As the students walk in, have several pictures depicting different workplaces scattered on the desks. Have some key words written on the front (or back) of the photos such as *wearing a harness, wearing a mask, sharpening a knife*.

The pictures will help the students to focus on the upcoming lesson. The pictures will probably elicit informal discussion before the official start of the class. The words written on the photos will help provide students with vital bits of language.

Begin with a few minutes of general discussion as a class: *Class, imagine you are the boss in this workplace in the photo. Is there some aspect of work safety that you would like to improve? If so, which aspect?*

Either using the same photos or projecting one photo on the screen, have the students, on an individual basis, fill in the following chart. It could be provided on standard-sized paper. Let them know they have three minutes and that you can provide language help. Circulate to show your availability. Write any expression a student needs on the board.

THE SAFETY PERSPECTIVE	
What is being done well? (correct behaviours/preventative measures)	Potential risks

An example of a picture could be:

After three minutes, ask the students to compare their results with those of the student next to them. Ask a few students what their partner noticed about safe work procedures or risks.

Activity 2: Learning outcomes (3–5 minutes)

Reshow the graphic organizer you used the previous day. The graphic organizer will serve to recall the previous day's learning. It can also be used to build a sense of continuity/linearity in the learning process. Then, discuss the envisaged outcomes for this class.

Student outcomes for this class

Content
- can articulate existing knowledge about work hazards
- can identify obligations related to the prevention of work hazards
- can differentiate work accidents from work hazards and establish a link between both concepts

Language
- actively use the opportunity to communicate in the CLIL language, even if only partially
- can correctly use key vocabulary related to occupational hazards and their prevention

Learning skills
- know when and how to interrupt and to ask for repetition and clarification

Activity 3: Reading text about prevention of risks at work and doing related assignments (25 minutes)

PREVENTION OF RISKS AT WORK

Introduction

Better safe than sorry is not a cliché, but a proven truth. The prevention of occupational hazards requires a commitment on the part of the company and employees. The commitment is to the health of the employees. This will bring benefits to all – employees, employers, the company and society as a whole.

Any system of management for prevention of occupational hazards aims to ensure the health and safety of employees and workers. It must take into account laws and regulations. In Spain, we have a Law on the Prevention of Occupational Hazards. The Standards for Prevention contained in this law must be complied with by all companies. Companies need to ensure that all the workers (full-time, part-time, subcontracted, self-employed, etc) are aware of these standards.

All companies, as well as their personnel, must use safe working methods. Workers must not incur (face) any unnecessary risks. Companies and personnel in charge of machinery and equipment will take responsibility for verifying their working order at regular, set periods of time. Companies have to ensure that all employees using machinery and equipment are properly trained and have the appropriate information. Workers must never modify or withdraw the protection systems on machines or equipment.

What the students do

Students work in pairs to cross out, at least, 50 per cent of the text leaving the bare facts, the most essential information. They eliminate all repetition. They create a précis.

After completing the task, each pair compares its results with those of another two students.

Why

This is a highly challenging task. It requires that the entire text be read closely and that key messages be determined. Students doing a précis are more likely to understand and recall more information than those who have simply read a text and answered a few questions.

Those in charge of subordinates will be held responsible for their safety. Managers must make certain that the people reporting to them have received adequate information to work safely.

Personnel must use the personal protection equipment provided by the company and be responsible for its maintenance and proper use.

1. Safety regulations
1.0 General standards
Reporting

All workers must report all dangerous situations that they detect during work to their immediate superiors.

Order and cleanliness

These must be maintained in order to prevent accidents.

Inspecting first

Before working for the first time in an area, it must be inspected and studied properly.

Cleaning up

Once the job is finished, all tools, materials and residues must be removed.

No unauthorized use

Those workers not properly authorized and trained must not use machinery, equipment or electrical panels, cables or connections.

Respecting rules

Danger warnings, prohibitions and obligations must be respected at all times.

Using safety devices

Machine and equipment safety devices must never be switched off.

Using protective equipment

Workers carrying out tasks requiring individual protective equipment must use it.

No alcohol or drugs

The consumption of alcoholic drinks and drugs on company premises is expressly prohibited.

Not moving safety equipment

It is prohibited to move fire extinguishers, hoses, alarms, fire

What you, the teacher, do

- find the authentic material and make it more accessible (see page 84)

- explain the task prior to handing out the text

- work through two paragraphs with the class. These two paragraphs can already be on the board, projected on a screen or distributed as a separate handout. Working through the paragraphs involves asking probing questions and having students explain their reasoning: *Is there any repetition in the first paragraph? Which part of the repetition would you cross out and why? What sort of information is essential? Was any essential information lost?*

- hand out the full text. The first two paragraphs are done for the students and will serve as a sample.

- explain the task again, showing where the instructions are posted

- circulate to provide support, primarily through asking questions that help students take another step forward: *Is there still some repetition of ideas in this paragraph?*

- partway through the task, interrupt the students to 'Split the atom' (see following page)

- upon completion of pairwork, have the pairs compare results. Pairs could rework 20 lines of text to come up with a common result.

- the exercise can be taken up and discussed with the whole class: *Does anyone have a different opinion? Why do you think so?*

hydrants, emergency lights, emergency exits and to block or cover signs for the same (for the aforementioned things).

Removing toxic residues

All residues toxic to people or the environment (paint, varnishes, solvents and their containers) must be removed by the companies who have used them.

Toxic materials

Must never be dumped in the drainage system of the company.

Stopping dangerous work

The staff must ensure the application of the safety regulations. Staff are authorized to stop any work they consider hazardous that is being carried out by company or non-company workers on the company premises.

Planning for safety

The company must have a plan for self-protection. The plan details actions to be undertaken in emergency situations. The company's staff are responsible for providing company and non-company workers with information and advice on what to do during emergencies.

Co-operation

All non-company workers must collaborate with the staff of the company and follow their instructions.

1.1 Personal protection

Keeping safety equipment in peak condition

Safety equipment must be kept in perfect condition. In case of damage, replacement of equipment must be requested.

Respecting clothing requirements

Working clothes must be properly buttoned and without tears. There must be no loose or hanging parts than can get caught or hooked. Working with clothes that are stained with grease, oil, solvents, etc is prohibited.

Using protective glasses

Eye protection must be used when carrying out or looking at tasks ejecting solid or liquid particles, or emitting hazardous gases, sparks, etc.

Using helmets

Helmets must be used when there is risk of falling objects and materials. It is advisable to wear a helmet at all times during the working day.

Splitting the atom

This activity is a key that helps unlock students' feelings about what they are doing. Feelings can both empower or disempower us all. This activity enables participants to identify and address feelings that may be obstacles to learning. Halfway through the précis exercise, ask for the class's attention: *Let's assess how we are feeling about this exercise. Those people who feel this exercise is like taking a walk on the beach on a beautiful Saturday afternoon go and stand by the door. Those people who feel like they are climbing a hill go to the window. Those who feel like they are trying to climb out of a hole go to the back of the room.*

If the class is finding the exercise difficult there are several options. Those that are confident can be asked to work with those who are feeling less secure. You can also work through a few more sentences as a class.

Other options

Students can work in pairs to develop:

- a safety plan;
- a safety brochure;
- a display on work safety.

These options would include first giving the students the grid to be used for evaluating the final result.

Using shoes

Workers involved in setting up and dismantling must use safety shoes with reinforced toes and rubber soles with adequate grip and without fittings, to avoid slipping and electrical contact.

Using gloves

Safety gloves must be worn for all tasks where hands might be damaged. For work involving possible electrical hazards, suitably insulated gloves must be worn.

Using safety belts

The use of safety belts with shock absorbers is compulsory for all work not protected by scaffolding, railings, platforms, etc. In general, safety belts must be used to carry out any kind of work at a height over 3.5 m and must be properly secured.

Using masks and filters

Masks, filters or respiratory equipment must be worn to carry out tasks involving risk of breathing dust, gases, vapours or any hazardous substance.

Using ear protectors

Ear protectors must be used in all tasks with potentially hazardous sound levels.

Making the text accessible

- sentences have been shortened
- long paragraphs have been broken in two or three
- additional subheadings were created (see underlined subheadings)
- synonyms were placed in brackets after unfamiliar words or expressions

Activity 4: (Back-up)

In the unlikely event that you have time left over, the students can use this graphic organizer to categorize which of the safety regulations in the text would apply to which category of hazard prevention strategy.

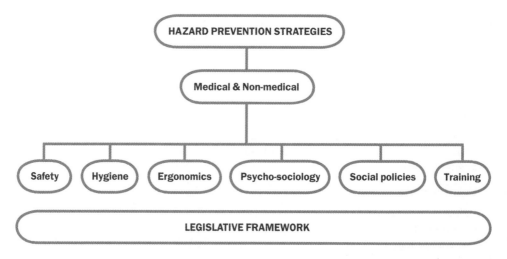

Activity 5: Achievement barometer (3 minutes)

You point to the board where you have written:

achieved

partly achieved

far from achieved

You return to the posted learning outcomes for the day, asking students whether each outcome was achieved, partly achieved or far from achieved. Relevant conclusions are drawn.

Day 3

Warm-up: (3 minutes)

Prior to the students' arrival in class, place the language support sheet (see below) on the students' desks. (If this is not possible, distribute it at the start of the class.) The sheet is provided to students to guide them in learning needed vocabulary. The sheet shows the students which words are high frequency and need to be retained. By categorizing words (similar parts of speech, antonyms, words describing procedures or attitudes), learning and recall are facilitated. When creating your own sheet, some particularly difficult expressions could be translated into the first language.

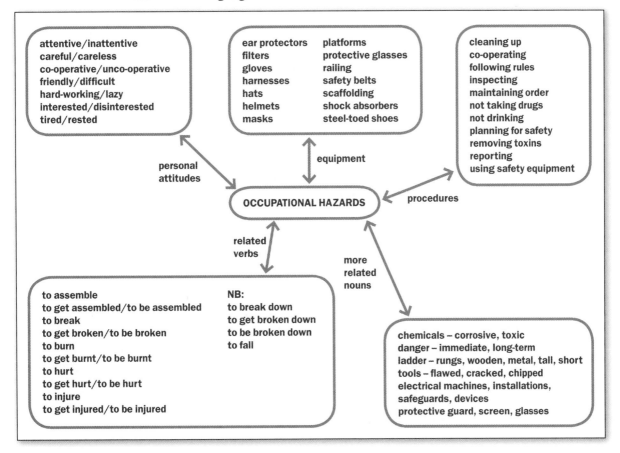

After taking time to greet students, ask them if anyone has noticed an accident waiting to happen over the last 24 hours. This may require more prompts such as: *Did anyone see someone driving dangerously, something at home in the kitchen, the way someone behaves at the gym, something you saw at work, some carelessness?*

If someone has trouble finding a word or expression in the CLIL language, if it is on the language support sheet, refer the student to it. If it is not on the sheet, give it to the students and have them add it. This will help build the habit of checking and building on the language support sheets.

Activity 2: Outcomes (5 minutes)

The following outcomes are discussed with the students. The lesson is a continuation of yesterday's lesson, using a continuation of the same text.

Student outcomes for this class

Content
- can articulate existing knowledge about work hazards
- can identify additional obligations related to the prevention of work hazards

Language
- actively use the opportunity to communicate in the CLIL language, even if only partially
- can correctly use key vocabulary related to occupational hazards and their prevention

Learning skills
- know when and how to interrupt and to ask for repetition and clarification

---

Activity 3: Setting the stage (10 minutes)

Watch a short film clip or two on workplace risks and accidents. These are easily downloaded from the Internet by searching YouTube™ or one of the general Internet search engines for:

- *safety in the workplace;*
- *occupational health and safety specialists' job description;*
- *accidents in the working place;*
- *occupational/labour risks.*

Students can be given a series of multiple-choice questions to look at prior to viewing the film. The questions can be answered while watching the film. As another option, students can be asked to list, in writing, risks that are shown or discussed in the film clips. After watching the film the students correct the answers to the multiple-choice questions. As you discuss what the students noticed, two students can write the main messages on the board, on chart paper or key them into a computer. Two students can be assigned the task of quietly correcting language errors. Ask the students to create a few summary statements.

Finish by asking students to recall from the work they did two days ago how many workers/employees in Spain:

- are injured per year;
- suffer a fatal injury/die.

You can also ask how many are blinded and how many are crippled in your own country, and provide the answers yourself right away. It helps, once again, to tie the topic to reality.

Activity 4: Reflection (25 minutes)

PREVENTION OF RISKS AT WORK (CONTINUED FROM YESTERDAY)

1.2 Working at heights/Scaffolding and platforms

Heights

People suffering from vertigo** must not carry out (do) work at height.

All those working at height must use a tool-belt.

When working at height, tools or material must not be thrown. They must be handed or passed using a rope or a container.

Assembly or dismantling**

Working platforms must have a minimum width of 60 cm.

Assembling or dismantling must be carried out (done) with maximum levels of safety, and the fixing of pieces to their definitive place will be made, if possible, before loosening them from supporting cables or ropes.

> **
> **vertigo**
> feeling dizzy, as though your head is spinning
>
> **to dismantle**
> to take apart
> …

Scaffolding must be firm and stable, set up by trained staff and have a banister, braces, railing and plinth base**.

The different levels and guard boards of the working platforms must be slip-proof, kept free of obstacles and provided with a draining system to eliminate all products capable of causing slipping.

Platforms with potential falls from over 2 m must be completely surrounded by railings and a plinth base.

The stairs to access the platforms must be placed laterally to the structure and never at the corners.

Checking before starting work

Prior to starting work, scaffolding or platforms must be checked to ensure that they are in perfect condition. Any anomaly** must be reported to a superior.

Before beginning work on wheeled scaffolding, the wheels must be locked.

SCAFFOLDING

Making text accessible

Provide a separate sheet with key terms organized in a way as to facilitate comprehension.

New vocabulary explained in boxes is inserted into the margins of each page, eg,

**

vertigo
feeling dizzy, as though your head is spinning

to dismantle
to take apart, to take to pieces

plinth base
a block or slab which acts as a base, stabilizing a structure

The underlined subheadings were added to the original for clarity.

Some sentences were shifted to a more logical place.

Long sentences were broken into two.

Some repetition was removed.

Usage of tools or materials

Only the necessary material to guarantee the continuity of the works must be stored on scaffolding and platforms in order not to overload them and keep the space clear.

Tools, utensils and materials used on the working platform must be placed in containers, minimizing the risk of fall.

> ★★
> **anomaly**
> something unusual, not normal
> …

Work procedures

It is forbidden for workers to be at different levels on the same vertical (in the same column).

No worker must be on the scaffolding when it is being moved.

When scaffolding is being used to access working platforms at a height of 3.5 m or more, a safety belt, harness or alternative protective measures must be used.

When carrying out work on mobile platforms, safety devices to prevent them from moving or falling must be used.

1.3 Portable ladders

Checking before starting work

Ladders must be inspected before beginning work, discarding those not offering sufficient guarantees of safety. The ladder must be made of one piece, and the rungs must be assembled and not merely nailed.

Before going up or down a ladder, workers must ensure all rungs are firmly in place.

Physical requirements

Ladders must have an anti-slip base, or securing devices at the top.

Wooden ladders must not be painted (except with a transparent varnish), as paint may hide flaws or anomalies which may be dangerous.

Procedures

Workers must face the ladder when using it.

Workers must carry out their tasks facing the ladder and holding it with one hand. Should this not be possible, they must use a safety belt secured to a fixed point, never to the ladder.

It is prohibited to connect two ladders.

Ladders must not be simultaneously used by two people.

What you, the teacher, do

Have students work in four groups. No more than five students in a group. The groups are called the:

- cookery sector group;
- building & construction group;
- aircraft maintenance group;
- ICT components manufacturing group.

If necessary, form two groups with the same name, distinguishing them by simply saying *cookery group one and two*.

Present instructions orally and post them (see below).

Posted instructions

These support students who are visual learners and those that are having trouble understanding everything being said.

- *read individually*
- *individually, mark with a star legal obligations unique to your sector*
- *individually, circle obligations common to all four sectors*
  - *cookery*
  - *building and construction*
  - *aircraft maintenance*
  - *ICT components manufacturing*
- *fill out the graphic organizer in a group*

Storage

When ladders are not being used, they must be stored away and protected from the sun and rain. They must never be left horizontally placed on the floor.

1.4 Tools

Choosing the right tools

Only tools suitable for each specific task must be used.

Inspecting first

Tools must be carefully inspected by the users prior to use, discarding those presenting flaws** and reporting them to an immediate superior.

To avoid the use of tools in poor condition, they must be labelled, indicating any flaws.

> **
> **flaw**
> a mistake or fault in something that makes it less effective
> …

Standards

Electricians' tools must comply with legislated standards.

Tools with handles must have suitable dimensions and be well secured without cracks or chips, and must, when necessary, have insulating material.

Maintenance

Tools must be kept clean of oil and grease.

Cutting or sharp tools must be kept suitably sharpened, never carried in pockets or loose within toolboxes, but always in their cases or special containers.

1.5 Machines

Key messages

Portable machines must always be kept in perfect working order. Neglect in this regard might be fatal.

Set-up

Compulsory protection for fixed grinding machines are: a protective screen for the observation of work; a protective guard covering ¾ of the grinding wheel; the machine must be secured to the ground at the same level as the axis or above it, with a maximum distance from the periphery to the grinding wheel of 3 mm.

What the students do

1) Individually read the text.

2) Individually, mark with a star, in pencil, legal obligations that are unique to the student's group/sector that was determined at the start of the activity.

3) Individually, circle legal obligations that are common to all four sectors established for the groups at the start of the class.

4) Individually, refer to the language support sheet as needed.

5) Once finished, share results with the other group members.

6) With the group, fill out the graphic organizer (follows).

Classroom management

Students evaluate groupwork dynamics, such as the equal sharing of workload.

Core features addressed

Multiple focus on content, language and learning skills by using language support and graphic organizers.

Building the learning environment by displaying needed language and providing a supplementary handout.

Authenticity ensured by taking texts currently used in industry.

Active learning through peer co-operative work, including by assessing one's own work against that of others.

Scaffolding provided through language support, including subheadings, graphic organizers and by providing peer feedback and support in completing the assignment.

Inspecting first

Prior to any work with a portable machine, its condition must be checked. Any detected anomaly must be reported to an immediate superior.

Before drilling, it must be checked that there are no cables or obstacles in the work area that might cause accidents when operating with the drill bit.

Working procedures

Pneumatic** machines must not be disconnected from their hoses or valves without first shutting down the feed and allowing the air to escape from the tool itself. The hose must not be bent to interrupt the airflow, except in cases of emergency.

> **
> **pneumatic**
> works using
> compressed air
> …

Riveting machines and similar pneumatic tools must always be used with the head or tool bit downwards when not in operation. After use, the tool bit or head must be removed from the machine.

It is forbidden to adjust the securing of the appliance when the grinding disk is working.

Side faces of the grinding wheel must never be used to sharpen tools.

Small items must be held with a clamp or pliers when grinding.

Standardized protective glasses must be worn when working on a fixed grinding machine.

Portable grinding machines must have a metallic protector and the operator must wear protective glasses or a face-guard at all times.

1.6 Prevention of electrical risks

Inspecting first

Before using an electrical apparatus or installation, check that it is in perfect working condition, comply with precautions to be adopted and respect them scrupulously**.

Before connecting an electrical apparatus, check that the electrical supply is adequate for the machine.

Check for dampness. Do not use electrical apparatus or installations if they have accidentally got wet or if the operator has wet hands or feet.

Procedures

While using an electrical apparatus or installation, use only the parts necessary for the purpose. Do not use or modify any security devices.

Do not manipulate or try to repair installations or electrical machines. In case of irregularity, report it to an electrician.

Never open the protective safeguard of electrical devices and respect all warnings and signs in order to avoid bodily contact with cables or electrical components.

Standards

All electrical installations carried out in the company premises must comply with Electro-technical Standards for Low Tension and be installed by electricians officially authorized by the Ministry of Industry.

Graphic organizer for previous activity

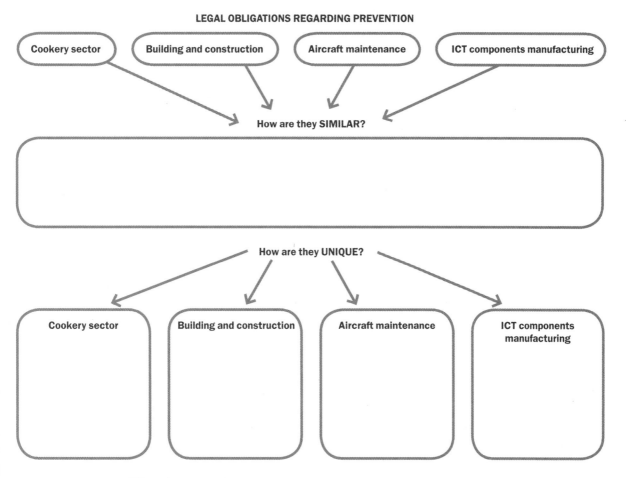

Day 4

Activity 1: Warm-up and summarizing (10 minutes)

Use the graphic organizer on the following page to summarize, through dialogue with the students, what they have been learning during the past few days (first two branches). The remaining branches show what remains to be done over the coming weeks. After a few introductory sentences that set the stage, the dialogue with the students might include questions such as:

Does anyone recall any hazards deriving from machines? What are some of the appropriate strategies for dealing with that hazard? Is there something more that can be done?

Has anyone here ever got a shock from electrical equipment? What happened? Which safety measure was ignored?

What worries you about safety or hygiene in your chosen field of future employment? How can you reduce those risks?

What are you doing to help you remember what we are learning this week?

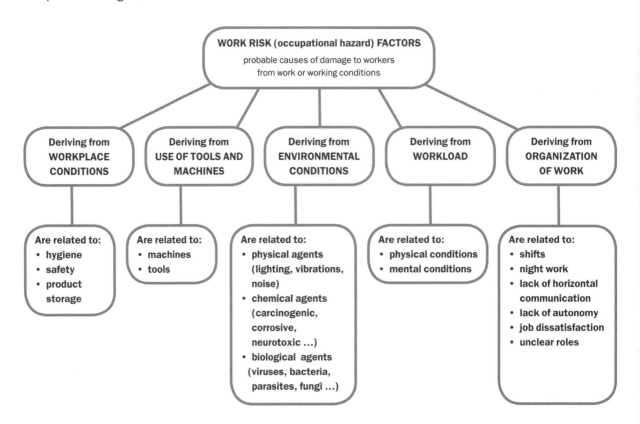

After the discussion, ask students to look at the following chart.

Areas of risk	Risk factors		
Hygiene	grease (floor, counters, machines)	dirt (floor, counters, machines)	debris (floor/working surfaces)
Safety	doors and gates	emergency exits	aisles
Product storage	shelves	cupboards	rooms
Physical condition	ergonomics	carrying	lifting

Ask them if this chart jogs their memories and if it helps them recall additional risks. Have them bring up one or two additional points that they recall. There is not enough time to work through the whole chart. Ask them why they think it was easier to recall more information thanks to the chart. Discuss the importance of systematizing information and breaking it down into chunks.

Activity 2: Establishing learning outcomes (5 minutes)

In today's lesson the students will practise systematizing information while learning about legislation related to hazard prevention. The learning skills outcomes for today are:

- being able to systematize information into organized chunks;
- asking for repetition and clarification as needed (sub-text: you can ask me for help).

The planned content outcome is:

- a prevention plan based on legislation for a given place of business.

The language outcomes remain:

- actively using the opportunity to communicate in the CLIL language;
- correctly using key vocabulary related to occupational hazards and their prevention.

> **Classroom management**
>
> Many students are likely to have a negative reaction to being asked to read legislation. However, being able to read legislation is an important skill in the working world. In pointing out this requirement without addressing student fears here and now, learning will probably be impeded. You can ask the students what concerns they have about these outcomes. Several students are likely to ask whether they have to read the laws in the CLIL language. The answer is yes, but that they do not have to read the whole law. Laws are also organized into chunks. They will have to look for specific information in specific areas. You will help them to do this and you can provide them with a glossary.

Show them the following graphic organizer to indicate which legislation they will be using:

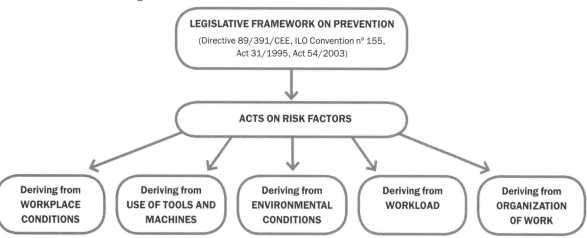

93

Activity 3: Using legislation to design a prevention plan (40 minutes)

Hand out a copy of one law that the students will be using. Ask them to scan the sub-headings and try to find the section entitled 'General and particular provisions'. Discuss the meaning of the title.

Ask if someone can identify one risk factor. Can someone find the required prevention strategy? Write this risk factor and prevention strategy on the board. Have the students pick one more risk factor that is explained in the law. Take one sample sentence from the law. Have all the students work individually on reducing that risk factor down to a few words. Take it up together.

Have several students help you to distribute the assignment. Go through it together.

The following is a sample one-page worksheet that would be given to students.

Designing a prevention plan

Type of work: Group assignment

Final outcomes:

- a computer presentation of seven slides.
  (NB: Transparencies and poster-sized paper are also options)
- a presentation of the seven slides that involves all group members.

First steps

1) Form a group (minimum four people, maximum five).
2) Pick a business (restaurant, hotel, electronic manufacturer, etc). Each group must choose a different workplace.
3) Inform the teacher, who will give you a group number needed when naming your electronic file.
4) Read the rest of the instructions and study the evaluation grid.

Content

Slide N° 1: Title. (During the presentation briefly state why you chose this workplace.)

Slides N° 2, 3, 4, 5, 6: **Some** key risk factors related to workplace and workers and proposed prevention measures.

Slide N° 7: Research resources (names of the laws used) .

Evaluation grid

Key elements (Have you included the basics?)	★ No	★★ Partly	★★★ Yes
Title			
Risk factors related to workplace			
Prevention measures related to those workplace risks			
Risk factors related to workers			
Prevention measures related to those worker risks			
Research resources			
Work process			
File copied to classroom desktop prior to class			
File named according to pattern (eg, Group One Aircraft Maintenance Hazard Prevention)			
Each group member presents a fair share			
Stayed within five-minute time limit for presentation			
Clarity			
Slides are easy to read			
Presenters can be heard			
Correct language usage (errors do not affect comprehension)			
Spoken text helps better understand slides			

Final mark – pass or fail
A pass requires at least nine ticks in the 'yes' column and no more than **two** ticks in the 'no' column.

Source documents and language support

Have one person from each group come and get a package of documents from a central point. Due to space restrictions the legislation is not reproduced here. The sources are the following International Labour Organisation and European Union websites:

* http://www.ilo.org/public/english/protection/safework/cis/legosh/esp/index.htm/
* http://eurlex.europa.eu/LexUriServ/LexUriServ.do?uri=CELEX:31989L0391: EN:HTML/
* http://www.ilo.org/public/english/protection/safework/cis/legosh/eec/index.htm/

The package of legislation should include a glossary of key terms. The one used for this lesson was downloaded from the Spanish Ministry of Labour and Social Affairs at http://www.mtas.es/insht/en/principal/tesauro_en.htm/

> **Classroom management tip**
>
> Explore giving up the responsibility of distributing papers. Options might include:
>
> * several students always help distribute without being asked to do so;
> * lay the same papers in four separate areas so they can be picked up quickly.

Mid-point discussion (halfway through the exercise)

What is the biggest challenge? It is likely to be the limited timeframe. Suggest having group members break up the task so each person reviews one law and develops one slide.

How many risks are you putting on one slide? If it is more than three, they are probably trying to pack in too much.

Activity 4: Evaluating outcome achievement (5 minutes)

Ask whether the students feel they are able to systematize information into organized chunks. How many feel *yes they are*, how many feel *no they are not*? Do they need to practise this skill some more at a later date?

Since the major outcome is a prevention plan, have the students use the evaluation grid to assess where they stand at the moment.

Some follow-up questions might include:

Who is ready to present their information?
What do you have left to do?
Who is responsible for getting the presentation on the class computer?
What have you done to check language?
Do you have all the required parts of the presentation?
Will you get together after this class to practise or before class tomorrow to practise?
Have you timed yourself?
Who needs help after class?

Day 5

Activity 1: Warm-up (4 minutes)

The goal is to see who can list the largest number of workplace risks and related prevention strategies in three minutes. They have to be passed on in a very noisy work environment. Let the students know that this is also a way of making sure their voices will carry during the upcoming presentations. Many actors and presenters do vocal exercises before speaking.

Have the students line up in two lines facing each other – lines A and B. The lines should be at the opposite ends of the classroom. People are partnered with the person in the other line that is immediately opposite. All of line A, all at once, begins to share one workplace risk for employees. The partner in line B repeats the risk and makes a suggestion about how to prevent it. The person on the other side repeats the prevention strategy and presents another risk, and so forth for three very noisy minutes. The exercise helps get rid of inhibitions. Students keep score themselves.

Activity 2: Practising for presentations (6 minutes)

Halfway through the six minutes tell the students they have three minutes left. Remind them when one minute remains. This will help you stick to your time schedule and help the students to use time more efficiently.

Activity 3: Presentations and discussion (45 minutes)

During the presentations, the rest of the students take notes individually on the prevention plans developed by the other groups. The outline for writing the notes is presented and posted. The notes are to include:

- name of business;
- five workplace-related risks and prevention strategies;
- five worker-related risks and prevention strategies;
- one suggestion for improving the presentation.

Each group is applauded. Immediately after the presentation, each group is asked to comment on what they did well and what they would do differently next time. Your feedback is given thereafter (verbal and by the evaluation sheet). Positive aspects are stressed.

Activity 4: Analysing progress in achieving the week's outcomes (5 minutes)

This is an opportunity to summarize and celebrate the students' accomplishments. Many will be highly critical of their language skills. They may need help in seeing that you value their efforts and risk-taking. This is an accomplishment worth celebrating.

Return to the week's outcomes, moving through them one by one, deciding on whether each outcome has been achieved or not. Students can use the 'thumbometer' to show the extent to which outcomes have been achieved. The thumb pointing upwards shows full achievement of each planned outcome and by turning the thumb downwards like a dial students can show lesser degrees of outcome achievement. After assessing the achievement of each outcome, mirror back to the students in summary statements what you feel the students are telling you. Ask if there is one thing they would like to do more of next week that would help them to learn more.

Teacher's personal reflection

Since this is the first week, it is important to assess what areas of language need to be worked on. The suggested grid below can serve as a vehicle for discussing with other colleagues those aspects of language you would all agree to focus on during a given week. This kind of coordinated approach can help foster more rapid development in language growth.

Language outcomes evaluation grid for teacher			
Oral production of CLIL language (presentation) ★★★ satisfied with result ★★ improvement needed ★ comments/plans	★★★	★★	★
% of CLIL language use during presentation			
Fluency			
Pronunciation			
Sentence structure conveys the meaning			
Presentation structure (introduction, core text, conclusion)			
Written production of CLIL language (summary)			
Use of verb tenses			
Use of irregular verbs			
Adverbs			
Adjectives			
Quantifiers			
Specific vocabulary			
Sentence structure			
Connectors			
Pronouns			
Numbers			
Summary structure (introduction, corpus, conclusion)			
Other			

Core CLIL features focused on during the first week in vocational education

The following chart highlights those core features of CLIL which were applied during the previous activities.

Multiple focus	Safe and enriching environment	Authenticity
• language learning in non-language classes • content acquisition in language classes • integrating several subjects • cross-curricular themes/projects • reflection on the learning process	• using routine activities • displaying language and content • building student confidence • using learning centres • accessing authentic materials/environments • student awareness of and growth in language	• students indicating language needs • accommodating student interests • connecting learning and the students' lives • connecting with speakers of the CLIL language • using current materials
Active learning	**Scaffolding**	**Co-operation**
• students communicating more than teacher • students help set learning outcomes • students evaluate progress in meeting learning outcomes • favouring peer co-operative work • negotiating meaning • teachers acting as facilitators	• building on a student's existing knowledge, skills, attitudes, interests and experience • repackaging information in user-friendly ways • responding to different learning styles • fostering creative and critical thinking • challenging students to take another step forward	• planning lessons in co-operation with CLIL and non-CLIL teachers • involving parents • involving the local community and authorities

Guiding principles focused on during week one

COGNITION
- content, language and learning skills outcomes are articulated in co-operation with students
- learning builds on a student's existing knowledge, skills, attitudes, interests and experience
- students analyse achievement of learning outcomes independently, with other students and with the teacher, and work to set new outcomes
- students can synthesize, evaluate and apply knowledge and skills acquired in several subjects

Community
- students feel that being members of a learning community is enriching
- students have the self-confidence and skills to work within a group and the local community, balancing personal interests with those of others
- parents, teachers and students are partners in education
- students can define their role within the classroom, the local and the global context

Content
- content is clearly linked to the community within and outside of the classroom
- students apply new content and develop related skills through experiential activities
- content is substantive without being overwhelming
- content from various subjects is integrated
- cultural content is integrated into all subjects

Communication
- students actively use the right to participate in activities and communication, in the classroom and in the community
- desk placement and displays on classroom walls and other available resources support learning and communication
- students and teachers co-construct and negotiate meaning
- language/communication skills are developed in all subjects

4 Putting CLIL in motion

Working through cross-curricular themes and projects

Setting your sights on successful CLIL

Supporting language learning in content classes

Teaming up with fellow teachers

Supporting content learning in language classes

Reflecting on learning

This chapter describes what is unique about setting learning outcomes for CLIL. Learning in CLIL is much improved when links are made between, and co-operation is increased among, various classroom subjects. This chapter explains how to support language learning in content classes and how to support content learning in language classes. It specifies the role of cross-curricular themes and provides examples. Assessment in CLIL is detailed. The chapter concludes with suggestions on facilitating co-operation among teachers.

Setting your sights on successful CLIL

Big dreams and big actions leading to big results – this is the aim of CLIL. The ultimate goal of CLIL is bilingualism or multilingualism and, as one finds in other educational programmes, academic and personal success.

Part of CLIL's winning game plan involves establishing learning outcomes:

- content-related learning outcomes;
- language-related learning outcomes that support the acquisition of content;
- outcomes related to general learning skills.

An outcome describes the enduring knowledge, abilities and attitudes that allow a student to exercise and apply learning in his or her personal and professional life. More simply put, it is what a student knows and can do thanks to what he or she has learnt.

From a *Dead Poet's Society*, standing-on-the-desk perspective, outcomes are a set of opportunities that help expand the student's repertoire of knowledge (about self and others), skills and options for making the most of life.

Learning outcomes can:

*   provide a focus for instruction;
*   provide guidelines for learning (knowledge, skills, attitudes);
*   provide targets for assessment (in other words they are measurable);
*   provide a vehicle for involving students in setting personal targets;
*   facilitate the communication of non-negotiable expectations;
*   convey instructional intent to others;
*   provide a framework for final evaluation of learning;
*   provide a framework for assessment of teaching (adapted from Gronlund, 2004).

Most importantly, involving students in setting learning outcomes helps them to develop a very important life skill: the constructive habit of goal-setting and outcome-planning that successful people use on a daily basis.

Sample outcomes

Students verify and apply rules and language required for measuring the area of rectangles.

Students find, select, analyse, synthesize and use relevant information for preparing to travel to another country.

Students analyse the conflict in Northern Ireland from three cultural viewpoints.

There are certain distinctive aspects to setting learning outcomes for CLIL:

Linking outcomes related to content, language and learning skills is challenging. In meeting with CLIL teachers, we have understood that planning for and focusing on all of these outcomes before and during a lesson has initially required considerable effort from students and teachers, but that once mastered, it quickly leads to greater student engagement and learning. In the long run, it saves time.

Taking into account that language is not the primary subject being taught. Content can be learnt with minimal language. This is counterintuitive. Moreover, focusing primarily on content helps to facilitate language learning. This is particularly the case when language learning in content classes receives regular and systematic attention.

Not compromising the quality of content due to a lack of language knowledge. Separating the essential from the non-essential is key. Content drives CLIL programming. It is the opportunity to use newly acquired content in a meaningful way that captures student interest.

Language outcomes are difficult to arbitrarily sequence, as these outcomes are driven by content, as well as student interests and needs. Providing students with the vocabulary and discourse patterns that they need to manipulate the content, when they need them, will help you exceed the demands of the standard language learning curriculum. You will just follow a different sequence.

There is a need for coordination of outcomes and learning activities development among teachers. If our students see teachers co-operating they will better assimilate that groupwork is a normal part of life and not just something that is done in class. Moreover, without coordination, CLIL is an uphill battle. By developing joint projects that are marked by several content teachers and the language teacher, or by building a unit around a common theme, learning becomes more relevant because it transcends one classroom and has a wider application. Therefore, learning is increased and, in the long run, a teacher's task is made easier.

Making links with native and non-native speakers of the CLIL language. Contact and communication are the payoffs for language learning. They help learning to take root and flourish.

Making links with the community so that content can be applied in community-based activities. Meaning-making is a social process and it is all the more meaningful if a project takes place in or is linked to the 'real' world outside school. These are the moments and lessons we do not forget.

Maintaining a balance between creating a psychologically safe learning environment and encouraging language growth. This is a tightrope act. You will know you are starting to see-saw if your students stop speaking or if errors are becoming fossilized.

Maintaining a focus on learning skills. CLIL is a bit of juggling act. Its multiple focus is better maintained if we keep a spotlight on learning skills. Moreover, we cannot accept responsibility for our own learning unless we have some idea of how we learn. This involves raising awareness of how we learn (eg, our preferred learning strategies and styles) and how we think (meta-cognition). This helps us to obtain the knowledge and tools to plan, assess and improve our own learning. It also helps us to develop mental habits that can contribute to success and happiness.

View from the field 5

My reality check

I am a science teacher, not a language teacher. I figured it was the language teacher who had to ensure that my students had sufficient language to handle the content. After all, just getting through the curriculum even with non-CLIL students can be a challenge. Reality started to sink in when the language teacher said she would try to use some of the vocabulary I was using, but did not really understand science very well. I realized I had to start helping my students to learn the language they needed. I used glossaries and lots of visuals such as charts. I started working to make everything doubly clear. After presenting a small piece of information, I kept checking to see if the students understood. I worked to get rid of anything extra and focus on the essentials.

Initially, I assumed too much responsibility and spent too much time explaining language. Eventually, I decided to do more pair- and groupwork and hands-on experiments. I still tried to support the students by making information available in clear, manageable chunks and by providing labelled diagrams and glossaries. I constantly checked for comprehension, providing language on a needs-be basis. Yet, above all, I found that if I tried really hard to make the topic relevant to the students, to somehow or other connect it to their lives, the students were motivated to learn the content. When motivated to learn the content, they seemed to learn the language. I did not so much have to teach the language, as provide language support and put the language to interesting use.

Marc Dumont, science teacher, Canada

Supporting language learning in content classes

Every subject has its own terminology – language that is common to scientists, mathematicians or actors. A useful first step is to decide what language the students absolutely must know (content-obligatory language) to master the content. The language that could be helpful, but is not absolutely necessary (content-compatible language) for learning the subject takes a back seat, although it needs to be accommodated. Content-compatible language comes to the fore as students try to express their own thoughts in relation to the topic under study. Consequently, content-compatible language is often language that truly interests the student. It can sometimes serve as the foundation into which content-obligatory language can anchor itself.

Cloud, Genesee and Hamayan state that content-obligatory language includes 1) technical vocabulary (taxonomy, numerator), 2) special expressions (least common multiple, common ancestral species), 3) multiple meanings of words (mass, table), 4) syntactical features (passive voice, embedded clauses) and 5) language functions which predominate in a particular content area of a lesson (informing, defining, analysing, classifying, predicting, inferring, explaining, justifying, etc). These language abilities are necessary for students to acquire concepts, ask questions, explain understanding, demonstrate mastery and prepare for future learning in the content area (Cloud et al, 2000).

Whether it is content-obligatory or content-compatible language, there need to be plenty of opportunities for oral interaction among students. We do not learn to speak a language simply by listening, reading or writing. For new language to take root, we need to use it in conversation before it can become a lasting part of our output repertoire. The multi-faceted nature of the CLIL approach involves an extra focus on student interests, peer co-operative work and the fostering of critical thinking, among other methodological strategies. These foster the learning of content and provide increased forums for discussing and otherwise communicating about content. Those increased opportunities support language learning.

This view is supported by feedback we have received from CLIL teachers in the field. When asked what they felt were essential elements in supporting language learning in content classes, the answers had little to do with specific language-learning activities or support materials. Nonetheless, some of those materials are found at the end of this section. However, first we summarize what CLIL teachers had to say. The following list was developed based on previous co-operation with a highly experienced CLIL educator named Lynda Boynton.

1. Create a psychologically and physically safe environment

Students must feel free to experiment with the language and not fear making mistakes. Students of all ages need to understand that they, too, must help create an environment where their classmates will feel comfortable – safe from ridicule, sarcasm or physical aggression. This is done through having the class establish rules and through adherence to those classroom rules; by dealing with problems through discussion; by providing positive reinforcement for efforts to communicate constructively; and by encouraging students to analyse and improve their own commentary, verbal and non-verbal reactions and behaviours. Above all, it is paramount to believe that your students will succeed and to demonstrate your faith in them.

2. Consistently use one language

Always strive to use the target language. Initially, when necessary, a student can summarize in the first language what was said in the CLIL language. A guest can be invited in to cover safety issues in the first language. However, these are bridging techniques normally only used sparingly at the start of an extensive programme.

3. In the beginning, it is acceptable for students to use the first language

Expect students at the primary level, who are at the start of a programme, to answer initially in their own language. They will often immediately verbalize structures taught to them in the target language; however, do not expect spontaneous self-expression in the target language before the third or fourth month. During these first months, the students are developing their receptive language skills. More and more, they will understand what you say to them, although they will not yet be able to express themselves easily in the target language. Expect primary students to mix languages during the first half of the year, in particular. Encourage the use of the CLIL language at all times.

In secondary and vocational CLIL classes, students will also mix languages. This facilitates communication. Give the students the needed phrases in the CLIL language and when possible write them on the board. Once an expression has been used, consider it to be part of the classroom repertoire. To help students avoid the temptation of relying on you as the only source of language, you can also ask individuals who are having trouble finding the right word how to get the point across in another way. You can ask other students for input or guide the student to a dictionary or a vocabulary wall. In anticipation of language needs associated with a new topic, some of the language can be posted on the wall or on the board in advance of a class.

Do not provide incentives, such as a redeemable classroom currency, for speaking the target language. It is counterproductive. This will create a situation where the student only feels motivated to learn the language in order to receive external rewards. Your goal is to develop your students' desire to learn and speak through their internal motivation and the intrinsic rewards their learning will bring. The primary incentive will be the learning of subject matter and the enjoyment of success in communicating in the target language.

4. Speak slowly and articulate clearly

Speak very clearly when introducing new language and structures. However, be careful not to overexaggerate words or speak unnaturally slowly. When planning, be aware of the number of new words or structures you are introducing the students to at any one time. They will need to be challenged yet comfortable, not frustrated or overwhelmed.

5. Use an appropriate level of language

Avoid structures that are too complicated for your students, but speak in a grammatically correct manner. In order to keep challenging your students, use a level of language in class that is one step ahead of theirs – enough to make them work at it without making it too hard.

6. Use facial expressions, gestures and pictures to reinforce meaning

Contrary to what is often common practice, have students listen carefully to the new words to try and discover the meaning in the target language before you show the visual aids. This way, the idea registers first in the target language.

7. Repetition is required

Repetition will help students to grasp meaning and create a sense of security. They will begin to repeat to themselves the new vocabulary as they develop their receptive language skills. When they become more comfortable with the language, they will begin to repeat the vocabulary out loud and express themselves somewhat more spontaneously. In particular, with younger students, this is where an established routine for the beginning of each day helps.

8. Make it meaningful

The language, themes and content of classroom lessons must be relevant and of interest to the students. Initially, this means focusing on the students themselves, their family, their school and the community. Later on, it can include music, local issues, school events, the environment, problems in the community, community workers, sports, fashion, healthy lifestyles, etc.

Also, by concentrating on solving problems that require critical thinking and co-operation with small groups of peers, students become more engaged and interested in learning. By tapping into the experiences, personal interests and background of the students, and by really challenging them to think, the work students do in school becomes more meaningful, authentic and relevant to their lives.

9. Provide a variety of language models

Students need to hear the CLIL language spoken by different people in different contexts. The language of school does not always suit everyday situations. Invite guests into the classroom and arrange field trips. Establish a buddy system between classes, pairing each younger student with an older student, and arrange for them to meet once or twice a week. Join international projects such as Science Across the World or set up a project with a school in another country with students for whom the CLIL language is a second or first language. Create assignments that require students to use native-language resources such as music, video clips, blogs or home pages.

10. Create a wealth of opportunities to use the language

Proactive strategies such as groupwork, pairwork and activity centres are more effective than having a class do primarily written exercises, which you then correct by having one student respond at a time. By understanding the students' current state of knowledge and their attitudes, by taking into account different learning styles, you can develop programmes and activities that meet a variety of their needs. Ideas, lessons and activities must be presented within contexts that are relevant to the students.

Students will learn the language by using it. Peer co-operative work (pair- and groupwork) that is focused on problem-solving activities can be particularly useful. This provides them with opportunities to develop collaborative skills and to gain confidence in presenting their own ideas and opinions to their peers.

11. Communication is of primary importance

It is more important for students to communicate than to worry about having perfect grammar. A student should receive positive reinforcement for speaking, and for speaking correctly. The teacher can model the right word or phrase, or correctly recast a faulty sentence. As students progress, you can prompt or guide them to self- or peer-correct. Once the student has corrected the error, continue the dialogue. Where possible, students can take the lead in conducting a conversation. This empowers them and supports the development of a classroom culture where students assume ever-increasing responsibility for their learning.

12. Create a wide variety of opportunities to develop all four language skills – listening, speaking, reading and writing

Each language skill reinforces the other. Look for opportunities to combine all four skills into one activity or a series of activities. For example, if you are discussing globalization, first have the students write down some of their own thoughts about the pros and cons of globalization. In pairs, each student could read what the other wrote. The two students can then combine their answers into one written statement. They can practise presenting their conclusions. One pair then presents to another pair. The two pairs discuss their differences and try to establish one common text.

13. Work systematically to build equal status for languages used in the school

All languages learnt and used in the school are deserving of equal attention. For example, opportunities should be taken to make announcements in the languages of the school. Student assemblies could include performances in the CLIL language. You can model the value of the CLIL language by speaking it with students and colleagues outside the classroom in the halls or cafeteria. Sheltered opportunities for communication with peers from abroad, who speak the CLIL language, and with non-CLIL students can help students understand the benefits of language learning. Most students perceive international communication to be exciting. Languages can further be brought into the school ethos by creating opportunities for bringing various languages, including the students' native language(s) such as Gujarati, into the school during assemblies and fairs.

The head teacher/principal of the school and other staff need to demonstrate their support for the CLIL programme. This is best achieved when CLIL and non-CLIL teachers co-operate and when both groups notice and publicly acknowledge each other's achievements, and look for opportunities to create these jointly. However, creating an elitist aura around the CLIL programme is usually counterproductive, undermining the status of the programme among the general population of students and staff.

14. Set high, but realistic expectations

Do not underestimate what your students or you can do. Have high, but realistic expectations. At the same time, students need to see those high expectations as attainable and fair. Also, search for the negative expectations about students that you carry in yourself and work to replace them with positive expectations. Above all, expect effort and dialogue from your students about the learning process. If students are having trouble meeting expectations, build scaffolds to support them in their efforts. High expectations help to reinforce the meaningful nature of school: they help students to concentrate on learning and to behave better. They lead to greater achievement.

For example, if students are writing letters to a politician, they would be expected to use the appropriate level of language and to make realistic proposals for solving an issue of concern. This may involve providing them with a general structure for the letter and typical discourse patterns. However, students would also be expected to polish language and style, as well as analyse the extent to which their proposals are logical and realistic. They can be asked questions such as where the money would come from for this proposed change, who would manage this change and what evidence they are using to back up their proposal.

15. Find ways of recognizing student effort and success

Reward effort. Also, reward co-operation, peer teaching, self-reliance, analysis of the learning process, task completion, progress in meeting planned outcomes, as well as achievement in all subject areas. Every student needs well chosen moments in the limelight.

Avoid constantly saying *well done* – the big pitfall of empty praise. Effective recognition is specific and consists of both analysis and some form of public recognition. Give students an opportunity to speak about how they achieved their result. Listening equates with recognition. Display student work in the classroom and hallways. Exhibit project work in the library. Invite someone such as the head teacher to see and comment on the work.

Separate praise from advice about how to move forward. The easiest way to do this is by banishing the word *but*. For example, skip the second half of the following sentence. *The graphs you used and the repetition of key messages helped make the presentation a real success, but you have to be careful not to get carried away with the repetition.* The word *but* cancels out the reinforcement.

Some samples of how content teachers can create language support for students follow. Many more are found throughout the book.

In history, for example, the past tense is often used. Assuming that the students have studied the past tense in language classes, they may simply be having trouble recalling irregular verbs. To support students, a verb chart can be created by choosing verbs most likely to be used in history. When students make a mistake with using irregular verbs in the past tense, they can be invited to self-correct by referring to the chart. See examples below:

Present	Simple past	Past participle
be	was/were	been
become	became	become
fall	fell	fallen
hold	held	held
steal	stole	stolen
take	took	taken
win	won	won
…	…	…

Phrasal verbs	Definition	Sample usage
hand down	• leave as an inheritance • pronounce formally	*He handed down the watch to his daughter.* *The decree was handed down from the head office.*
hand over	• yield control of • give something to someone who is usually expecting it	*She handed over power to her son.* *After a 40-day siege they handed over the castle to the Goths.* *He handed over the evidence to the police.*
come across	• find by chance	*I came across the oil spill as I was hiking along that isolated stretch of coastline.*
come along with	• accompany • make progress	*He came along with us to the party.* *How is she coming along with the project?*
come down with	• become ill with	*My brother came down with a cold and won't be joining us.*
...	...	...

A select corner of the board or the classroom wall can be reserved for a word wall that contains 10 to 20 words that students feel they most need to retain during a given week. Every day, students can be encouraged to add to or subtract from the word wall. Students can be asked to explain why a word is so important that it should be put on the wall. Some students will want to write these words in their personal dictionary for a given subject. (Can be expanded to include expressions.)

Another option is to bring out key content and vocabulary at the start of a reading passage or before giving a written assignment with a graphic organizer such as the one that follows.

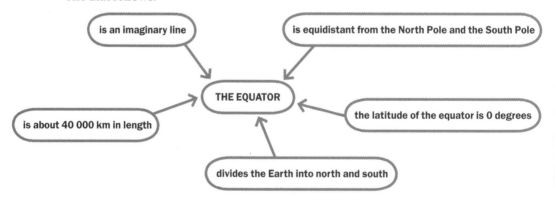

By grouping words according to categories (eg, verbs, nouns, idioms; tools, indoor materials, outdoor materials; grains, fruits, vegetables, poultry, red meat, fish) comprehension can be facilitated. An example can be found in Chapter 3 on page 85.

Students can also be given some 25 words associated with a topic on a handout. They can be asked to cut or tear the handout into strips horizontally and vertically so that each word is on a separate piece of paper. Students then work to categorize words according to key concepts in the given subject. These word groups serve as a review of both vocabulary and key concepts.

Guiding students to pictorial dictionaries is particularly helpful as they usually group vocabulary according to concepts, themes or objects. Moreover, written words are supported by illustrations.

In science, when studying the atmosphere, the following illustrated and written text with a sample of how to do the exercise supports both language and content acquisition.

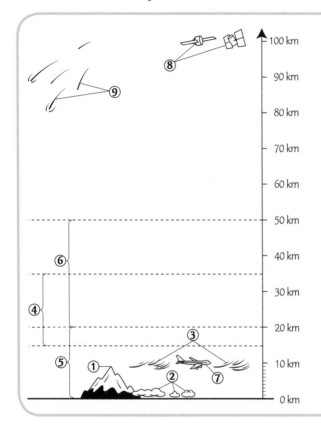

Look at the illustration and create sentences. Use the comparative, eg, *higher than, lower than, faster than, thinner than.*
1) tallest mountain on earth (8 850 m)
2) rain clouds (0.5–3 km)
3) cirrus clouds (8–11 km)
4) ozone layer (15–35 km)
5) troposphere (up to 20 km)
6) stratosphere (up to 50 km)
7) plane flying at a height of 10 km
8) satellite (100 km)
9) meteorites burning up in the atmosphere (80–100 km)

Example:
Planes fly at a lower elevation than satellites.

Supporting content learning in language classes

Hold the horses! Stop the show!

Q: If comprehensible and meaningful content are what drives language learning, what do we do about teaching vocabulary and grammar?

A: We keep teaching vocabulary and grammar, but we try to dress it up a little differently. Language teachers have always worked to create meaningful contexts. CLIL provides an expanded window of opportunity for teaching language. Since we know that students are, generally speaking, most motivated by content and less interested in language for the sake of language, it is worth exploring how to make the most of the content opportunity in language classes.

In CLIL programmes, students' language develops quickly. Content teachers are partners with language teachers. They provide students with additional opportunities for language learning. CLIL students almost inevitably understand and master a language much faster than those who only learn it as a subject. Nonetheless, the language curriculum still needs to be taught and often enriched.

It is good practice for language and content teachers to agree on weekly language goals/outcomes. Content teachers commit to helping students achieve these goals/outcomes. Thus, human nature being what it is, content teachers will also expect some support from language teachers in helping students to learn the content curriculum. However, most language teachers can realistically only manage to support the teaching of one or two content subjects at a time.

On a practical level, a shift in thinking and practice takes place. The language teacher uses the language textbook more as a reference tool, and works regularly with material from content classes to teach language. Most often, these content materials would be content-compatible as opposed to content-obligatory. The materials are often provided by the content teacher, or they are proposed by the language teacher. The materials would sometimes need to be rewritten to help stress a given point on, for example, syntax or grammar.

For example, if the language curriculum requires that the conditional be taught, a text from science class about climate change can be incorporated into the language class by rewriting it in the conditional. For example:

What measures will the government need to take?

What measures would the government need to take if temperatures were to continue to rise?

What will be the impact on the local tourism industry?

What would be the impact on the local tourism industry?

What will need to be taken into account when assessing the potential costs of climate change?

What would need to be taken into account when assessing the potential costs of climate change?

Similarly, if students are studying in biology class the consequences of overeating, and if *if* clauses are the focus of the language curriculum, students could be asked to use those clauses to write about the potential risks of overconsuming given foods.

If I were to drink excessive quantities of orange juice, it could contribute to obesity and tooth decay.

If the language skill being developed involves comparing and contrasting, the content teachers could provide diagrams and charts for written and verbal analysis in the language class.

Another option would be to jointly organize a language and content (eg, history, geography or civics) class project for students. In this case, the history teacher, for example, marks the final product based on history and learning skills outcomes. The evaluation criteria might include the use of a minimum number of sources, accuracy of facts, presentation of evidence, presentation of several perspectives, the logical construction of arguments and following the agreed-upon structure and format. The language teacher would mark for the achievement of language outcomes, for the correct use of any number of grammar points and linguistic features that have been under study during the week. For example, students might have to use a certain verb tense at least ten times, at least ten phrasal verbs, *if* clauses or gerunds.

Should complex sentences and subordinate conjunctions (*while, after, although, wherever,* etc) be the focus of a given week's language curriculum, they can be used to tie together short sentences provided by a content teacher. For example:

Starting point:

The planet Saturn may be seen by the naked eye. The rings of Saturn may not be seen by the naked eye.

First step:

The planet Saturn may be seen by the naked eye; however, its rings may not be seen by the naked eye.

Taking it a step further:

The planet Saturn may be seen by the naked eye; however, one requires a telescope to see its rings.

If vicious circles are the focus of a given week's language curriculum, the science or biology teachers could be asked to provide some examples on an issue under study such as HIV. You can begin by drawing a circle on the board with a directional arrow on it. Ask the students to imagine that this circle represents a typical day in their lives. Ask them how that makes them feel. Their ideas can be put on the board: *feels safe and secure, boring, doesn't get you anywhere, not exciting, feels like a rat in a cage, feels pointless, have no control.* Ask them what would happen if an unexpected temptation or problem was introduced into the circle. For example: *What would happen if your parents worked in a chocolate factory and brought home a big, free box of broken bits of chocolate every night? What would you do if you came home every evening to a noisy neighbour who only turns down the music for five minutes each time you ask him to do so?* Ideas generated by this type of questioning would also be added to the board, and eventually, you can identify a vicious circle.

As a next step, the students can be provided with the following words on the board.

fear not saying no embarrassment intoxication infection
lack of knowledge illness
desire poverty peer pressure not using condoms HIV
wanting to be popular STD (sexually transmitted disease) being cool

Ask the students to work in groups of four to create a chart illustrating a vicious circle about HIV infection, using four of the above words or phrases. Each group will be expected to present their charts explaining each of the four terms. Each group member is expected to present part of the chart.

One chart is selected and coping strategies/solutions are brainstormed for how to deal with each element of the vicious circle. An example follows:

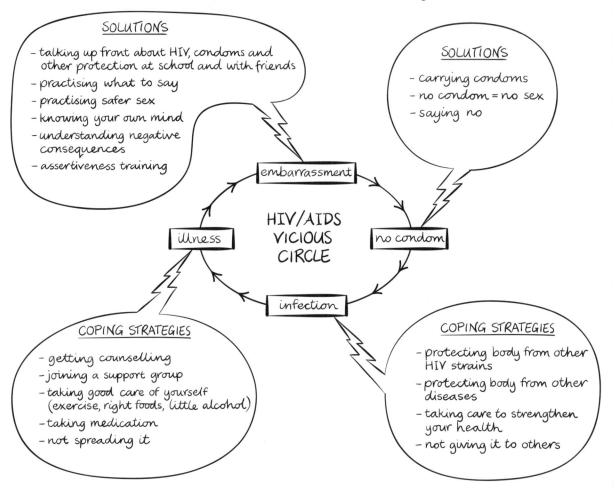

There is also an opportunity here to discuss the difference between coping strategies and solutions.

Students could also explore vicious circles in their lives. Key words such a *tobacco, destructive relationships, shopping* or *lack of exercise* can help trigger thoughts. The assignment would be to create a similar organizational chart as above. As a second step, students would write six paragraphs: an introduction; one paragraph on each element in the circle, first explaining the element in one sentence and then proposing solutions or coping strategies; and a conclusion. The assignment could be marked by the language teacher for language and composition skills, whereas the biology or science teachers could mark for accuracy of statements and depth of critical thought.

When preparing to discuss literary works with students, the language teacher can work with the history and geography teachers to look for historical links or geographic connections. Both disciplines often impact heavily on how stories unfold.

A lexis for linking language and content

Class, what does this remind you of?

Is there a link here that can be drawn to another class?

How can you use these verbs to describe something you have learnt in geography or history?

Compare the use of adjectives on a page in this novel with their use on a page from your science textbook (frequency, tonality, originality, repetition).

You studied bones in science this week. We are focusing on creative writing. Imagine that people in different countries have different bone structures. In each country people have a few bones that are much, much longer or much, much shorter than the average person's bones. Describe how people would look in two of those countries and how their other bones would need to change to support those longer or shorter bones. Then describe a scene where two people from the two different countries meet and try to accomplish a task together.

We are learning how to make recommendations. Take figures from history. State something positive that they have done and use that to make a recommendation, eg, *Napoleon, you have created some excellent laws. Spend more time writing laws and less on war.* Now take your recommendation and change the register of language so that you will not be arrested for impertinence and so that you might be listened to, eg, *Your Excellency, you are a brilliant lawmaker. The world is a better place thanks to you. You will be remembered forever for your laws. Might it be wise to consider putting more national resources into law-making?*

Language teachers can find electronic support materials about content topics that can easily be adapted for language learning. For example, by typing the word *animation* with a content topic such as *acid rain* or *carbon footprint* into any major Internet search engine, one can access many animations or pictures. Some animations consist of short videos or slides that have no words, but may contain sound effects. These can be used for teaching in any language. Students can create narration for these. Those animations that contain text or speech can be used as an exercise in adapting language for different audiences. For example, students can change language into a different register such as MSN communication, into the words of young people, or into a brochure for the public at large. In the language class devoted to the first language, students could use a CLIL language animation to speak about the same topic in the first language. This will help ensure terminology is learnt in both languages.

For language teachers, the key is to take the time to plan for integration with content teachers so as to discuss themes being studied and the linguistic resources needed to study these themes. Ideally, this is done with the whole CLIL team. However, if this is difficult in your working environment, much can be accomplished by one language teacher and one content teacher working together. Students will learn more language in a language class if they are working with information from content classes and using that information to create and express something they consider meaningful. Also, that learning is later more easily retrieved and used as needed.

Working through cross-curricular themes and projects

> *An integrated whole is greater than the sum total of its parts.*
> **Heino Liimets**

Learning too often takes place in separate compartments or silos for each school subject. Cross-curricular themes and projects create bridges between the various subjects taught. In school, we work to help students to gain the knowledge and skills they need for success in the real world. The real world is usually not safely compartmentalized. In our daily lives, we often need to apply skills from several subject areas simultaneously. Cross-curricular themes and projects better reflect the reality of daily life.

Cross-curricular themes and projects usually require social, affective, cognitive and personal interactions with one's surroundings. Thus, these themes and projects make learning more meaningful. Students are likely to be more engaged and learn more about the subjects involved. Moreover, young people become better placed to apply learning from school to their own lives.

> **GETTING STARTED**
> Start small.
> For example, do a joint project with just one of your colleagues.

In primary school, themes often include: *all about me, my day, school, my family and home, autumn, winter, spring, summer, friends, my country, food and drink, holidays, good health, the media, the environment, my hometown, information, culture, legends, castles and fortresses, our continent, adventures on the seas* and *treasure hunts.*

Under the theme *treasure hunts* in civics, students would analyse what they value in life, the difference between price and value/values. They might look at learning about the treasures of their own country. Students could also look at holidays that various cultures around the world celebrate in a given month. In science, they might learn about scale, symbols used on maps and how to use a compass. They might also learn about islands and peninsulas, elevations and the implications of elevations. They might go to the local museum for an active learning experience looking for public treasures. In mathematics, millimetres, measuring distance and converting to and from scale could be at the centre of studies on the treasure theme. A multicultural maths fair could look at contributions made to mathematics from around the world. In physical education, students could be required to use a map and a compass to find a place in the playground where they will complete a series of physical tasks (eg, jumping, climbing, doing squats).

In history, students may focus on what different peoples have treasured throughout history. In language classes, students could read excerpts from Robert Louis Stevenson's *Treasure Island*, Astrid Lindgren's *Six Bullerby Children* or folk tales from various countries such as *The Fisherman and the Goldfish* from Russia or *Two Ways to Count to Ten* from Liberia.

An orientation game or treasure hunt could require students to apply skills learnt in different subjects. They might develop a plan, predict measures and compare those with actual results, answer questions and get the teacher to sign off on the completion of work at various stations on the hunt. For extra points, students could analyse how to improve results next time.

A sample, small-scale history, civics and art project follows. Students would be likely to invest considerably more time in polishing the language if the language teacher is involved. Overall results are likely to improve as well. The language teacher can separately evaluate the same project.

This exercise incorporates the following critical features of the CLIL methodology:

- planned outcome stated;
- several subjects integrated;
- key term (moral authority) explained at the start to scaffold both language and content learning;
- connection to the students' interests by speaking about someone they respect and how they themselves have been influenced by someone;
- builds a bridge between the students' own lives and history;
- requires higher order thinking, comparing, analysing, evaluating and creating;
- reinforces the value of peer co-operative work through evaluation instruments (the project could include a presentation of the results phase).

Combined history, civics and art project

Outcome: A four-page booklet on the topic of moral authority.
You will be able to explain why and how some people influence you.

1) Describe two people that you consider to have moral authority. Choose someone you know personally and a major figure from history. Use three to five sentences each to explain both of your choices.

2) Write two questions you would ask the individual you know personally and whose opinion you respect. How do you think he or she will answer? Write three sentences for each answer.

3) Write two questions that you would like to ask the famous figure from history. How do you think that person would answer, if he or she could? Write three sentences for each answer.

> Someone with moral authority often has the power to influence you, but he or she does not necessarily have the right to order you to do something.

4) Actually ask two questions of the person you know and respect, and write down what he or she says. Write a maximum of three sentences for each answer. Explain any differences in what that person said and what you thought he or she would say.

5) Describe a situation where someone influenced you to do something that you did not want to do. Why did you do it? What would you do differently next time? Write ten to twelve sentences about your experience.

6) Sketch one of the two people in question for the cover of your booklet (tips: How will you portray that person's authority? What are some symbols of authority?).

Evaluation scheme – 100 points

10 logical organization

10 a rough copy of the assignment with suggestions for improvement from a fellow student

20 creativity

20 artwork and layout

20 depth of thought

10 grammar and spelling (checked spelling, correct use of the simple past and the conditional)

10 varied vocabulary (synonyms)

In secondary school, themes could include *climate change, globalization, trade, people who have changed the world, Nobel laureates, conflict resolution* or *environmental issues such as wetlands.* The following diagram shows how the wetlands theme can be used in several subject areas, and to support school-wide goals. Work done in each subject is complementary, but quite different. One project is used to try to connect all subjects.

BUSINESS

Current and potential benefits
- tourism
- agriculture
- environment/biodiversity

Current dangers
- disease
- birds affecting air traffic

Drainage of wetlands
- benefits of draining
- direct and indirect costs

SCIENCE AND BIOLOGY

Listing and categorizing resident and migratory species

Defining the contribution of wetlands to water quality, prevention of erosion, migratory species, etc

Germination and lifecycles

Risks for humans (eg, disease-carrying mosquitoes)

Observing, recording and analysing

Testing water

MATHS

Measuring and graphing the probability of seeing various birds in wetlands

Analysing numerical data about species

Graphing current trends

Projecting future trends

Creating geometric models

CROSS-CURRICULAR PROJECT

Developing a local wetlands management plan

Developing a plan to restore a former wetland

Developing a plan for the co-habitation of an airport and a wetland

OTHER CONNECTIONS

Connecting with the school development plan by involving the local community, including parents. Students could survey local community leaders and their parents.

Part of the project could be done in the CLIL language and part in the first language

WETLANDS

DRAMA/DANCE

Roleplaying different perspectives:
- the mayor
- the student
- a local resident
- a homebuilder/developer
- mother nature
- future generations

Exploring through dance the behaviour of wetland creatures

HISTORY

Reading about societies that have collapsed because of environmental degradation (eg, Easter Island, the Norse colony in Greenland and the Maya in the Yucatan Peninsula)

GEOGRAPHY

Classifying different types of wetlands (eg, bogs, marshes, reefs, estuaries) and their characteristics

Analysing Haiti versus the Dominican Republic to find links between how the lack of respect versus respect for the environment have translated into higher and lower standards of living

LANGUAGE

Reviewing great quotes about nature and biodiversity

Reading about people versus nature

Reading passages from great works such as Nobel prize-winner Gao Xingjian's *Soul Mountain* that depict the beauty and fragility of nature

Reading poetry about nature

In vocational education cross-curricular themes might include client-centred service, entrepreneurship, consumer awareness, media literacy, sustainable development, safety and security, marketing, career path development or respect (eg, for oneself, for clients, for the environment).

A major cross-curricular project might involve establishing a company. This could include innovation, maths, accounting, planning, law, funding, as well as advertising and marketing. Another project could be the reorganization and refurbishment of, for example, a municipal playground. This could involve laws and regulations, planning requirements and permissions, lobbying and communications including writing press releases, finding out client needs, evaluating risks, planning and construction of playground equipment and evaluating results.

One theme that cuts across many topics in vocational education is information and communication technology (ICT) and the individual.

What ICT skills will employers expect of students? Key concepts can include email communication principles and protocols, existing software and hardware, upcoming technologies, integration of new technologies, data networks, efficiency, personal wellbeing and opportunities for professional advancement. By exploring some of these issues in several classes at once, students can better understand their importance and application.

The theme of the individual's relationship with ICT cuts across almost all subjects in different types of vocational education. For example, in training cooks or electricians, students can develop a display covering five of the concepts detailed above. If one of these concepts is the integration of new technologies, the student displays might show the various types of skills expected from employers and the related moral and ethical issues. Students provide examples of how those skills might need to be applied in the work environment.

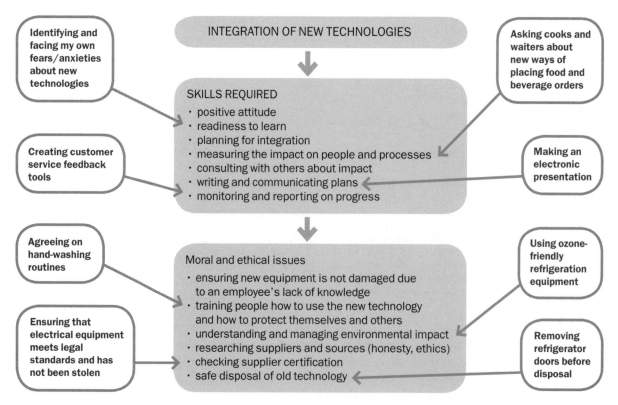

Benefits and challenges of cross-curricular work	
Potential benefits	**Challenges**
· connects learning to the world outside school · helps create bridges between subjects · helps synthesize information · develops unified perspectives · builds the habit of transferring knowledge and skills among school subjects · engages the individual and fosters co-operation · promotes constructive interaction · leads to improved outcomes · can foster healthy competition among groups · builds respect for others · promotes active learning/teaching · accommodates different learning styles · accommodates different ability levels · promotes in-school agreement on learning outcomes, values and evaluation	· takes extra planning time · difficult to agree on common content, language and learning skills outcomes · can create turf wars about project focus · scares some staff · may require an investment in terms of training · hard to establish right level of difficulty · difficult to get staff to co-operate · some parents and students may not see it as work · hard to agree on assessment · some students may go along for the ride, but not really work

Reflecting on learning

Reflecting on learning feeds cognitive development. It is by determining what we know, by establishing benchmarks, setting goals, assessing progress and looking at how we are learning that we can make informed decisions about the whole process.

Five key reasons for organizing assessment are:

- to determine existing student knowledge so one can plan teaching better;
- to determine student achievement levels (benchmarks) for measuring progress in achieving content, language and learning skills goals;
- to understand student interests, attitudes and learning styles (what inspires them);
- to involve students in taking greater responsibility for their learning;
- to obtain information needed to make decisions about how to deliver on improving learning.

Assessment is not only the reality check that helps us teachers and our students to keep grounded and to stay on the straight and narrow, but is also the launch pad for taking us to greater heights. Assessment is not an island in itself. It is an integral part of every lesson. Teachers are always checking to see whether students have understood the material or instructions, if the class is engaged, whether the students are speaking less or more than the teacher, if planned content and language outcomes are realistic or whether there are obstacles that need to be removed from the path of learning. Teachers also guide students to assess their own progress on an ongoing basis. And that is no small task.

Planning for learning by doing or by construction goes hand in hand with planning for assessment. Most CLIL teachers intuitively assess progress made in meeting outcomes associated with language, content and learning skills as they proceed through a lesson. However, advanced planning is also required.

As learning outcomes are established, it is important to decide how their achievement will be assessed. Moreover, learning is likely to improve if students are involved in planning for assessment. At the very least, at the start of every lesson, planned outcomes need to be posted and discussed. Time needs to be taken at the end of each lesson to analyse progress made in achieving those outcomes.

There are some distinguishing characteristics of assessment in CLIL. Progress students make in the following areas is assessed:

- achievement of content and language goals;
- achievement of learning skills goals;
- use of language for various purposes (ie, academic, social, business registers);
- ability to work with authentic materials, as well as with native and non-native speakers of the CLIL language;
- feeling safe to experiment with language and content;
- ongoing growth (avoiding plateauing).

Further, the following are also assessed:

- effort;
- level of engagement;
- preferred learning styles;
- day-to-day work;
- all four language skills (listening, speaking, reading, writing);
- day-to-day communication;
- oral presentations;
- projects;
- planned and spontaneous assignments;
- partner and groupwork;
- social and emotional development;
- balance between co-operation and self-reliance.

Temptation tango/Senseless samba

Giving an assignment without also giving the evaluation criteria.

Giving a pop quiz or threatening with tests, as opposed to trying to make testing a positive learning experience.

Teaching something new during the last five minutes, as opposed to assessing progress in meeting goals and ending on a positive note.

Assessment takes place:

- at the programme start-up to establish benchmarks;
- daily, through observation;

- daily during and/or at the end of each lesson with the students;
- at the end of each unit;
- at intervals, such as formal reporting by means of the report card;
- when learning appears to be hindered.

Assessment is done:

- based on planned curriculum outcomes;
- based on pre-established criteria that have been shared with the students in writing and discussed thereafter;
- by collecting anecdotal information about each student;
- through student portfolios;
- through files of student work;
- by using evaluation grids;
- by means of checklists, eg, level of participation;
- through peers (editing, reading buddies);
- through student self-evaluation;
- through student conferences with the teacher about a specific assignment.

Assessment instruments are used throughout this book. One assessment technique which embodies many aspects of the CLIL method is the use of portfolios. A detailed explanation follows. Olga Little was our original source for many of these ideas.

PORTFOLIO ASSESSMENT

WHAT IS A PORTFOLIO?
A portfolio is a presentation of a student's most valued work. It is evidence, collected over a considerable period of time, of a student's knowledge, skills and of progress made in achieving learning outcomes. It is a tool for learning.

SELECTION CRITERIA FOR STUDENT WORK

- linked to learning outcomes
- made based on results achieved and/or progress made
- collected at regular intervals (eg, once a month) and representative of a student's most valued work, demonstrating progress, effort and results

AIMED AT HELPING STUDENTS

- to develop learning and critical thinking skills
- to build the capacity to examine knowledge, attitudes and learning skills
- to become independent learners
- to build educational partnerships with peers, teachers and parents
- to work with peers, parents and teachers in seeing learning as a holistic, cross-curricular and longitudinal process
- to receive helpful feedback and positive reinforcement
- to assess personal growth/progress
- to set realistic goals
- to build self-confidence, as well as develop presentation and dialogue skills

FOR DISCUSSION AT/OR/ DURING

- student–teacher meetings (eg, once a month)
- parent–teacher meetings (eg, once every three months)
- preparation for exams
- report card time
- when students want to share their work with others
- end of project, year, etc

Warming students to the idea

The word *portfolio* can be broken down. Its roots can be found in the verb *portare* (to carry) and *foglio* or *folium* (sheet of paper). Younger students can speculate on what a portfolio is, what it might contain or be used for. Older students can be encouraged to share what they know about portfolios and what they feel and think about using a portfolio.

In addition to actors, artists, designers and architects, many people in a large range of professions keep a portfolio. For example, some school districts require educators seeking promotion to present portfolios. Closer to the student's world, some colleges and universities include the development of a student portfolio as a graduation requirement.

Guests can be invited into classes to show students their own portfolios. These guests can be encouraged to speak about how they put their portfolio together, what they learnt through the process and how it helped them achieve their goals. For vocational students, it would be helpful if the guest also spoke about how the portfolio was used when applying for work.

CLIL connection

In CLIL, portfolio assessment calls for a three-fold approach. Progress made in mastering and applying content, language and learning skills development is always assessed. Plans and strategies for meeting learning outcomes are also viewed through the same three-fold focus.

Moreover, portfolio assessment is an effective tool in supporting the application of several core features of CLIL methodology. For example, portfolio assessment lends itself well to taking into account and discussing different learning styles and strategies. It encourages students to take ownership of their work through reflection and discussion about the learning process and results. Portfolio assessment provides a forum for challenging students to take another step forward and to set realistic personal goals. It is also a vehicle for involving parents and a student's peers.

Integration

In primary school, students usually have one portfolio that integrates all subjects. In secondary, students ideally have one (a maximum of two) portfolio(s) that integrate(s) several subjects. Based on the expectations of potential employers, vocational students may need some highly focused portfolios – for design or modelling, for example. Ultimately, having one portfolio will help students to synthesize and integrate knowledge and skills developed in various subject areas.

A portfolio that focuses on language learning has been developed by the Council of Europe. The Council's European Languages Portfolio is an excellent tool for helping students and teachers to focus on the development of all of the languages a student is learning. See www.coe.int/portfolio/.

SELECTING PIECES

Students can be asked to rate their work in one subject or category (such as essays) from the weakest to the strongest. Analysing why they work well in certain areas and not in others helps to get students thinking. Was there a difference in how they prepared for making one piece over the other? Were there other differences in the process they followed? What problems or challenges did they face in doing these assignments? The strongest or best work is placed in the portfolio.

Portfolio contents (further reflections)

Portfolios can be used to collect:

- a range of student work (eg, pictures or projects, essays, compositions, reports);
- scanned versions or photocopies of work when the original is in an art show or in a notebook;
- best work or favourite pieces from all subjects;
- electronic files (Word, PDF, PowerPoint, Media Player, emails);
- DVDs (digital photos, video clips);
- CDs (digital photos of projects/models/experiments, sound recordings of interviews or presentations);
- biannual parent or teacher messages (notes, emails, video clips, sound recordings containing positive feedback to the student that also explain the reasoning behind that feedback);
- plans for the upcoming months or year.

Portfolio organization

All entries are dated, as portfolios are used to measure progress over time.

Portfolios can be completely electronic or completely in hard copy form, or a combination of the two. Students are increasingly media literate and often have a decided preference for electronic communication like blogging and text-speak. Electronic portfolios can facilitate storage, help build IT skills and support students in understanding what should also be preserved in hard copy. Moreover, electronic portfolios can speed up access as separate audio-visual equipment is not required for viewing or listening to recordings. Electronic portfolios kept on a school server can facilitate access by all teachers.

A sample table of contents follows:

1) Letter of introduction

   Usually written at the end of a term and finalized at year-end. The letter is used by students to introduce themselves. Students summarize accomplishments as reflected in the portfolio, assessments/reflections and future plans.

2) Table of contents
3) Review of last year's accomplishments and plans
4) Key samples of work from the previous year

   A maximum of three pieces of work of which the students are proudest.

5) This year's best pieces

   5.1 Work number one (title of work and subject(s))

   5.2 Reflections on work number one

   5.3 Work number two (title of work and subject(s))

   5.4 Reflections on work number two

   5.5 continues …

6) Interviews and reflections
7) CDs/audio tapes and reflections
8) DVDs/videos and reflections
9) Parent response sheet
   Completed at the conclusion of a teacher/student/parent interview.
10) Peer response sheet
    Completed after a sharing session with a classmate.
11) End of term reflections
12) Plans

MAKING IT HAPPEN: WHAT THE TEACHER DOES

GOAL-SETTING
Decide on your focus in using portfolio assessement – the purpose

PREPARATIONS
- seek opportunities to co-operate with other teachers
- invite guests
- develop student self-assessment criteria
- decide on a table of contents
- decide on portfolio storage
- develop a matrix for year-end evaluation of the portfolio
- develop parent- and peer-reflection sheets

TEACHING STUDENTS
- what portfolios are
- related routines
- how to assess work
- how to use evaluation criteria
- how to establish goals/outcomes
- how to organize portfolios
- how to lead a student–parent conference
- learning skills
- criteria for assessing knowledge and skills development
- criteria for assessing language growth

SUPPORTING IMPLEMENTATION
- have students illustrate their portfolios
- regularly refer to the portfolio
  (eg, what would you include in your portfolio this week)
  and support its development
  (eg, using class time for planning, assessing progress re selection of work, reflections, goals-setting and roleplaying student-led conferences)

Classroom management

Typical pitfalls:
- not taking enough time to discuss this method with students and parents. People need to be given the information about the 'how' and 'why' behind portfolio assessment. They need to see the benefits of the method and understand their roles and responsibilities.
- trying to apply all portfolio assessment best practices at once. It takes time for all those involved to adjust to this method. The key is to get started and not to try to do too much at once.
- over-emphasizing portfolio assessment. It rarely counts for more than 20 per cent of a student's final mark.

View from the field 6

Snapshot from a student-led conference

When I was first told we had to start doing portfolio assessment I remember getting tired just thinking about it. I could not figure out where I would get the time to prepare or how I would squeeze something else into the curriculum. I had visions of sitting with parents and students and going through a feel-good exercise that would not change much of anything. I was wrong, not that it has been easy. In the long run, student-led conferences and portfolio assessment, in general, have saved me time because students have assumed greater responsibility for their learning and parents have become more adept at supporting their children.

I always start out each student-led conference by thanking the parents for coming. I explain that we are here to listen to the student. I really think this helps establish the right dynamic – one where the student is in charge. I also state that we are here to learn what the student has accomplished, to discuss his or her learning goals and strategies and to see how we can work together to support his or her accomplishment.

I give the floor to the student. Senior students begin by thanking those present for taking the time to meet. The student, based on a learnt routine, says he or she would like to give an overview of some of his or her work, explain what he or she has learnt (language, knowledge, learning skills, attitude) and what he or she has accomplished. The student also states that he or she wishes to receive feedback from us and to discuss next steps or plans.

The student begins by highlighting one piece of work, assessing the result and explaining why he or she chose this piece. After the student has finished this, I model a positive comment about the piece. The parents usually say something positive without being further prompted. Some parents start criticizing right away, so I try to rein them in by saying this is the point where we are focusing in on the positive.

After discussing the best piece, the student summarizes what his or her goals were for the year and how he or she has achieved them, and how he or she has progressed or improved. The portfolio is used as evidence. The student asks for feedback from his or her parents and from me, and a discussion ensues. Personally I have had to work really hard at remembering not to take over from the student. The conferences also help parents hone listening skills and to be less prescriptive.

Finally, goals and plans/strategies for achieving the goals are presented and discussed. The first few times students can be pretty stiff and not really enter into a dialogue, but as time goes by, during successive conferences the students are more and more comfortable with the idea. Roleplaying these conferences in class really helps students to feel comfortable and to take charge. During the conference, if the student forgets to explain how he or she thinks his or her parents could support goals achievement, I will prompt the student.

I have seen these conferences help students develop a new understanding of their own learning. As the students learn to evaluate their own work and learning process, they more easily take charge of their own learning and become more adept at problem-solving. Goal-setting becomes more realistic. Increased self-confidence and improved communication skills are also by-products.

Moreover, students' comments help me to understand what the students feel is important and how I can best help them. I have even received a few real 'wake-up calls', or blunt messages during these conferences. Once a student said to me that he found it very difficult to do presentations in front of the class, particularly when people constantly interrupted with comments and questions. That was a surprisingly diplomatic and direct reference to me. I apologized for interrupting and promised not to do so again during future presentations. This exchange contributed to building a meaningful and a more respectful dialogue between us, to building a more balanced student–teacher relationship, and to helping the student gain a greater sense of control. It also forced me to take a look at my own practices and habits.

Mary Harris, class teacher in Australia

Guided reflection

Students need considerable guidance in how to reflect on their work. Frameworks for reflection can focus on:

- thoughts/feelings about the piece of work;
- the student as a learner;
- achievement of learning outcomes (language, content, learning skills, attitude);
- plans for future learning.

In year two of primary school a student may be asked to complete four of the following sentence fragments each month and six to nine at year-end. As students progress through school, the number of sentence fragments chosen for completion from the list below may increase to as high as ten to twelve.

Thoughts and feelings	Student as learner	Plans
The best part of this work is … *Next time, I want to improve …* *I most enjoyed …* *I was worried about …* *I want you to know that …* *This is my best piece of work because …* *I wish I had remembered to …* *My parents will like the way I …* *I want people who look at this work to know …* *When I finished this piece of work I felt …* *The hardest part of this piece of work was …*	*I am getting better at …* *When I look at other pieces of work I have done …* *When I did this work I learnt …* *I would like help with …* *I don't understand …* *I am having problems with …* *I think I did a good job because …* *If I could do this piece of work again, I would change …* *What this work says about me is …* *My strength in … is …* *My work in … is changing because …*	*I want to improve …* *Next time, before I start writing I will …* *It is important for me to …* *I must remember to …* *I want to practise …* *Next, I want to learn …* *I need to use …* *It is important for me to …* *I'm going to think about …* *I will …* *In maths, science, (etc) I need to …* *My parents can help me to …* *My friends can help me to …*

Achievement of learning outcomes
My language goals were …   *My subject goals were …*   *The attitude I worked to develop was …*   *I achieved my goals (fully, in large part, to some extent, not at all) because …*   *… is a goal that I did not completely achieve because …*

In secondary and vocational the following framework is suggested.

Thoughts and feelings	Student as learner	Plans
The best part of this work is …	Analysing samples of other people's good work I learnt …	I want to improve …
Next time, I want to improve …	I referred back to the evaluation criteria …	Next time I will …
I most enjoyed …		It is important for me to …
I was worried about …	When I did this work I learnt …	I must remember to …
I want you to know that …	I am having problems with …	I want to practise …
This is my best piece of work because …	I am getting better at …	Next, I want to learn …
I wish I had remembered to …	I would like help with …	I need to use …
My friends will like the way I …	I don't understand …	I will plan by …
I want people who look at this work to know …	If I could do this piece of work again, I would change …	Before I start next time, I will …
When I finished this piece of work I felt …	What this work says about me is …	In maths, science, (etc) I need to …
The hardest part of this piece of work was …	My work in … is changing because …	My parents can help me to …
		My friends can help me to …

Achievement of learning outcomes
My language goals were …
My subject goals were …
The attitude I worked to develop was …
I achieved my goals (fully, in large part, to some extent, not at all) because …
… is a goal that I did not completely achieve.
I need to pay more attention to the following evaluation criteria: …
My reflections are tied to my goals/learning outcomes (to a great extent ——— not at all)
My portfolio is well organized and easy to follow (to a great extent ——— not at all)
Evidence/sources is/are given to back up content claims (to a great extent ——— not at all)

Suggested criteria year-end portfolio assessment

- completeness, correctness, neatness, organizational logic
- demonstration of achievement of curriculum outcomes
- demonstration of progress in quality of work
- link between reflections and curriculum outcomes
- inclusion of knowledge, skills and attitudes in reflections
- quality of thought (awareness of meta-cognition, productive mental habits, critical thinking)
- demonstration of progress in the quality of reflections
- creativity (variety, visual appeal)
- completeness and clarity of presentation during student-led conference
- extent to which plans are realistic

The following is a grid for year-two or year-three students in primary. Students can fill in the boxes on the ten-point grid to show what level they have reached.

Portfolio assessment grid

Date: _____   Name: _____

Organization

Student's assessment | 0 | | | | | | | | | 10 |

Teacher's assessment | 0 | | | | | | | | | 10 |

Quality of thought

Student's assessment | 0 | | | | | | | | | 10 |

Teacher's assessment | 0 | | | | | | | | | 10 |

Realistic plans

Student's assessment | 0 | | | | | | | | | 10 |

Teacher's assessment | 0 | | | | | | | | | 10 |

Language

Student's assessment | 0 | | | | | | | | | 10 |

Teacher's assessment | 0 | | | | | | | | | 10 |

General appearance

Student's assessment | 0 | | | | | | | | | 10 |

Teacher's assessment | 0 | | | | | | | | | 10 |

Teacher's comments:

_____

_____

Parent's comments:

_____

_____

Student's comments:

_____

_____

The following grid is intended for evaluating a portfolio that would be presented to a potential employer. It can be simplified according to the needs of secondary or vocational students. To increase relevance for students, the grid includes specific references to the employer's perspective.

Criteria	1) BEGINNER	2) APPRENTICE	3) NEW HIRE	4) EXPERIENCED EMPLOYEE
Summary statements	Employer may not take you seriously. You do not leave the impression that you are serious about learning. Insufficient preparation. Organization of work is weak. Work includes many inaccuracies.	Employer will want to see rapid improvement. You have an elementary grasp of all the issues such as the subject matter (content), language requirements and how to improve learning. This is hopeful. However, you have some serious work to do.	Competent new employee. Employer will still expect you to improve. You have an understanding of all the issues such as the subject matter (the content), the language requirements and how to improve learning.	Outstanding work of a prized employee. Your work is consistent in quality. It has a high degree of precision. It is well organized, visually appealing and demonstrates depth of thought.
Organization of portfolio	No table of contents. It is difficult for the reader to find things. No page numbering. No apparent system of organization.	Table of contents does not accurately reflect contents. Uneven level of organization. Some sections well organized while others are disorganized.	Shows a good understanding of how to organize work in a reader-friendly way. Generally good quality, but somewhat uneven with certain shortcomings.	Material is user friendly: · table of contents reflects actual contents. · pages are clearly titled and numbered. · diagrams and charts are clearly labelled. · each section is organized in a similar fashion. · each section can be found quickly.
Appearance	Cover and title pages are not illustrated. Portfolio looks sloppy.	Cover and title pages are illustrated, but show little effort and thought. Links between illustrations and content unclear. Lack of neatness distracts reader. Excessive use of varying fonts.	Portfolio is relatively neat, but in need of improvement. Cover and title pages illustrated in a logical fashion. Clear link between illustrations and content. Some inconsistent use of fonts.	Varied use of illustrations (clear computer-generated or original art, pictures, good use of colour, balanced used of fonts). Visually reader-friendly (text is not too dense or sparse). Demonstrates creativity (has a personal, unique touch).

Criteria	1) BEGINNER	2) APPRENTICE	3) NEW HIRE	4) EXPERIENCED EMPLOYEE
Language usage	There is a considerable number of spelling errors. Vocabulary is simple and full of repetition. Includes incomplete sentences. Punctuation errors. Reader has difficulty understanding what the writer is trying to say. Messages in the letter are disorganized: · no bridges or transitions between paragraphs. · lack of logical progression. Does not reflect an understanding or those writing concepts that have been taught.	Several disjointed sentences. Vocabulary is simple and repetitive. Shows signs of organizing thoughts, but much remains to be done. Uneven quality. Several punctuation and spelling errors. Meaning is unclear in a few places. Uses only some of the writing concepts taught.	Language register is appropriate (vocabulary is suitably formal, appropriate for age level, non-repetitive, not too simple). Quality is relatively even. Messages in the letter or analyses are mostly in a logical order with proper transitions. Reflects a relatively clear understanding of those writing concepts that have been taught.	Language register is appropriate. Meaning is clear. Vocabulary is precise and varied. The covering letter is structured logically: · there are bridges between paragraphs and/or they follow in a logical order. There are very few language errors and these do not impact negatively on comprehension. Reflects a clear understanding of those writing concepts that have been taught.
Content relevancy	Pieces chosen are not linked to learning outcomes. Pieces chosen do not show progress made in learning. Pieces chosen do not meet vocational standards for the profession.	Few links are made between sample work and learning.	Most pieces chosen are linked to learning outcomes and reflect vocational standards for the profession. Most pieces chosen clearly show progress made in learning.	Pieces chosen are clearly linked to learning outcomes. Pieces chosen meet vocational standards for the profession. Pieces chosen clearly show progress made in learning.
Analysis of learning process	Does not reflect on the development of learning skills. Only quotes what others say without analysis of that commentary. Does not explain why the chosen work is relevant to his/her learning.	Little effort is made to go into depth. Little understanding of personal strengths and learning needs. Goals and plans are sketchy and unrealistic or not aligned to real needs. Approach is unsystematic.	Shows a good understanding of personal strengths. Has a sense of what needs more work. Has set some goals and made plans, but these could be more practical and systematic.	Gives concrete examples as evidence of learning. Analyses own work and the opinions of others in a systematic manner. Reflections regarding work try to get to the bottom of work habits, learning styles and needs. Draws logical conclusions. Sets challenging goals. Makes realistic plans.

Teaming up with fellow teachers

> **Method and mates**
>
> Methodology and teamwork go hand in hand. Teaming up with colleagues can maximize the impact of CLIL. Through teamwork, content and language knowledge can more readily move out of the confines of one classroom and find their application in another context. This is not only a relevance-builder for students, but for teachers as well.
>
> A new common space and greater sense of community is created that can feed the learning of all involved – teachers and students.

There are two primary reasons for teachers to co-operate:

1) It feels good and can lead to the birth of a team or a professional learning community that can support professional development and personal wellbeing.
2) Effective co-operation contributes to improved student achievement. [1]

CLIL is a challenge, both for teachers and students. Teaming up with other teachers to plan lessons, joint activities or strategies, or to adapt and develop materials is a way of creating the synergy for more easily meeting the demanding CLIL challenge. It can help us to lower stress, to work more efficiently, to be more precise in our goals and to avoid duplication. Above all, linking subjects makes learning more meaningful for students and prepares them better for a life that is not neatly organized into subjects.

As you start with CLIL, we suggest weekly meetings that include CLIL teachers and others involved with the same student groups. For example, the teacher of the first language can be a particularly supportive ally. This would be the place for planning and risk-free open and frank discussions that help lead to increased options for all involved. Suggestions for what to focus on during these meetings follow:

establishing commonality – recognizing the different contributions that all teachers are making to help students achieve planned outcomes.

recognizing achievement – taking the time to celebrate what you, your colleagues and your students have achieved.

agreeing* on learning skills outcomes – one learning skill can become the central focus of the entire school for a one-, two- or four-week period. You agree on who will teach what and how you will reinforce the skill.

[1] Hargreaves (2007) reports that '… professional learning communities have a systematic and positive effect on learning outcomes (Louis and Marks, 1998; McLaughlin and Talbert, 2001; Anderson and Togheri, 2002; Bolan et al, 2005)'.

* NB: By writing out key points that have been agreed upon, the participants' plans and commitments are likely to become clearer and are more likely to be implemented.

problems – everyone is going to have problems with CLIL, just as all educators face problems in their classroom. A team culture that makes it legitimate to have problems and that focuses on solving them will help everyone to move forward successfully and feel good about what they are doing.

agreeing on language outcomes – decisions are made about which grammar point(s), discourse patterns or vocabulary will be the focus of the week. Participants agree on who will do what.

creating cross-curricular projects – for example, a project that includes several CLIL teachers could also include the mother-tongue language teacher. Students might produce a précis of the project in their mother tongue. This hits several nails on the head at one time – it involves a non-CLIL teacher, that teacher gets a better understanding of what is being done in CLIL and it can support the acquisition of the needed terminology in the mother tongue.

sharing self-selected video clips of lessons – the teacher whose lesson was filmed chooses to share part or all of the lesson with colleagues. The discussion focuses on identifying what was done well. The teacher chooses one moment he or she would like to talk about improving and asks for ideas. Criticism is not aired in the discussion. Sharing of personal difficulties by all is encouraged, as are constructive suggestions.

make and take – a session where teachers meet to prepare materials for a given unit. As an alternative option, these sessions can be led by an expert in materials development. Teachers are provided with the resources and guidance in how to produce certain types of materials.

discussing at-risk pupils – teachers establish a joint strategy, report on progress and suggest needed changes.

sharing techniques – once a month at a staff meeting a teacher shares a technique that he or she has used in class and that has worked particularly well.

marking one project by several teachers – helps equalize values and standards. Encourages students to work extra hard and to better understand the skills and effort required for success.

revisiting standards, previous agreements or indicators of good teaching – occasionally revisiting these helps one to recall important principles and to stay on track in meeting common goals.

centrally organized district meetings – administrators create a forum and arrange for a short professional development session. Without the presence of administrators, a facilitator helps teachers to share experiences.

summarizing group achievements and deciding how to inform management – it is wise to blow your own trumpet from time to time. If you have been working hard to improve learning, other people should know about what you have done. This will build credibility and better position you to influence the channelling of needed resources for your work.

In addition to meetings, there are numerous other options for teaming up with colleagues. The following strategies have been gathered from teachers in the field:

observation – one or two teachers observe(s) a colleague's entire class. Afterwards, the lesson is discussed. This tool can be particularly effective when teachers first agree upon a specific focus for their discussion, such as getting the maximum number of students to speak or fostering critical thinking. This helps take the pressure off the person whose lesson is observed. It supports the sort of in-depth dialogue that fosters professional growth.

school exchanges – a teacher from one school switches classes with a teacher from another school for a day or a week. The new students and difference in school cultures can help give professional development an important boost.

team teaching – two teachers work together during a whole class to engage all pupils, thereby also modelling their favourite strategies to each other.

success stories – once a week, via email, one teacher shares a success he or she had with his or her class and explains what made it work.

posting new or adapted materials on the school intranet – done anonymously or signing one's work. This requires a little thought about how to archive and share work. Once people get in the habit of producing and storing all their materials on the intranet a vast world of resources opens up for everyone.

creating an idea bank – this is created on the school server. It is used to share ideas about, among others, discipline, projects, activities, evaluation and professional development material.

chat rooms – setting up a specific time once a week on the school website where school teachers and teachers from neighbouring schools can chat about concerns, solutions or successes, etc.

skype-ing – this free software makes it possible for small groups of people to converse with one another at a specific time every week without leaving home or the office. It works particularly well for small groups, up to three people.

working with target groups – the content and/or language teacher and a teaching assistant concentrate on helping a specific group of pupils to move forwards.

roleplaying an inspection – two colleagues use education authority criteria or an observation checklist to assess a lesson and then roleplay the dialogue between the inspector and the teacher.

Co-operation killers

Co-operation is not without its dangers. As you voluntarily team up with your fellow teachers, avoid the following like the plague:

1) Having managers hijack your agenda

   Managers are always under pressure to deliver, especially in environments that are driven by national test results. Stick to your guns in controlling your own agenda. In the long run, it will help improve student learning and probably test results as well.

2) Playing the blame game

   Administrators, students and parents are easy targets. Instead of blaming others, the focus needs to be on solutions, finding ways to raise the awareness of and influence on each of the groups.

   Avoid having your meetings digress into a self-indulgent wallowing about what is going wrong. Meetings like that just feed into depression and despondency. Look to understand causes and discuss scenarios that address the issue at hand.

3) Not understanding groupwork dynamics

   Knowledge about group dynamics will help give you the tools to better understand and manage your co-operation. This will help you to assess your progress in moving from the initial stage of forming your team, to dealing with the inevitable conflicts, to setting parameters and making it through to a more productive phase.

4) Only relying on your own team's resources

   At some point, you will begin to recycle your own knowledge. New learning needs to be brought to the group through reading, professional development courses, visiting other schools and so forth.

5) Forgetting to celebrate the short-term wins

   Take the time to enjoy and recognize the small victories. Otherwise, people get tired!

Head teachers/administrators are part of the teaching team. However, they may need help in fully understanding the needs of the CLIL students and the teaching team. In particular, at the start of a CLIL programme, you may need additional funds for teaching materials and extra time for planning. It may be helpful for head teachers to learn how some of their contemporaries have supported CLIL teachers in finding the time to plan together – adapted from Cloud et al, (2000):

- the head teacher takes three classes of pupils to the auditorium and shows them a content-related film. Thereafter he/she leads a discussion.
- the head teacher takes five or six classes of students and gives a lecture. Students are told that this format is common in post-secondary education. Before the lecture, they are given tips on note-taking. After the lecture, the students analyse their notes against a model using an evaluation grid to determine how many key points were taken note of and if subheadings were created, etc.

- one teacher takes two groups of students for an hour so one teacher can be freed up.
- teaching timetables are scheduled so that several teachers that need to co-operate have their planning periods at the same time.
- teachers are released from hall or lunchroom duty.
- one or two supply teachers are hired to come in for one day a week. If students are assigned individual work, or even groupwork, a supply teacher can handle two classes at once.
- a block of elective subjects is scheduled at the same time of day and taught by experts from the community.
- funds are sought for curriculum, course or learning materials development work during the school year or in the summer.
- student teachers are regularly received at the school, which will allow some teachers, on some occasions, to leave the classroom for planning sessions.
- during assemblies of the entire student body, one teacher can observe two classes, thus releasing half the staff.

5 Opening windows for personal achievement

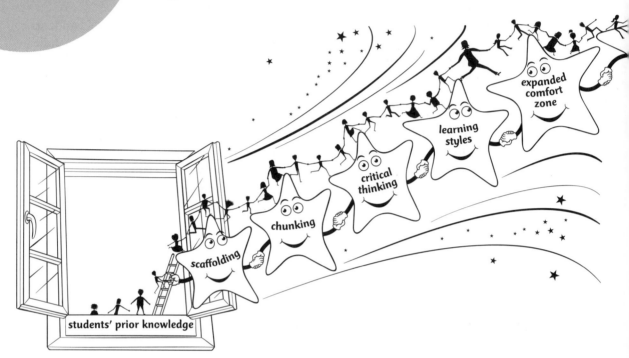

This chapter is about erasing limitations and increasing opportunities for personal achievement. Actions described here enable teachers and learners to take greater control over the learning process and to improve learning results. Scaffolding, anchoring into previous learning, chunking and repackaging knowledge, fostering creative and critical thinking, as well as challenging students to step just outside their comfort zone all expand learning opportunities for students. These are achievement builders for CLIL.

Hold the horses! Stop the show!

Q: Scaffolding, chunking, repackaging and fostering critical thinking are all characteristic of general good practice in teaching, aren't they?

A: Yes, they are!

Q: So tell me again, what are they doing in a book about CLIL?

A: CLIL cannot be divorced from good practice in education. Learning through a second language is cognitively demanding. CLIL methodology fuses both standard good practice in education and features that are unique to CLIL. The strategies discussed in this chapter are considered an essential part of daily CLIL practice. They can be used systematically to support the achievement of content, language and learning skills goals.

Building scaffolds

> *He who would learn to fly one day must first learn to stand and walk and run and climb and dance; one cannot fly into flying.*
>
> **Friedrich Nietzsche**

Just as we put up scaffolding to repair a building or to add another storey, scaffolding is used in education to access, improve and add to current knowledge. In education, scaffolding is akin to a temporary supporting structure that students learn to use and to rely on, in order to achieve learning outcomes.

Many of our parents unknowingly used scaffolding as they taught us how to ride a bicycle. They probably prepared us by first speaking to us about bicycles and about the importance of balance. It is likely that they helped us to address our fears or to think about related dangers. Later, we were given a tricycle, next, a bicycle with stabilizers added to keep us from falling over. And then, our parents removed the stabilizers and ran alongside us, holding the seat of the bike to keep us steady. Progressively, they would let go of the bike for a few seconds at a time until, finally, we managed to cycle proudly on our own, to the cheers of our parents. We learnt hand in hand with our parents, slowly assuming ever greater responsibility and gaining ever greater independence.

Meaning for the individual is created through a social process. 'What and how we learn, depends very much on the company we keep' (Gibbons, 2002). Scaffolding can be described as a partner-assisted, social rather than strictly individualistic learning process. It 'leads learners to reach beyond what they are able to achieve alone, to participate in new situations and to tackle new tasks' (Gibbons, 2002).

Scaffolding helps students to access previously acquired learning, to analyse it, to process new information, to create new relational links and to take their understanding several steps further. Moreover, it helps students to better understand the learning process, to build momentum, to save time and to enjoy short-term wins. It lowers frustration and builds success. In short, scaffolding is a sheltered learning technique that helps students feel emotionally secure, motivates them and provides the building blocks – such as language or background knowledge – needed to do complex work.

Scaffolding is not a permanent crutch. As one set of scaffolding is slowly removed, another set is quickly built up to support the next topic at hand. Taking into account that the ultimate goal of scaffolding is to help students take yet another step further in their understanding, scaffolding is constantly in a state of being rebuilt.

> **SCAFFOLDING SMARTS**
>
> Remove scaffolding bit by bit, but build it up quickly where needed.

Scaffolding can be built by teachers, other learners (groups, pairs, students who have mastered a topic, older students helping younger students), by materials, by structured tasks, by parents and by other members of the community.

There are a host of different scaffolding structures or strategies. Most teachers intuitively use some of these strategies even before exploring literature about the scaffolding technique. Strategies include:

- initially providing reinforcement for attempting to speak, then for a partially right answer and then for the right answer;
- explaining a point using the register of language used by students;
- brainstorming a topic to determine the existing level of knowledge;
- providing language immediately, as it is needed;
- avoiding the use of synonyms when referring to key terms;
- inserting synonyms or definitions in parentheses into the original text;
- placing notes in the margin of handouts;
- shortening sentences;
- breaking material into chunks;
- using graphic organizers such as Venn diagrams, tables and charts;
- reducing the number of tasks one gives to a student at one time;
- assessing obstacles to learning;
- highlighting the most important text in a passage;
- having students develop their own definitions for terms;
- having students explain to the class how they solved a maths problem;
- using pictures and realia;
- having students sum up a text by writing headings for each paragraph;
- having students sum up a reading passage by writing a newspaper headline;
- having students cut out 40 to 60 per cent of the original text (précis);
- giving clues and asking follow-up questions;
- providing key phrases or words used in writing introductions, bridging paragraphs and conclusions, together with a writing assignment;
- helping students to better understand and manage the learning process.

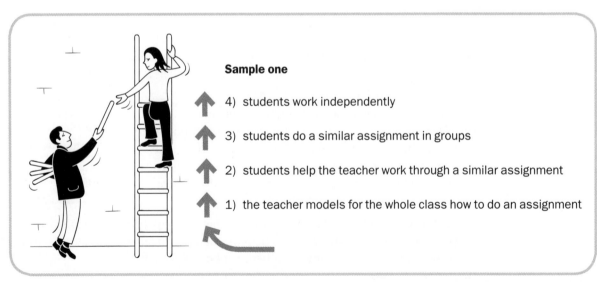

Sample one

4) students work independently

3) students do a similar assignment in groups

2) students help the teacher work through a similar assignment

1) the teacher models for the whole class how to do an assignment

Sample two

7) students read an additional passage alone and answer questions for homework

6) discussion on where the errors in logic were made

5) students read a text on logging and compare their educated guesses with accurate information

4) students work in groups to identify false statements

3) students read a concept map that contains three false statements about logging

2) a classroom discussion on the pros and cons of logging in national parks, with key ideas and vocabulary recorded on the board

1) students close their eyes and envisage one thing of beauty they have seen, smelt, touched, heard or tasted in a forest or in a national or city park. These thoughts are shared in pairs. A few students also share what their partner said with the entire class.

The remaining sections of this chapter can be used as elements of scaffolding. At the same time, each can be seen as a teaching strategy in its own right.

Anchoring into previous learning

Proficiency is not developed by compensating for lack of ability, but rather by extending related knowledge and skills that the student already brings to the classroom.

Every Student Succeeds

Just as scaffolding surrounding a building needs to be on a firm foundation, so does scaffolding in education. To make progress in 'understanding' means 'linking to prior learning' (Petty, 2006). Just reproducing something is not evidence of understanding, of learning. 'Relational links are the glue that fixes learning in memory' (Petty, 2006), and the first relational link that needs to be made is to one's prior learning. It is our existing knowledge base and our current level of understanding that provide the underpinning for new learning. Our existing knowledge base and our current level of understanding serve as a foundation and as an anchor for new learning.

This applies not just to the learning of content, but to language learning as well. Students can be asked to recall language they feel may be useful for the topic at hand. This language can be posted on the board. However, new language needs a firm place to anchor. Although prior language is part of that firm foundation, so are the student's own attitudes, opinions or experiences related to the topic under study.

Language also takes root when there is an authentic context and students can immediately put the language to use. Providing language out of context prior to a

A USEFUL RETHINK

There is strong evidence that just-in-time language teaching can be more effective than pre-teaching vocabulary.

(Gibbons, 2002)

lesson is likely to be less effective than first creating the personal connection and the context, and then providing the language immediately or just in time, as it is needed, as it can be immediately applied.

Language and content acquisition go hand in hand. New language is best acquired while assessing one's current state of understanding and while acquiring new content knowledge that is used in class to achieve new levels of understanding.

The following is an example of how a content teacher might begin to introduce physics. It connects to and helps bring out existing knowledge, and uses other scaffolding techniques to begin to further the student's understanding of physics.

Provide students with the following descriptions in writing:

Descriptions

Chemistry, biology and physics have been described as follows:

a) you know it's **chemistry** if it **smells**;

b) it's **biology** when someone/something is **green and squirming** and

c) it's **physics** when something doesn't **work**.

Read through the above definitions together and present your own story in writing and orally, checking for comprehension.

My (the teacher's) story

I used to have a car with one tyre that used to go flat slowly. Once a month, I had to pump up the tyre with air.

What was involved: chemistry, biology or physics?

My explanation: Option 1

The tyre was flat. I could not drive the car.

The car was not in **working** order. That makes it physics.

My explanation: Option 2 (process of elimination)

The tyre going flat isn't related to smell or someone/something turning green or squirming, so it must be physics.

Your (the student's) story

Describe two incidents from everyday life.

Decide **with a partner** if each of these incidents belongs to the domain of chemistry, biology or physics.

Sharing

As these personal stories are shared with the whole class, students are encouraged to explain their reasoning. You ask follow-up questions such as: *Very good, a roller coaster is a good example of physics at work. If the engine only pulls the roller coaster cars to the top of the first slope, what makes the cars keep moving after that? What makes the ride work after the first big slope, after the big peak?*

CONNECTING PHYSICS TO EXISTING KNOWLEDGE

- language that students understand and use in their lives
- examples from everyday life
- builds a foundation for new learning

FACILITATING COMPREHENSION

Key concepts and words in bold

Example from everyday life

CONNECTING TO OTHER SUBJECTS

Developing relational links facilitates comprehension

Explaining one's reasoning

CHUNKING

- subheadings used
- each step presented

CONNECTING TO EVERYDAY SITUATION

easily grasped example

Connecting to and analysing student's OWN experiences

STUDENT-BUILT SCAFFOLD

Pairwork provides support before trying something on one's own.

Student-shared examples may be more easily retained than those presented by the teacher.

FOLLOW-UP QUESTIONS

Take thinking one step further

One of the most common and effective ways of anchoring into previous learning is through brainstorming. Brainstorming is an exercise in free association. A topic is raised, such as elephants, safety issues at school, alcoholism, how to make hotel clients feel welcome or how to solve conflicts. Participants say whatever comes to mind in relation to the given topic. Once the initial brainstorming session is completed, the results are analysed. Students are usually encouraged to see if they can group or categorize the points raised during the session.

In CLIL, brainstorming words or expressions needed to do an assignment is a common pratice. The result of a brainstorming session can be a word bank. The words or expressions can be categorized as nouns, verbs, phrases, expressions for bridging paragraphs, etc.

As a first step, the rules for brainstorming are discussed with the students. These include:

- no verbal criticism of any idea;
- no non-verbal (grimaces, gestures) criticism of any idea;
- no compliments;
- body language is neutral;
- all ideas are recorded;
- wild and zany ideas are welcome;
- 'piggy-backing' on already recorded ideas is welcome;
- quantity is more important than quality.

Classroom management

Despite the rules, students are still likely to comment on the ideas being generated during brainstorming. Many will refrain from saying something but may groan, laugh, grimace or otherwise express their opinion through body language.

Try the following:

- do a brainstorming session on why some students are afraid to contribute;
- do a brainstorming session on how to control the natural desire to comment;
- repeat the rule out loud as it is infringed and then encourage students to keep going with the brainstorming;
- have the students assume responsibility for saying *no criticism* when someone infringes the rule.

Instead of simply listing words on the board during a brainstorming session, a web can be created (see the following pages). Any given circle in the web can be used to start brainstorming a new subset.

Another option is to structure thinking prior to beginning a brainstorming session by using a framework. We propose the diamond. The students are provided with the topic, in the centre of the diamond, and four subheadings. Students brainstorm one category at a time or all four at once.

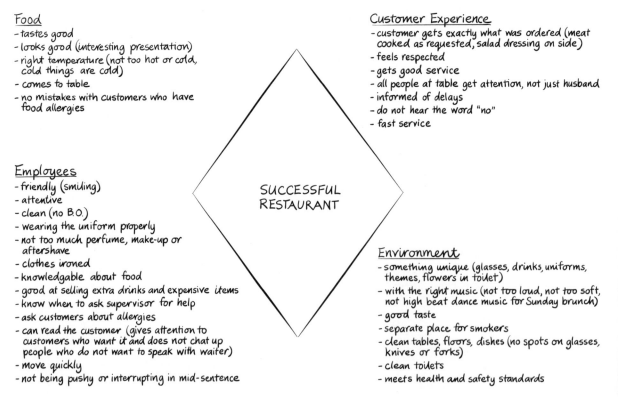

Previously acquired knowledge can also be accessed using a variety of graphic organizers. For example, provide your students with the following partially completed fishbone organizer. The one presented below is about elephants. All or most of the subheadings are provided. Students can provide some of their own subheadings. The subheadings will probably help students to recall more information than can be obtained during a simple brainstorm.

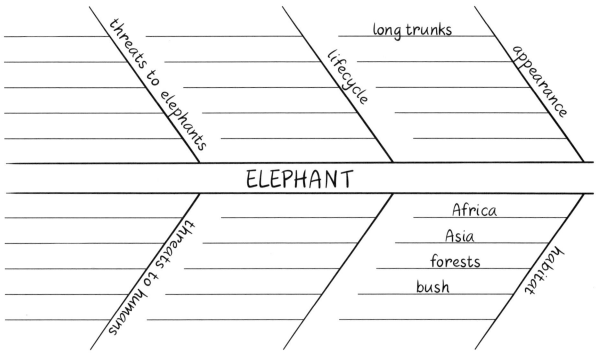

The 'Getting ready to learn' framework on the following pages helps not only to anchor into previous learning, but also provides a forum for talking about feelings and attitudes. If the student's attitude vis-à-vis a new topic is negative, it is best to know about it, so it can be addressed. If a student says a topic is stupid or useless, no judgement need be made. It is important to ask probing questions to find out why a student feels that way and to check with the student whether you have properly understood the reasoning given by mirroring back the student's statements.

> *Attitude is a little thing that makes a big difference.*
> **Winston Churchill**

Some students can share why they feel the topic is relevant. Those opposed to the topic and the rest of the class can be asked for ideas about how to make the topic more relevant to them. Since the topic is likely to be part of the curriculum, it cannot be skipped. As fear of failure is often behind a negative attitude, it is wise to explore with the students what would help him or her get through this less pleasant part of the curriculum. The following chart can be helpful in doing this.

What I know	How I learnt this	How I feel about this topic	What I want to learn

Chunking and repackaging knowledge

A king had three sons, whom he loved. He also loved his country. The king had to choose the right son to succeed him. The country had to be ruled wisely. The king thought long and hard about how to make the right choice. Finally, he tied some branches into a small bundle. Then he called his sons and told them that the son who could break the whole bundle would inherit the throne. The eldest son tried and tried, but he was not able to break the bundle. The same thing happened to the second son. When his turn came, the third son untied the bundle and broke the branches one by one.

The moral of this Spanish folktale, based on one of Aesop's fables, is that breaking big bundles into smaller pieces helps one to succeed. In this information age, we have probably all experienced being overwhelmed by the sheer amount of information thrown at us. For most of us, information is better absorbed when it is packaged into digestible bites. For example, telephone numbers are usually grouped into two, three or four numbers to facilitate reading and retention. Sometimes letters are used.

12 24 78 48 22   or   (416) 577-3472   or   1-800-FAB-PIZZA

It is commonly believed that the average person can hold no more than seven pieces of information in his or her short-term working memory. So there is little point in presenting large amounts of information quickly. Our minds unconsciously reject excess information.

To move information into our long-term memory so it can be recalled at a later time, we need to anchor it to prior knowledge by defining relational links and contrasting new knowledge with old. We need to put the new knowledge to use, organize it, assess it and consider it relevant.

When written material or oral information is presented in clear chunks that do not contain more than seven pieces of well organized information, the short-term memory can usually process it. A sense of confidence and emotional security can develop. As each small chunk of information is worked through, the student is likely to experience a feeling of success. There is an almost immediate sense that the material is 'doable'. This positive reinforcement makes it easier to stay on task. If the student's mind wanders, it is easier to return to the material when chunks are clearly delineated.

For educators, chunking can facilitate communication with students and can further the use of scaffolding. As soon as learners have worked through one chunk of text or material, you can ask questions such as:

- *What is the key question this chunk/section/paragraph poses?*
- *What is the most important thing you need to remember here?*
- *What is the key message?*
- *What are you going to highlight (with a marker) in the text?*
- *How does this contrast or link with what we learnt about topic 'X' last week?*
- *What are the key words or expressions you need to remember?*
- *How are you going to help yourself recall this information?*

As students become more adept at answering some of the above questions, they can create their own scaffolding by working in groups or pairs to answer questions about key chunks. As it becomes clear that students are coping well with the written material, the scaffolding can slowly be withdrawn. As the students proceed through the text, some key paragraphs can simply be spot-checked to ensure that everyone is on track. At this point, the activity may have become an exercise in independent reading.

There are numerous tools for chunking. They include graphic organizers such as tables, charts, graphs, diagrams, mind maps, webs and pictures. Chunking also involves using analogies, mnemonic devices or groups of words and numbers. Samples of these tools for chunking are presented below. Finally, a full lesson is described.

JAPAN TODAY: Five categories – Five facts				
Major cities and their population figures	**Major exports**	**Major imports**	**Education system**	**Major historical events still having an impact on the country**

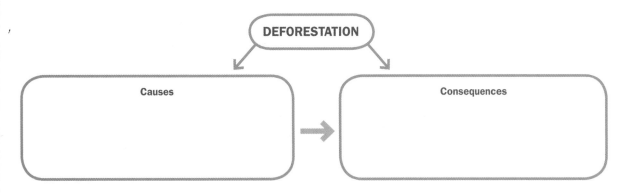

STORY MAPPING

TITLE: The Little Prince

AUTHOR: Antoine de Saint-Exupéry

MAIN CHARACTER: THE LITTLE PRINCE

OTHER CHARACTERS: THE PILOT
THE ROSE
THE FOX
THE SNAKE

CLIMAX

10. The prince decides to return home and lets the snake bite him.

9. After telling his story, the prince sets off with the pilot to find water.

8. The prince refuses.

7. A snake offers to send the prince to the heavens with poison.

6. The little prince arrived on Earth.

5. Travelling to Earth, the little prince visited six planets. He doesn't understand why people behave as they do.

4. The little prince explains why he left his home (Asteroid B612).

3. The pilot and the prince become friends.

2. A little prince arrives.

1. The pilot crashes in the desert.

11. The pilot fixes the plane.

12. Next day the prince's body is gone.

13. When pilot sees stars, he hears his friend laughing.

14.

15.

CONFLICT: The little prince catches his beloved friend the rose in a lie and leaves home to cure his loneliness.

SOLUTION: The little prince dies and hopefully goes to heaven, to his asteroid in the sky.

LOCATION: The Sahara desert

MAIN IDEA: The important things in life are only visible to the heart.

Based on Buehl, 1995

CONCEPT EXPANDER

term → → related words → summary statement → → → consequences → → → summary statement

| GLOBAL WARMING | radiation emission trap atmosphere ultraviolet | Global warming results from emissions being trapped in the atmosphere, which increases ultraviolet radiation. | drought (East Africa, 2007) migration (Darfur, 2007) extreme weather (Asian Tsunami, 2004) famine (Horn of Africa, 2007) | Global warming will lead to more drought, migration, famine and extreme weather across the world. |

term → → related words → summary statement → → → consequences → → → summary statement

| CARBON FOOTPRINT | responsibility damage choice lifestyle sustainability | Each person can choose to live a sustainable lifestyle and can take responsibility for reducing damage to the world. | ecological balance (less extreme weather) more secure future (cleaner air) global citizenship (thinking globally, acting locally) wellbeing (fewer respiratory illnesses) | The citizens of the globe will have a more secure future if they work to reduce each person's carbon footprint and increase ecological balance and wellbeing. |

Expanding the expander

Once a topic has been organized and systematized using the concept expander, students can be supported in developing a series of sentences on any given example from the consequences they listed. This can be done by simply asking for a five-line report on, for example, the drought in East Africa. Another option is to help students think through several aspects of an issue such as the impact of environmental damage on the economy, people and international relations. Students could also develop a series of recommendations for reducing their own family's carbon footprint.

Mnemonic devices

Using catchy sentences, phrases or jingles can help us all to recall information. We favour having students invent their own. For example, each week, two students can be responsible for developing a mnemonic device that they share with the class on the last day of the week that helps their classmates recall a point learnt during the week.

Some examples of mnemonic devices used in the English-speaking world for generations, as well as more recent ones, follow:

Thirty days hath September,
April, June and November;
All the rest have thirty-one,
Excepting February alone:
Which hath but twenty-eight, in fine,
Till leap year gives it twenty-nine.

In fourteen-hundred and ninety-two, Columbus sailed the ocean blue.

Please excuse my dear Aunt Sally.
This helps recall the order of maths operations (parentheses, exponents, multiplication, division, addition, subtraction).

My very earnest mother just served us nine pickles.
Mercury, Venus, Earth, Mars, Jupiter, Saturn, Uranus, Neptune, Pluto.

Pluto is no longer considered a planet and as new planets are discovered the list changes:

My very entrepreneurial mother Cheryl just sold us nine cheap Xenons!
Mercury, Venus, Earth, Mars, Ceres, Jupiter, Saturn, Uranus, Neptune, Charon, Xena.

Two old angels skipped over heaven carrying ancient harps.
This one is used in maths to remember the equations for tangent, sine and cosine.
O stands for opposite, A stands for adjacent and H stands for hypotenuse.
Therefore, tangent = opposite/adjacent, sine = opposite/hypotenuse and cosine = adjacent/hypotenuse.
See http://712educators.about.com/b/a/141766.htm/

Kings play cards on fat green stools.
Tells us the order of taxonomy in biology: kingdom, phylum, class, order, family, genus, species.
See http://www.mnemonic-device.eu/biology/

Chunking and repackaging in maths: sample lesson

The following is the first maths lesson of a new unit on Pythagoras' theorem. It begins by accessing prior knowledge and connecting with the personal interests of the students. The lesson takes into account the following aspects of anchoring into previous knowledge, providing scaffolding and chunking information:

- it starts with students explaining their own preferences;
- it includes a human interest story (connects with the underdog in all of us);
- the story connects with a widespread interest in the Olympic Games;
- it provides explanations for difficult vocabulary;
- the work process helps build learning skills such as guessing meanings from context or reorganizing information;
- students organize information according to a graphic organizer – categorizing and thereby chunking;

- the chunking exercise is initially interesting and easy, yet gets progressively more difficult, requiring more critical thinking;
- the assignment is provided one step at a time so as not to overwhelm students;
- it helps students to organize information;
- it builds a bridge to individual work through pairwork;
- it provides an additional framework (an organizational guide) for the most difficult part of the assignment.

As a first step, a few minutes are devoted to asking students:

- *Who watches the Olympic Games?*
- *What are your favourite competitions?*
- *Is there an athlete that has partcularly impressed you? Why?*

Have the students read the following text about an Olympic athlete. Afterwards, discuss it briefly.

> During the early years of the Olympic Games, organizers did not want to let this stubborn, young hawk-nosed brawler* enter the competion. They said he was too small. But the young man persisted*. He was eventually allowed to compete. He beat everyone. If this had happened in our time, Pythagoras would have made the headlines of all the papers: 'Unkown Greek wins gold medal in fist fighting'. As you know, nowadays, fist fighting is not an Olympic sport. However, in those days, there were no newspapers or medals. Had there been newspapers and medals, they are unlikely to have survived for thousands of years. Legends, however, seem to have a long life. Pythagoras's life is the stuff of legends.
>
> *Adapted from Studies of Famous Mathematicians, Heino Koppel, Tallinn 2000*

* brawler
someone who is always ready to fight

* to persist
to keep working at something, to not give up

As a third step, have students look at pictures of Pythagoras in encyclopedias or on the Internet. It helps to put a face to the person being studied. Students are also likely to gain further information from their search. Ask them to describe the man.

Tell students they will be creating a poster about Pythagoras. This establishes the learning outcome.

Next, have students read a text individually to find facts about Pythagoras. Due to limited space, we are not reproducing the text here, but many are available on the Internet by searching for *Pythagoras biography*. Of course, most would need to be simplified by shortening sentences, eliminating the less important information and by explaining difficult terms, expressions and words.

Have the students scan the text for unfamiliar words. Work through a maximum of five words or expressions together. Provide clues and encourage the students to guess the meaning from the context. Tell the students that as they are working on their own, they do not need to understand every word as long as they get the main ideas.

Next, have the students work individually to search for facts in the text. Each student writes each fact he or she finds on a separate card, sticky note or small piece of paper.

Next, students form groups of four or five and compare facts. This allows students to see what they have missed and to self-evaluate achievement.

The students continue to work together to group the ideas into categories. The categories are given names such as 'discoveries', 'famous sayings' or 'personal life'.

Provide the students with large pieces of paper and remind them that they are going to create a poster about Pythagoras. The facts are glued onto the sheet of poster paper according the scheme below, which is provided to the students as a handout. Students write in the names of the categories they have determined.

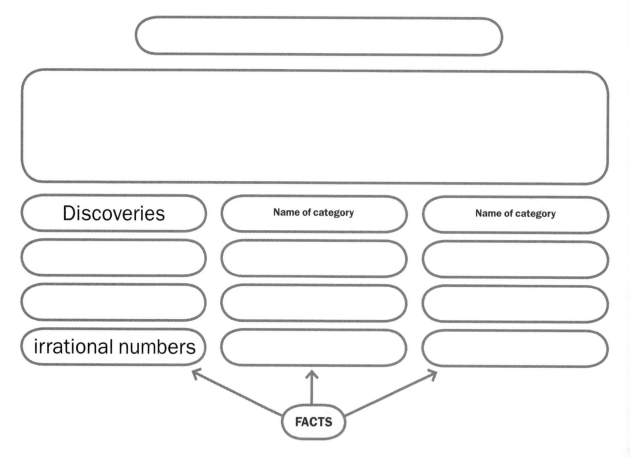

NB: The graphic organizer does not label all of the boxes. Some steps in the assignment are unknown. This allows the students to concentrate on each step of the assignment without having to worry about what remains to be done.

Next, each group gives the text a title, writing it in the upper box of their poster. Students then develop a summary statement in the box below the title, the second box from the top. This may seem very difficult for some students. By suggesting that the summary statement include information from the title, the names of the categories and some examples from the facts, and by writing this clue on the board, students are more likely to be successful in doing this difficult part of the assignment.

Fostering creative and critical thinking

In the days before television, Albert Einstein often travelled on lecture tours with his chauffeur. Once, as they were arriving at the next small town on the tour, Einstein complained to his driver that he was getting bored of repeating the same lecture over and over. The driver responded by saying, 'anytime you want to change roles ...'. Einstein took him up on his offer. As the driver had heard the lecture over a hundred times, all went well. He was even able to answer the typical questions asked after the lecture. Then someone asked the driver a question that he could not answer. Einstein sank in his seat, thinking they were about to be caught in perpetrating a hoax. However, the driver, continuing to pose as Einstein, responded by saying, 'you know, that question is so easy I'll bet even my driver, who is sitting over there, could answer it.'

The moral of the story? Creative and critical thinking can get you out of a pickle and even help you out-think a genius.

Creative thinking involves the creation/generation or further development of ideas, processes, objects, relational links, synergies and quality relationships. Critical thinking involves the evaluating of all of the above.

On a practical level, in the context of education, critical thinking can be described as mental processes that learners use 'to plan, describe and evaluate their thinking and learning' (Moseley et al, 2005). It is self-directed thinking and, thus, fundamental to learning. By working to improve the quality of our thinking, we improve learning.

Yet creative thinking, as well, is an essential element in effective planning or, at the very least, has the potential to improve planning. As we try to analyse and solve problems in our everyday lives, we often imagine various solutions. Creativity can be used to better explain our ideas to others and even to evaluate our plans and results from unique perspectives. It is difficult to separate creative thinking from critical thinking. Both are inextricably intertwined.

Moreover, our values, attitudes and feelings have an impact on our thinking. Thus we need to examine the influence of these elements on our thinking processes. For example, having a negative attitude about a topic will ultimately affect our capacity to learn. Our minds are more likely to reject information about which we have negative feelings.

Our feelings are our most genuine paths to knowledge.
Audre Lorde

Our emotional state of mind can contribute to or hinder learning. Positive emotions 'enhance the ability to think flexibly and with more complexity, thus making it easier to find solutions to problems' (Goleman, 1995). Conversely, 'when a concept struggles with an emotion, the emotion almost always wins' (Sousa, 2001). It is difficult to think rationally when one is emotionally overwhelmed by negative feelings or insecurities. Thus, 'learners in positive, joyful environments are likely to experience better learning, memory, and feelings of self-esteem' (Jensen 1996, as cited by Wright, 2005).

Since meaning is co-constructed through a social process, critical thinking is also tied to social processes. The understandings we reach and the solutions to problems we propose need to match on some level with the understanding of others. At the very least, others have to be prepared to accommodate our views.

Most educators operate on the premise that quality of thinking can be improved with the support of others, be they teachers, mentors, peers or parents. Ways of supporting students in honing critical thinking skills follow.

There are dozens of frameworks for thinking. These frameworks make it easier for us to analyse our thinking. They make it easier to understand meta-cognitive processes and to manage our own thinking. They are a learning skill for better managing thinking. As educators, we can use them to support students in becoming independent learners who more effectively manage their own thinking and memory.

In education circles, perhaps one of the most widely known models of critical thinking is Bloom's taxonomy. He states that all learners need to develop both lower and higher thinking skills. The six levels of difficulty start with practical lower order thinking (eg, labelling a diagram) and move upwards to more abstract and complex higher order skills (eg, critical evaluation). However, not all teachers have found all levels of Bloom's model easy to use. Working in concert with Bloom and his colleagues, Anderson and Krathwohl (2000) posited a modified version of Bloom's taxonomy.

A word to the wise

Of the approximately 80 000 questions asked on average annually by teachers, 80 per cent are at the lowest level of thinking – factual knowledge.

(Gall 1984, Watson & Young 1986, as cited by Echevarria et al, 2000)

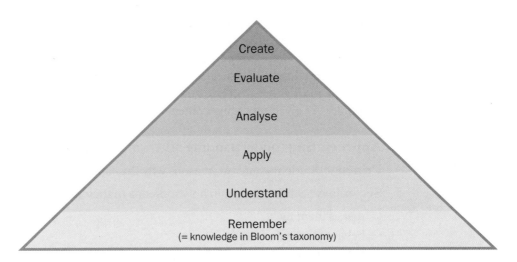

We find this modified taxonomy particularly useful as a checklist. It is our belief that if the majority of lessons are based on tasks associated with:

- applying one's new knowledge and understanding;
- analysing the effectiveness of the application of new knowledge and understanding;
- evaluating progress in task completion and learning; and
- creating something new;

this will lead to greater levels of learning. It will also lead to greater recall of facts, for we learn best through experience. In fact, the 'remember' and 'understand' levels are embedded into activities such as analysing, evaluating and creating.

Both Bloom's taxonomy and Anderson and Krathwohl's updated version of that taxonomy provide a series of verbs, in addition to those in the pyramid, to help educators to use the pyramid. For example, for the pyramid verb *analyse*, other verbs are provided which help educators to plan learning activities. These include *differentiate, organize, attribute, sequence, subdivide*, as well as *distinguish between* or *among*. The lists are easily found on the Internet by typing *beyond Bloom* or *Bloom's taxonomy* into one of the many search engines.

There are many other frameworks for fostering critical thinking. The non-hierarchical list of verbs on the following pages can be considered as one of those frameworks. It is not so much a systematic whole as a general guide for developing activities that foster high order thinking skills. It includes some overlap. It was created in large part based on Stahl and Murphy's framework for thinking and learning, combined with elements from other models for cognitive (and affective) development such as those by Quellmatz, Presseisen, Halpern or Perry (as presented by Moseley et al, 2005). The verbs constitute a checklist, a sort of treasure trove that can be drawn upon to expand one's repertoire of strategies for developing critical and creative thinking. It can also serve as a 'spiceometer' – it helps one to keep in mind the old adage that *variety is the spice of life*.

What follows are some examples of how we can use this list of verbs to foster the development of creative and critical thinking in the classroom. These verbs help bring out facts; look at various processes including the learning process; analyse attitudes, emotions and values; and support the development of thinking skills and emotional intelligence to create new knowledge and experiences for the learner. Examples are given regarding content, language and learning skills.

Appreciating (understanding others and yourself)

Primary: Students state two reasons why they appreciate key people in their lives.

Secondary: Students explain how someone in their lives that they admire:

- makes them feel;
- behaves towards them;
- helps them see things more clearly.

Vocational: Students explain five things that they like about their vocational field.

Students name five attitudes they would appreciate in their colleagues at work.

Assigning (setting items apart for a particular purpose)

Primary: Students describe human traits found in animals and vice versa.

Students analyse the dangers of assigning labels to people.

Secondary: Students assign responsibility for the current state of the environment to various stakeholders and propose solutions.

Students assign mathematical values to letters in formulas.

Vocational: Students assign roles and tasks in a group, and afterwards weigh up how fairly work was divided.

Associating (connecting items together)

Primary: Students make birds by fitting together pieces of a teacher-created bird puzzle. In particular, pieces for the necks and heads are cut in such a way that any head will fit on any bird.

One student gives a definition and the others guess the word or expression.

Students match answers with questions.

Secondary: Students create analogies of how the body and the world's ecosystem are similar, eg, by identifying the impact of the failure of one key component.

Vocational: Students interview working people to find out how soft skills such as teamwork and positive thinking can increase performance and production.

Classifying (putting items into categories)

Primary: Each child places one shoe in a pile. Students decide how to sort them, eg, by size, boys', girls', sport, leather, plastic, sandals, running, dress shoes, colours, etc. This activity can be used to integrate maths into language lessons by creating and analysing graphs or tables. (*How many leather shoes are there?* Sentences making comparisons with *more, less, fewer*; sentences that express preferences.)

Students sort vocabulary into 'difficult words' and 'easy words'.

Secondary: Students classify the ecosystem in a local park according to producers, consumers, decomposers, predators and prey. They identify dangers to each group that could disturb the natural balance and suggest prevention strategies.

Students sort vocabulary into 'difficult words' and 'easy words'. They can also brainstorm effective and ineffective studying strategies.

Vocational: Students studying nursing classify ethical issues they are likely to face in a job. They develop response scenarios and analyse potential consequences.

Key phrases, nouns and verbs needed to discuss a given topic or classification can be listed.

Combining (putting items into a single whole)

Primary: Students look at patterns and decide on pattern blocks that constitute a whole unit. For example, things that are circular and layered, eg, trees and the solar system.

Students combine seemingly disjointed words into a sentence: (*photosynthesis, planets, morning, pills, Paris, mouldy, fashion show*).

Photosynthesis, pills and planets provided the inspiration for this morning's fashion show in mouldy old Paris.

Secondary: Students discuss how diverse factors contribute to a single social problem, such as vandalism.

Students imagine what the result would be if two famous and very different people worked together, eg, a portrait painted by two very different artists from history such as Leonardo Da Vinci and Andy Warhol, or a plane invented by the Wright Brothers and fashion-conscious footballer David Beckham.

Vocational: Students list the serious physical or mental consequences of taking various combinations of drugs.

Students are provided with a list of nouns, verbs and/or adjectives that they combine into instructions for using equipment (eg, *measure out, area, dig, test, lay, pattern, supervisor*).

Measure out the patio area. Dig out a test area. Lay the bricks into a pattern. Ask your supervisor for approval. Start work.

Committing (understanding and accepting responsibility)

Primary: Engage students in projects that foster commitment, such as volunteering in homes for the aged or at an animal charity. Students then write about the experience.

Secondary: Explore in groups the implications and commitments of the school sponsoring a child in another country, eg, short-term and long-term responsibilities, costs, activities, leadership, lobbying, reporting and checking the emotional and physical wellbeing of individuals involved.

Vocational: Students analyse the reasoning behind an industry's ethical code and think about the implications of not following such a code. For example, aircraft mechanics agree not to use spare parts without serial numbers. Uncertified parts may be of substandard quality and cause serious accidents.

Comparing (identifying similarities and differences)

Primary: Students compare the type and quantity of waste produced by one classroom with another.

Students compare similarities and differences in descriptions of the same event by various people or authors.

Students compare language used in blogs and magazines.

Secondary: Students draw the night sky and compare it to a drawing in a textbook.

Students compare text messaging with emails, describing differences in the use of vocabulary, abbreviations, punctuation, style, greetings, length and purpose.

Vocational: Students watch video clips and compare interpersonal styles across cultures.

Students compare the language of someone working in customer service to the language of someone working in a warehouse.

Condensing (distilling the essence of a text)

Primary: Students reduce a story into a series of subheadings.

Students condense a definition into one word.

Secondary: Students write about an important historical event in the style of a contemporary newspaper article, as though it were a piece of breaking news.

Vocational: Students reduce employee rules and regulations into a series of generalizations, eg,

- wash hands before touching food
- separate cooked and uncooked food

Hygiene needs to be maintained on personal and work levels.

Converting (changing the features of an item or information)

Primary: Students convert mixed numbers into fractions.

Students convert sentences written in common speech into a different register. For example, a student's oral description of a science experiment could be written up as a scientific report.

Secondary: Students convert the class's energy use during one week into a carbon footprint.

Vocational: Students convert a recipe for 5 servings to 500 servings.

Students convert sentences used in the kitchen amongst staff into sentences that could be shared with clients, eg, *That's bloody hot!* versus *It is a rather spicy dish, madam.*

Defining (determining key qualities and/or characteristics)

Primary: Students define terms related to weather.

Students guess a word or expression that someone is thinking of by asking yes and no questions.

Secondary: Students develop their own definitions for terms in maths, science, literature and geography.

Students solve riddles.

Vocational: Students define work processes such as frying, poaching, checking, testing, cutting, grinding, milling, mixing, weighing and measuring.

Describing (reporting the features of an item or information)

Primary: A student describes an object or concept and asks the other students to guess the word.

Student A and B both have a picture or a drawing of the same animal. The animals are virtually identical, but a few features are slightly different in each of the photos or drawings. Without showing each other the pictures, the students work together to discover the differences. (This activity is also an act of comparing.)

Secondary: Student A describes a painting to student B, without showing it to his or her partner. Student B draws a picture based on student A's description. Student A looks at the result and describes what changes need to be made. Then the two students compare the drawing with the original, assessing their collaboration and drawing conclusions. This activity can also be used to draw a series of geometric shapes, or in maths to describe the measurements of various objects.

Vocational: Student A describes an electrical scheme, which student B then draws. Student A looks at the result and describes changes to be made. The students compare the drawing with the original, assessing their collaboration and drawing conclusions. Students then complete the task with a visual, an auditory and a kinesthetic learner. They assess whether the task was completed as desired. This is followed by an analysis of where the instructions could be improved.

Designating (assigning a name, a title or a function to an item)

Primary: Students analyse various popular board games to determine which ones require a greater level of skill. In groups, they create their own board game requiring several higher order thinking skills.

Secondary: Students study aerial photographs and provide land use designations (eg, agricultural, industrial, recreational, nature reserve). They justify their designations.

Vocational: Students name every tool they use, elements in an electrical circuit, in a microscope or in an aircraft wing.

Students listen to dialogues and designate the register of language being used (formal, casual, professional, non-professional, etc).

Discriminating (treating some items of information differently from others)

Primary: Students explain how they behave with someone they trust, distrust, like or dislike, and how they behave with a friend, a stranger or a bully.

Secondary: Students discriminate unhealthy patterns of behaviour from healthy patterns of behaviour in relationships with their classmates.

Students analyse differences in how two newspapers treat the same topic.

Students separate essential information from the non-essential information in a chapter in a book, a report, a manual or a presentation.

Vocational: Students define how to tell the difference between high-quality and low-quality products.

Students establish criteria for measuring products created in vocational classes.

Students establish the differences between a safe and unsafe working environment.

Students distinguish various types of damage on the fuselage of aircraft or on the body of a car.

Extending (taking ideas a step further)

Primary: Students write a continuation of a fairy tale they have just read.

Secondary: Students give an extended explanation of a definition, eg, if a historical figure is referred to as a *right-winger*, the students might explain what sorts of policies this person supported and fought against.

Vocational: Students are provided with a dictionary definition of the word *professionalism*. They then define what the word means to them personally and describe how they think professionals behave in the workplace.

Identifying cause and effect (defining what was at the root of an event and what result it produced)

Primary: When a student is upset in class, stop and ask him or her to identify what he or she is feeling. He or she should also describe what happened. This usually calms the student down, as it requires some thinking. If the student is upset because of the actions of a classmate, identify one reason why that classmate may have behaved in the way he or she did. Then propose two possible solutions to the situation.

Secondary: Students analyse the domino effect and look for examples from history where it has occurred. Students could also look for instances where the domino effect was predicted to produce one result, but in the end led to another.

Students look at paintings and identify geometric shapes such as squares, circles, triangles, trapezoids and parallelograms within them. Then they analyse the effect of these shapes on the artwork.

Students identify the cause of unproductive behaviours and their consequences.

Vocational: Students look at ten workplace problems and decide how each one relates to the other nine problems. For example, students could determine whether each of the following problems is a cause or consequence of the other problems:

- a lack of time
- too great a workload
- a dissatisfied client
- tensions among staff
- low morale
- unfilled positions
- lack of turnover in sales
- low profitability
- old equipment
- no parking

Students then decide in which order the problems should be tackled.

Imaging (forming a mental image)

Primary: Students lay their heads on the desk and close their eyes. Have them imagine they are a virus living on a door handle and looking for a body to enter. Which points of entry would they try? How would they enter the body? Where would they move to in the body? What problems would they cause for the host?

Students imagine they are Aztecs. They see tall, four-legged beasts and unusually dressed men (Cortés and his men) moving rapidly towards their temple. They write a journal entry on what they felt and what happened on that day.

Secondary: Students lay their heads on the desk and close their eyes. Guide them on a journey to a lush and beautiful tropical island. The island has a freshwater river and many birds. They have been marooned with little more than pocket knives. How do they find food, create shelter and organize their lives?

Have the students imagine what the world would be like today if Britain had encouraged all its colonies from the very start to establish independent parliaments with equal representation of indigenous populations.

Vocational: Students lay their heads on the desk and close their eyes. Ask them to imagine themselves ten years from now. What community are they living in? Are they living in a house, on a boat or somewhere else? How big is it? With whom do they live? What do they do on weekends? What food do they eat most of the time?

How do they earn a living? What are the people like who they work with? What do they do well? How do people treat them? How do they treat others? What are the steps that need to be taken to achieve this – education, personal development, etc?

Linking (finding relationships)

Primary: Give students cards featuring pictures from fairy tales. Ask them to combine pictures according to verbal instructions. Try unusual combinations to create new stories. For example, Little Red Riding Hood can visit the wolf.

Students analyse how they studied for a given assignment or test and what the result was, with the aim of pinpointing effective learning strategies.

Secondary: Students look at a theme such as beauty, war or family through art. They study works from different ages and find commonalities.

Students identify relationships between castle architecture and location, local resources or enemy strengths.

Vocational: Students group together elements that form units, eg, *nuts and bolts*, *Petri dish* and *agar*.

Observing (looking in detail at someone or something)

Primary: Students observe how two plants grow, and note observations. One plant is turned 180 degrees every day, the other is not. One receives more water.

Secondary: Students observe colour changes or other changes resulting from biochemistry tests. Students note their observations.

Vocational: Students observe one task on an assembly line (on a video or in real life) and describe all the steps involved in completing the task.

Predicting (anticipating what is likely to happen)

Primary: Have students put some lentils or beans on humid cotton and then water them. They predict what will have happened by tomorrow. The next day they observe what has happened and compare this with their prediction. The same process of predicting, observing and comparing observations with predictions continues for a week. The students assess whether their predictions are becoming more accurate each day and why.

Secondary: Students are given information on the circumstances before a historical event, such as the enactment of an unpopular law that changed history, and predict what the effect will be in terms of politics, the economy, literature, art, etc. Ask students to decide whose predictions they think are most accurate and why. Study the event and compare the predictions with what really happened.

Vocational: Students read five different pastry dough recipes and predict the type of pastry each will produce. They then bake the pastry and compare the results with their predictions.

Students predict the results of leaving ingredients out of a recipe.

Students predict the taste of unusual combinations of food.

Reconciling (putting opposing items together to form a consistent whole)

Primary: Have students look at pictures or drawings of living creatures eating other living creatures. Ask questions such as:

What size is the animal doing the eating?
What size is the animal being eaten?
Is this always the case?
How can we combine these drawings into one? (food chain)

Secondary: Have students estimate how many metal paper clips will fit in a half-litre glass that is full to the brim with water, without spilling any water out of the glass. (Hundreds of metal paper clips fit into a full glass of water without spilling a drop.) The students reconcile how the seemingly impossible is possible by analysing how the water and the paper clips interact with one another.

Vocational: Groups discuss ways of accommodating different customer expectations in order to create a profitable plumbing or carpentry business.

Roleplaying (thinking like someone else and communicating and acting as that person would)

Primary: Students pretend they are a leaf that falls from a tree, breaks down and re-enters the tree.

Students act out attending a dinner or a meeting with a famous person.

Secondary: Students conduct a television interview (in pairs) with a historical figure such as Confucius, Hannibal, Shakespeare, Eleanor of Aquitaine, Mbande Nzinga, the Angolan Queen, Socrates or Mother Teresa. A student begins a monologue and impersonates a historical figure or a character from literature. The other students guess who is being impersonated.

Vocational: Students pretend to carry out a cardio-pulmonary resuscitation manoeuvre.

Students roleplay dealing with a customer complaint.

Teams are formed and each team plans how it would deal with an emergency. After ten minutes, each team picks an emergency from a hat and roleplays the agreed response. The roleplays can all take place at the same time. The students can then share their work with the class group by group.

Separating (taking things apart to identify specific components)

Primary: Students chart the food preferences of their classmates.

Students chart foods under headings such as *meat, fish, vegetables, fruit* and *dairy products*.

Students separate some given words and expressions into two lists: low-frequency words and expressions and high-frequency words and expressions.

Secondary: Students separate opinion from fact in articles.

Students separate fantasy from typical daily reality. They analyse a popular TV programme and compare it with their lives and the lives of their friends and family.

Vocational: Students separate tools according to function (testing, drilling, fastening, etc).

Selecting (making a preferred, imperative or needed choice)

Primary: Students select healthy foods from a menu.

Students choose correct spellings or word order from several options.

Secondary: Students choose five careers that they find attractive. They analyse investments required to qualify for these positions, and the possible returns. Students also analyse the positive and negative aspects related to each of these careers. Finally, students put the careers in order according to preference.

Vocational: Students review a list of tasks and select tools and/or equipment for each task.

Students choose key phrases from a list of high-frequency phrases so they can order supplies.

Triggering (something that sets off another thought or an event)

Primary: Provide prompts such as:

- *We learnt that yesterday* … Analogies that trigger and connect with previous knowledge. (Caution! Analogies, although powerful learning tools, can provide an incomplete picture. Discussing the similarities and differences between the analogy and the question under study and/or having students define their analogy will help avoid this pitfall.)
- Say a word and ask students to describe the images it triggers.

Secondary: Students analyse ten world conflicts to find common triggers.

Students make up chants or songs that could help recall formulas or other key information.

Vocational: Students are in teams of five. One team at a time, each team is given a word and must come up with another word related to it (eg, *drill > hole, screw, nails, electric, professional, dentist, construction, fire*). If a team fails to suggest a related word after, say, fifteen seconds, the next team tries. If that team succeeds, it gets a point. From here on in, each team gets a point when it answers. No point is awarded if no answer is given.

Variation: Students can come up with words that are related by meaning (*bolt, nut, hub, wheel*, etc), field of study or sound.

Utilizing (demonstrating how things could be, are being or have been put to use)

Primary: Students imagine new uses for paper clips, eg, earrings, fingernail cleaner, backscratcher. (Caution! To keep this exercise on a strictly intellectual level, do not actually provide the students with the object.)

Secondary: Students think of new uses for discarded products.

Vocational: Students think up new uses for chocolate or industrial by-products.

Verifying (specifying how information should be accepted as valid or true)

Primary: Students compare a draft with the evaluation grid.

Students verify a composition three times: once for logical flow of ideas, once for spelling and once for punctuation.

Secondary: Students give a correct or incorrect hypothesis, such as for the boiling point of water, and measure for accuracy.

Students welcome feedback from others and analyse their emotional reaction to that feedback. They also measure the extent to which they take into account feedback from others.

Vocational: ICT students verify that every chunk of the computer software programme actually takes the user to the next level/step.

Students verify the validity of biochemical test results by testing infected and uninfected samples.

QUESTIONS FOR ENCOURAGING CRITICAL THINKING DURING DIALOGUE WITH STUDENTS			
Process	**Logic/Analysis**	**Justice/Different perspectives**	**Language**
How did you come to that conclusion? Should we consider doing anything else before we start building/writing/presenting?	What would you have done in that situation? Why do you think that person/character did that? What is important to that person? If that actually happens, what will be the consequences?	What will your supporters say about this argument? What will your critics say about that argument? What would your parents say? What would your friend say? What is the proof? Why do you think that is so? Are you being fair? Can you trust that source? Is this relevant to us? What made you change your mind? You are getting close, but how can you develop that thought? Is there any disharmony here?	Can you say that more clearly? Can you say that with fewer words? Can you say the same thing in another way? How would a scientist say the same thing? How would a street kid say that? How would a really polite person say that? How would a nasty person say that? How would a political leader say that?
Linking to prior knowledge/attitudes	**Summarizing**	**Facts/Content**	**Values**
How is that tied to what we are studying? What does that remind you of? Can you give us an analogy? How is this different from what we have learnt? How does that make you feel?	What is the most important point you are making? Can you say that in five words or fewer? If you were a reporter, what kind of headline would you use to sum it all up? Can you create a mnemonic device to recall key information?	What information are we missing? Can you explain that further? Can you give an example? Is that your opinion or a fact? What makes this such a complicated issue? What can you use to back up/prove what you are saying? What are your sources?	What do you feel when you have gone against something you value or believe in? What values are driving this issue? Does this set off any warning bells for you? What would you have done if you were in that character's place?

What about me?

What is the percentage of teacher-talk versus student-talk in my classroom?
What percentage of my questions or assigned tasks require higher order thinking (applying, analysing, evaluating, creating)?
What do the methodologies I use say about my dominant learning style?
How do students with different learning styles from mine feel in my classroom?

To answer these questions, you could have someone observe your lesson and use a stopwatch to record the amount of time you speak. Also, an observer can simply mark off on a sheet whether a question required higher order thinking or whether the student was simply asked for content knowledge. Another option is to record a lesson and to take these measurements yourself while listening to or viewing the playback. The final question is best put to students, who can be given an opportunity to answer anonymously.

Learning styles

If students are from Mars, Venus, Saturn and Jupiter, we teachers want to be interplanetary citizens that can communicate with all of them, no matter what planet they reside on. Moreover, students want to communicate with us as well, no matter what planet we are living on. We certainly want to avoid the situation that Anne Marchant (2002) refers to as 'Students Are From Mars, Teachers Are From Venus'.

Individual preferences clearly exist regarding how we like to communicate and learn. When these learning style preferences are taken into account, they can act as bridges that enhance communication and learning. Numerous frameworks exist for classifying learning styles. Several of these distinguish between visual, auditory and kinesthetic preferences. No matter which framework one uses, awareness of different learning styles enables teachers and students to better identify the ways teachers teach and students learn. Using these frameworks can also facilitate dialogue about the overall learning process. Raised awareness of learning styles can help students take greater control of their own learning, and can serve as a first step in expanding a person's learning styles repertoire. It can facilitate further matching of teaching styles to learning styles.

An expanded repertoire of teaching and learning approaches improves learning. Students who approach the learning process with a wide range of strategies have more options available for meeting curriculum expectations. Moreover, increased student awareness of differing learning styles builds multiple perspectives. These multiple perspectives not only develop one's capacity to think critically, but help students to better understand others and to work within their learning community, while also building communication and teamwork skills.

> *Expecting all children the same age to learn in the same way is like expecting all children the same age to wear the same size clothing.*
> **Madeline Hunter**

On a practical level, CLIL students can be provided with a wide range of ways of manipulating, synthesizing, assessing and evaluating data, information and knowledge. For example, instructions can be given orally and visually through writing and pictures. Students can be asked to write instructions themselves for an activity or rewrite unclear instructions. Ensuing activities can also be designed to accommodate and develop diverse styles. In learning how to plan for survival in cold weather, students might:

- watch films on Amundsen's and Scott's expeditions to the South Pole (social, visual, auditory. If students can control the multimedia operating system, the film itself can become a kinesthetic tool.);
- brainstorm items to take on a winter hike (social, visual, auditory);
- work alone to pick the ten most important items to be carried on the hike (individual);
- look at and touch some of the actual items without any discussion (kinesthetic, visual, individual);

- work alone to reassess their personal list of the ten most important items for the hike while noting reasons for any changes made to the original list (individual);
- work in a group to pick the ten most important items for the hike (social, auditory);
- analyse how one's own previously developed list differs from that of the group (individual);
- spend an hour outdoors using the ten items or substitutes, and later writing observations and drawing conclusions (experiential, kinesthetic);
- research how Scott and Amundsen prepared for their expeditions to the Antarctic (visual, auditory);
- analyse why Amundsen survived and Scott died (individual).

When starting CLIL, it is particularly important to go beyond the standard exploration of personal learning styles by focusing on preferred language learning styles. This exploration can help students gain access to a wider range of language learning strategies particularly suitable for CLIL. It will also facilitate content acquisition. We also believe it is helpful for educators to assess their own learning styles and what impact those preferences have on their teaching; we are most likely to teach the way we learn the best. Consciously increasing the use of those learning styles with which we are least comfortable is likely, in the long run, to help all students to learn better.

SELECTED LEARNING STYLES AND STRATEGIES		
Visual	**Auditory**	**Kinesthetic**
Learner preference · Learning through seeing and visual stimuli **Student strategies** · scanning pictures, headings and charts before reading a text · developing flash cards with key concepts or language · posting sticky notes with key information in highly visible places · creating visual analogies · visualizing facts · relating key concepts to visual images such as symbols · repackaging texts as graphs, charts or pictures · writing or drawing a skeletal summary when reading, listening to lectures or doing pairwork · using colour to highlight main ideas (colour code opinions, facts, formulas) · using static and animated visual representations through multimedia	**Learner preference** · Learning through listening, speaking and auditory stimuli **Student strategies** · problem-solving through peer co-operative work (eg, orally summarizing a topic for a peer and having him or her fill in missing pieces or make corrections) · sharing notes and asking peers for feedback · making audio-recording notes and listening to them · using Voice Over Internet Protocol (VoIP) technologies such as Skype to do assignments and solve problems · verbalizing answers first in one's head before writing them down · orally summarizing and discussing short fragments of a reading passage · having someone read to you, or reading to yourself aloud	**Learner preference** · Incorporating physical activity into the learning process **Student strategies** · learning a series of facts while doing some form of exercise · modelling scientific or mathematical concepts or processes · engaging in activity-based roleplays · using total physical response (TPR) exercises · carrying out an experiment or developing a plan based on step-by-step instructions · linking language to learning through processes involving physical activity · reordering information on cards to reconstitute processes or formulas · developing rhythms for learning language or a series of facts · physically highlighting key language and pieces of information

Challenging students to take another step forward: Stepping just outside the comfort zone

> *You gain strength, courage and confidence by every experience in which you really stop to look fear in the face. You must do the thing which you think you cannot do.*
>
> **Eleanor Roosevelt**

Scaffolding and critical thinking strategies are tools for extending learning, for helping students to step out of and expand their comfort zone. In so many ways, those strategies are about helping students to operate in what Lev Vygotsky has called the zone of proximal development – the zone which lies between current knowledge and that which can be accomplished with the assistance of teachers and peers. These strategies help students to move from their current understanding of content and attitudes to a new level of understanding, and then to take another step forwards right back into the zone of proximal development. These strategies have been discussed in the previous sections of this chapter, particularly with respect to content. This section will focus primarily on how to facilitate language growth, but will also touch upon content and learning skills development.

The balancing act

One of the best ways of helping students to step out of their comfort zone is to do it yourself. As Albert Schweitzer said, 'Example is leadership'. Moreover, it is through the assessment and articulation of our daily practices that we establish our current level of understanding. It is this foundation on which we too build our own learning.

As a first step, you might assess the percentage of time you devote to content learning, the percentage devoted to language skills and the percentage devoted to learning skills development. If you are a content teacher, it is probably worth considering how you could increase your focus on form, even by a small amount. This should lead to increased accuracy of language usage among students and, in the long run, save you considerable time. More accurate language usage will lead to more precision in expressing and working with content. As a language teacher, great returns can be gained by working with a content teacher to teach the language curriculum using materials from a content subject. Content learning motivates students. Both content and language teachers have much to gain from teaching learning skills, particularly when it is done as a coordinated effort throughout several subjects areas.

Those suggestions are inspired by the counter-balance hypothesis put forth by Lyster and Mori (2006). The counterbalance hypothesis takes into account how teachers encourage students to increase accurate language usage. Lyster and Mori speak of recasts, explicit corrections and prompts.

In recasts, a teacher restates the student's sentences using accurate language. The student repeats the recast sentence. According to Lyster and Mori, it appears that recasts are particularly effective language learning tools in classrooms where students have learnt to focus on form. Recasts are much less effective in classrooms

Recasting strategies

1) **Shorten it.** Recast only the key part of the student's reponse.

2) **Focus it.** Vocally stress the needed change.

3) **Write it.** (on the board)

4) **Check for change.** Is recasting bringing results?

5) **Don't overuse it.**

A plunkety-plunk pitfall: Ending the dialogue with a student after he or she corrects a language error.

This can have the unfortunate unintended side effect of saying to the student: 'I am not interested in what you are saying'.

where the students have not learnt to do so, because the message regarding language repair is rather covert, as opposed to being clearly stated. Nonetheless, recasts are helpful scaffolding tools when students lack the language needed to discuss content. This is particularly true when starting CLIL. By providing the student with the phrase that he or she is lacking, it allows you to maintain the pace of classroom interaction and continue to focus on content.

Consequently, recasting is a very seductive and possibly an addictive tool that many of us educators unconsciously use to maintain pacing. Thus, it is a strategy that is often overused or ineffectively used and that may not lead to sufficient language growth.

Prompts include giving students clues and asking questions that help to point them in the right direction, be that in improving accuracy in content or language usage. Prompts about language are particularly helpful for students who are used to focusing on content. The ultimate goal of the prompt is to support student self-repair.

Particularly in language classes, the dialogue with the student has a tendency to end after the student successfully repeats the recast or achieves self-repair. This can have the unfortunate effect of undermining classroom communication, for the implicit message is that the language is more important than the content. For the student, it is the thoughts being expressed, the content, that is usually the primary motivation for speaking. Language for language's sake can be demotivating. Thus, we strongly recommend continuing the dialogue after the student repairs the language error for at least one sentence.

Following Lyster and Mori's advice, it is wise to integrate both prompts and recasts and to provide 'a balanced provision of both'. For example, a recast can be shortened and a prompt can be provided to help bring out the corrected language. We suggest placing that correction on the board during the dialogue with the student, while maintaining the pace of the conversation. Growth in language increases within the context of a meaningful discussion about content when attention is given by content teachers to form, and by language teachers to content as well as form.

That pet peeve and preventing plateauing

As students progress through CLIL, they seem to make certain errors over and over again. The errors become fossilized. Language growth seems to reach a kind of plateau and come close to halting. This may be due to the fact that in CLIL, there is often greater emphasis on communication than on complete grammatical accuracy. After all, if everybody understands each other, why fuss with detail?

However, language that is sufficient for classroom communication may not be considered sufficient for the world of employment. Fossilized errors can also drive the teacher round the bend, even making one feel peeved. We suggest discussing these fossilized student errors with your colleagues and deciding to pick a pet peeve. That pet peeve or set of fossilized errors become(s) a priority for the next week. Any time that pet peeve of an error is made, in any class, the teacher will prompt the students to self-repair. If change is not apparent, you can announce that five points on the upcoming test or essay will be given for the correct usage of this grammar point.

Another strategy is to help students to understand the relationship between language and power. Interviews with various people in one profession can be analysed to determine the register of language used and to assess the clarity of expression. Comparisons can also be drawn between various professions. Students can draw conclusions about what distinguishes one register of language from another. Further conclusions are drawn about how language can open or close doors in one's professional life. Finally, students discuss ways of increasing language awareness and of developing habits that support language growth.

Using silence

If you ask a question and pick the first student who shoots up his or her hand, other students understand there is no need to think further. It is worth taking the extra time to make sure that the majority of hands are in the air.

In CLIL, some students may be silent in class because they have not acquired the active language skills for speaking or because they lack the required confidence to experiment with language in front of others. In primary-level CLIL programmes, this phase may last for months. Students can nonetheless answer by raising their hands to indicate preferences. They can do mix-and-match exercises where the written word is matched with a picture, and they can initially provide one-word answers. Many language patterns can be posted on the wall and referred to so as to support the student in answering. Routine activities such as the morning circle, discussed in Chapter 3, where there is considerable repetition from day to day, can help build the confidence to speak.

With older students, we tend to leave them alone until they are ready to speak. It is often easier, both for the student and the teacher, not to call on them. The danger is that the students may cease to be engaged. Some strategies for supporting student engagement and their verbal contribution to classroom interaction follow.

Examples of teacher elaborations in response to student silence*

I can see from your eyes that you know something about this, and I would like to hear what you have to say.

Can you show us what you know by acting it out or drawing it?

I'm going to come back to you in five minutes. Please get ready to speak to us. After thinking by yourself, you can ask one other person in the class for help for a minute.

In private: *I want to hear from you during this lesson. Please get ready with one answer or a question. I will not ask you any more questions during this period. Let me know when you are ready to give an answer.*

Ask a question that requires a yes or no answer or that allows the student to pick between two answers.

You and your students provide reinforcement for the attempted answer.

Allow for peer explanations.

Allow for peer prompts to support a student in answering.

---

* adapted and expanded, based on Mohr and Mohr, 2007

6 Making CLIL come alive

This chapter is about connectivity. The tools used in CLIL to connect to learners, their world and the wider environment hold the potential for creating powerful synergy. Synergy is the energy that comes from good connectivity. A goose will fly much further and use less energy when flying in close formation with other geese. It has been estimated that a 'connected' flock flying in a V shape will be able to travel some 70 per cent further than if each goose were to fly alone. This chapter describes tools that can be used in CLIL for connectivity, making meanings matter and learner self-management. These can serve in building efficiency through coordinated effort.

Creating the classroom climate

We all want to feel physically and psychologically safe and that our lives are meaningful. CLIL students who feel respected, who feel free to think critically, who are willing to experiment with language and who feel that learning is challenging and meaningful are likely to learn the most. The following help to accomplish this.

Agreeing on classroom norms and rules

Students can better manage their own behaviour when they develop and agree on classroom norms, rules or principles of behaviour to help them learn. You might introduce the topic of classroom norms by first relating a memory of an uncomfortable moment you faced as a student. Students can then in pairs or groups share with each other a moment when they or a friend felt uncomfortable in a classroom situation. After the pairwork or groupwork, students can be asked if anyone is willing to share one of these personal experiences with the entire class.

The sharing of personal experiences is a stepping stone to brainstorming ideas on valuable guidelines that the group could agree on. With younger students you may need to provide direction by asking whether there should be a rule about listening to others and so forth.

The results of the brainstorming session are analysed to eliminate repetition and to establish priorities. A maximum of five to seven rules are agreed upon. Once an agreement is reached, it is posted on the wall. At the beginning, it is good to refer to these rules regularly. It is also advisable to evaluate, from time to time, progress made in respecting the agreed-upon rules to ensure that students are feeling safe and focused on learning. This could be an opportunity to celebrate the students' capacity for co-operation. The rules are adapted as new needs arise.

In secondary and vocational programmes, students may get tired of establishing these rules in all their different subject classes. One option is to co-operate with other teachers. For example, teachers could first meet to discuss their expectations and needs. This can be followed by having one teacher working with any colleagues who happen to be free during that lesson to discuss and create the rules with the students. These rules would apply to all classes. Each teacher could raise any issues that may be tied specifically to his or her class. For example, with science or some vocational subjects, students may need to agree that chemicals and equipment are never used without following precautionary procedures and having a teacher present.

Physical safety

Lack of language knowledge must not compromise safety. For example, in CLIL science and vocational classrooms many risks regarding equipment, chemicals, procedures and storage need to be managed. Although safety requirements may be explained and worked on in the CLIL language, students can be asked for written feedback in their first language about these requirements. Another option is for students to model safety procedures or work processes taking into account safety protocols. They can use coloured water instead of chemicals to practise mixing substances, or use blunt as opposed to sharp instruments to demonstrate their understanding of procedures or processes. They can also use the CLIL language to describe work processes that reflect safety procedures before undertaking the actual work.

Encouraging and rewarding risk-taking

All learning and communication involves some element of risk. CLIL students face an extra risk. Linguistically, they live in an ambiguous world. They do not always understand every word they hear or read. They are often missing vocabulary and discourse patterns needed to say what they want. They are expected to guess or deduce meaning and to get across complex ideas with simple language. They are asked to take risks in interpreting new material and in expressing themselves.

Students will take these risks if they are rewarded for their attempts, whether they are successful or not. They will not take the risk if they are criticized or ridiculed for their efforts in using content or language. Thus, effort receives greater attention than the perfect response. Talking openly about the role of mistakes in learning, and analysing how a mistake can lead to personal and academic growth can help foster a culture where learning through mistakes becomes the accepted norm and part of the classroom culture.

Nothing is more powerful than leading by example. When teachers take personal risks by using new methodologies or activities, and when they admit in class to their own mistakes, students see that this form of risk-taking is a normal part of life. This can even apply to the teacher's lapses or slips in using the CLIL language. In fact, taking and managing risks is a mental habit that supports life-long learning.

Quiet and noise

Studying in a second language is generally more demanding than studying in the first language. The same applies to those of us teaching in a second language. A few minutes of quiet time can help everyone involved to recharge and to collect thoughts. This could take the form of individual work. It may involve a short (eg, ten-minute) silent period where every student and the teacher read something of their choice in the CLIL language.

> **TENNIS, ANYONE?**
>
> Noise from shifting tables and chairs can be reduced by making X-shaped cuts into tennis balls and placing them over the bottom of chair and table legs.

Even moderate noise levels will hinder the comprehension of unfamiliar words and discourse patterns. CLIL classrooms are best located away from noisy areas such as gyms or busy roads. Also, supporting students in developing listening skills and in their ability to monitor noise levels, as well as in developing strategies for influencing others to reduce noise levels, will contribute to the improvement of the learning environment. For example, during groupwork, students can be interrupted and asked to assess how many people are finding the noise level tiring, how many are finding it difficult to hear everything being said in the group and how many think the noise level is fine and not hindering learning. Simply asking the questions will usually bring down noise levels and eventually increase the number of times where students self-assess their own noise level and ask their peers to reduce noise levels.

> **TRAFFIC LIGHTS / NOISE MANAGEMENT**
>
> Large circles in red, yellow and green are cut out. Green is posted on the board at the start of groupwork. Anyone can post yellow or red circles. Anyone can say *red light*, which is a signal to reduce the noise level.

Students can also be given the right to opt for silence. If they feel they cannot contribute to a discussion, they can say *pass*. If the pass rule is presented as a privilege to be used on rare occasions, most students will only use it in a moment of panic or when feeling lost. At the end of an activity, after someone has used the pass option, you can ask if anyone would like to add anything. Those who have said *pass* may be ready to answer.

Noise is inevitable. It is not a monster that must always be fought to the ground. It can be an opportunity. It tells us that students are excited by the topic, or that they may be lost or becoming disinterested. They can be asked to analyse why the noise level is rising, and on the basis of their response, the teacher can adjust the lesson accordingly. By creating opportunities for movement and noise, even senior students can release energy, re-energize and move towards a quieter mode of learning.

> **NOISE-INDUCED HEARING LOSS**
>
> **Hearing loss is an occupational hazard for teachers and students. High noise levels created by either of these two groups can damage hearing. Moreover, they are unnecessary and particularly tiring in a CLIL environment. Some teachers are unaware of the permanent damage they can do to their own hearing by speaking too loudly.**

Consistency and fairness

Consistency is a major building block in establishing trust. Lack of trust damages the learning climate that is crucial in CLIL. Trust is developed slowly and lost quickly. Moreover, rebuilding trust is particularly difficult. Students want to know that they can count on how the teacher will react to any given set of situations.

Previously agreed-upon norms will cease to carry any weight if a teacher's own behaviour is not consistent with what has been agreed upon. Disruptive student behaviour always needs to elicit the same response. Students will consider consistent consequences fair. Strong emotional reactions to student behaviour are discouraged as they create a climate of confusion and fear. Students will not know what to expect.

Using routines so students can predict what will happen is an attribute of CLIL. With young children, creating a pattern for the day and following it consistently helps the students concentrate on their learning, as they are able to anticipate what comes next. With older students, knowing there will be a warm-up, time for setting goals, the main activities and then evaluation of progress also provides a pattern for the average lesson. This gives students a feeling of control over their environment and allows them to be more relaxed.

Consistency in classroom management is most effective when it is in line with the school-wide culture and policies. In effective schools, staff meet regularly to discuss how best to manage classrooms. They develop common strategies for dealing with disruptive behaviour and look for ways of helping students to work towards and enjoy success. Policies and strategies are jointly determined and applied.

Associating the unfamiliar with something pleasant

It is natural to be suspicious, if not threatened, by what is new. As CLIL students are learning in a second language, they face greater levels of unfamiliarity. Actively seeking opportunities to associate new learning with current knowledge, with

something interesting and challenging, while still feeling safe, will decrease time wasted on resistance to new learning and increase student success.

For example, students can begin a new topic by creating a board game about a historical event for history class, or about interplanetary travel for science. To start with, information about the topic is provided to the students in well packaged chunks, and facts are presented in a distilled form. Students work in groups to study these materials on their own with the aim of using them to create the board game. This requires them to work through and gain an understanding of the language and the content within these materials. Normally there is an element of competition, or at least a desire to impress other groups with the newly invented board games. By presenting the games or by having the various groups play each other's games, the topic is reviewed. At this point, students will have gained considerable new knowledge about the topic and language related to the topic. They will have put that information to use and will have a solid foundation from which the topic can then be expanded.

Today, in much of the world, many students are very familiar with information and communication technologies. In a maths class, students can warm up for a topic by playing related maths games that are freely available on the Internet. Instead of teaching some new terms to a class, younger students might search for the meaning of those terms at the start of a lesson by using, for example, Jenny Eather's *A Maths Dictionary for Kids*, which is available on the Internet (http://www.amathsdictionaryforkids.com/). *The Visual Geometry Dictionary for Kids and for Kids' Teachers*, created by students at an American University, is also easily accessed online (http://www.math.okstate.edu/~rpsc/dict/Dictionary.html/). It can be used by students to look up a few key terms at the start of a lesson. The dictionary provides written and visual explanations by students of such terms as *an obtuse triangle*. The dictionary not only defines and illustrates what an obtuse triangle is, but what it is not.

Whatever way new material is introduced, students want to know they can cope with it. This involves teachers avoiding words such as *right* and *wrong*, by focusing on the processes used to get to the solution and by extending student thinking. In maths, this could include giving groups of students various problems and having them first prepare a description for another group about how they would solve the problem. The groups could then try to follow the described process. Explanations are adjusted until both groups understand the processes and successfully solve the problems.

Pacing to maintain positive tension

There is no point in doing an activity if involvement constitutes only superficial compliance, and there is no point in talking if no one is really listening. Some level of what Jean Piaget calls cognitive conflict is needed for engagement. The pace needs to be challenging enough to make students expend effort and sufficiently moderate to allow students to stay on track. The attention span of any given student or group can vary greatly from day to day.

Most CLIL teachers are very adept at intuitively setting the right pace. However, it is still useful to actively monitor student understanding and attitudes. For example, students can be asked to individually write a summary statement about a point under study. These can be checked at a glance, as they are being produced to get a sense of how many students have understood and can express a given point. One or two summary statements can be discussed as a class. Also, doing a quick survey by having students anonymously write one of the following expressions (*fighting my way through a bush, smooth sailing, looking for help*) to express how they feel about the topic under study will quickly provide a sense of how to proceed. This means that planned activities take a back seat to planned outcomes and student needs.

Valuing each student

A rule of thumb from psychology is that we like people who like us. All students need to feel important, liked and valued. Seeing and listening are the most powerful tools of recognition. These can include a personal hello, eye contact, a smile and asking a follow-up question about something a student has said. In particular with younger students, opportunities to help out the teacher can foster a sense of belonging and allow students to gain recognition for their contribution. Moreover, students can help ease the burden on the teacher.

Students helping and enriching one another

The teacher is only one person in a classroom of many people. It is often difficult to notice and/or attend to each student's needs as they arise. Encouraging students to assist one another and share with one another takes some of the pressure off the learner and the teacher. It helps bring new perspectives to bear and makes it easier for students to stay on task. It also fosters independence and encourages students to help one another. It contributes to building the co-operative and supportive classroom culture needed for CLIL.

As a first step, students can be guided to learn about each other, about their strengths and weakness. This helps build empathy.

Providing recognition for students helping others encourages this type of positive behaviour. For example, when drawing conclusions about learning at the end of a class, you can ask who received support during the class from another student. Students can describe the benefit gained. Above all, you listen, but provide reinforcement by demonstrating interest through asking a follow-up question, as opposed to just saying *well done*.

From a classroom management perspective, fostering student mentoring requires allowing for quick and relatively quiet exchanges between students at times when someone else is speaking. Body language (giggling, serious faces, pointing to learning materials) will usually signal whether students are on task or in need of being encouraged to return to task.

Displaying student work/Recognizing and celebrating success

First and foremost, displaying student work is a way of valuing the individual student and his or her contribution to learning. Students tend to take greater care and pride in their work if it is displayed. Discussions about what to display, where and for how long will help students to understand what they are trying to achieve with their work. Students are more likely to seek and incorporate feedback into their work if they know that others will see it. In general, it is likely to lead to a greater investment in the quality of the final product.

When students have finished a major project, guests could be invited to class to view their presentations. Milestones need to be established and marked. Getting halfway through a term, having everyone pass a test or improve their score and having a successful meeting with other speakers are all noteworthy events. Celebrations of academic achievement by the class foster belonging, a positive attitude towards learning and show that the teacher recognizes and values the time and effort put in by the students to accomplish the many tasks set before them.

Empowering students

When given a voice in the teaching and learning process, students are more likely to take charge of their own learning. Many of the strategies under the points above describe how to empower students.

Other simple steps might involve having students choose the order of activities, or choose one activity over another. For example, independent learning centres for reading, writing, listening, art, maths or civics can be set up in a classroom. Students choose the learning centre they want to visit. In each centre, they might be asked to accomplish a series of five independent assignments from among eight tasks.

Students can also be encouraged to take on a leadership role. For example, in groupwork the leadership role can be rotated. By rotating this responsibility within each group, they become more conscious of supporting one another, as each individual knows that his or her turn is just around the corner.

Older students can be asked to fill in a chart listing up to five things teachers can do that would improve classroom learning. Students can be given a voice in assessing the whole class or the programme, and can be invited to make suggestions for improvement.

Classroom set-up

Flexible seating arrangements are favoured in CLIL. Student desks are arranged in clusters of four or five or in a circle or a V shape. The old-fashioned rows with the teacher's desk at the front are only recommended for examinations or when students need to be working on a project alone. Rows create opportunities to hide, can create discomfort for students in feeling that they have someone behind them and do not facilitate communication or support the development of a democratic culture.

Drawing a floor chart can help you plan according to the space available. Students can also be encouraged to draw floor charts, which can be analysed from the perspective of how they support learning. With younger students, where classrooms may be larger, it is wise to designate areas for quiet, individual work, learning centres and groupwork areas.

Any attempts to personalize a classroom will help build an atmosphere that is conducive to learning. With senior students, posting some photos taken during class and simply printed out on a standard printer will liven up the classroom and help build a sense of group. Students could be asked to write captions that are glued onto the pictures. A vocabulary wall or a graphic organizer that helps students with new material will also facilitate learning.

Storage is an important consideration. Materials that students should have access to can be stored in different areas to prevent bottlenecks. Labelling in the CLIL language will help students to put things back where they belong and will reinforce language. Students can help with the labelling and be asked once a term about how classroom storage could be improved.

Maintaining a focus on learning

Successful CLIL programmes ensure that content learning standards are maintained. CLIL students and parents see language learning as an added value. They are generally not willing to compromise on content learning.

Connecting learning to learners' lives

> *We are each other's harvest; we are each other's business; we are each other's magnitude and bond.*
>
> **Gwendolyn Brooks**

Connecting with learners' lives presupposes that we create a safe and enriching learning environment, where students gain new knowledge about themselves and the world they live in. Through communication with others, students negotiate and create meaning and decide on the relevance of what has just been learnt. If we can engage students in applying new learning through the creation of a meaningful result, they are more likely to consider the learning relevant. What is considered relevant is more likely to become established in long-term memory for future application.

Connectivity (with oneself, one's community and the world) creates a sense of relevance. This means:

- first, connecting new learning to the individual by exploring his or her current knowledge and experience base and interests, and by building the capacity for self-analysis;
- second, connecting the individual students to the community around them by experiencing the power of working with others and by exploring the students' own impact on the community and the community's impact on them; and,

- third, connecting students to the world at large by developing an understanding of how acting locally is linked to global processes and how global processes are linked to the local community, and by experiencing the benefits of international perspectives.

These connections cement ties between learning and the individual, the community and the world at large. When students believe that new learning is applicable on a personal level and in the real world, it becomes relevant to them. Anchoring information in this way leads to learning and helps avoid students filtering it out as extraneous.

Taking into account students' interests

A first step can involve getting to know one's students better by surveying them about their interests. They can be surveyed about these interests directly or indirectly by enquiring about what they watch on television, their favourite humorous YouTube™ video, which sports they like or how they spend time during weekends. They can be asked about technologies they use, websites they frequent, the title of a book or magazine article they have read, what they look for in friends, what types of people they do not like, chatrooms they visit, what they talk about in chatrooms and their favourite applications on Facebook™.

Another option is to tell students that tomorrow you will be asking them about their interests. They can be encouraged to bring to school illustrative materials about their hobbies and pastimes that can be shared with the class. Students are encouraged to question each other about their hobbies. A variation of this would be to have five students a week create displays about their interests. The remainder of the students could question these students about their displays.

As students are often interested in information and communication technologies, by integrating them into learning we are taking into account student interests. For example, students can write text messages, an email, an analysis of someone's online profile or create their own online profile in the CLIL language. In secondary level history, they can create an online profile entry for a well known historical figure. They can include details about the historical figure's achievements, allies and enemies, disappointments, lessons learnt and future plans. The assignment can be extended by creating another online profile for the historical figure's main foe.

In geography, students can imagine that they have a 20 000-euro budget to spend on a dream one-year trip. They can be asked to analyse travel costs such as transportation, accommodation and food. They can also describe locations and sights they would like to visit, dangers, terrain, places of topographical interest, weather considerations and modes of transport. Students can place salient points from their research into charts and/or tables to bring out similarities and differences between various locations.

This geography assignment can be tied to science by measuring the carbon footprint of the traveller. It can be connected to maths by developing budgets and showing several different ways of looking at figures – costs per day, costs per month and costs per category such as transportation, food and miscellaneous expenditures. This could even extend to comparing the cost of living in different countries and regions.

In primary school, students can survey each other to find out about preferred foods, interests, qualities looked for in friends, favourite singers and bands or habits. Students can draw a scale model of their bedroom and plan how they would use a 1000-euro budget to remodel it. This may involve listing bedroom functions such as studying, sleeping and receiving friends. Possible dream designs can be created. The cost and quality of furniture and equipment as offered by at least three different manufacturers can be compared in a table. A final scale design is drawn up and a written description of plans is turned in to the teacher. As a follow-up, students can compare their personal living space with that of students in other countries using, for example, Internet forums. Students can use an evaluation scale to rate the creativity, clarity and precision of each other's work.

At vocational level, students in tourism, restaurant or other client-centred programmes might begin their studies by first analysing how they or their parents receive special guests at home. They could answer questions such as: *How do you guide your guests to the location? What do you wear? How have you prepared the home in advance? How do you open the door? What do you say at the door? What sort of body language do you display? What types of food and beverage do you commonly provide? How are these prepared and presented? In what circumstances have you or your guests felt uncomfortable? How do you say goodbye?* Students can also explore how they have been received in various social situations and how that has made them feel.

Vocational students could invent a new pastry, prepare a CV for working abroad or investigate work placements in the CLIL language. Once a work placement that interests them is identified, students could develop a strategy for obtaining the placement. The strategy might include investigating criteria used by employers for selecting work placement candidates, researching successful and unsuccessful work placements, readjusting one's CV for a specific work placement, writing a covering letter, making a presentation, roleplaying the interview and lobbying for the placement.

Students could also plan to establish their own business. In the case of a restaurant or a car servicing garage, they would describe the customer experience they intend to offer, their staff recruitment plan, the staff training programme, the budget and the legislative requirements involved, including licensing and health and safety regulations. As opposed to teaching all this material, students are guided to sources. Their investigations help them to learn for themselves as they work to complete the assignment. Later, teachers help guide students in filling in missing pieces essential for ensuring that curriculum outcomes are achieved.

Giving students opportunities to lead conversations

Taking into account student interests does not just have implications for how content is taught; it also has an impact on language learning.

In CLIL, language is driven by curriculum requirements and by the students' interests. What is truly unique about CLIL and what requires a shift from standard classroom practice is that, for a few minutes a day, language needs are determined by having students take the lead in communication.

It is by speaking about what is important to them that the language that students most want to learn will be revealed. We all like to speak about what is important to us. As students struggle to express their personal thoughts, it quickly becomes apparent which vocabulary and discourse patterns are missing from their repertoire. When teachers immediately provide students with these building blocks, our experience says that students retain this vocabulary and these discourse patterns with remarkable ease and put them to future use.

Taking the cue from the students

As she often did, one morning Maire asked her ten-year-old students in Estonia how they were feeling. This is what transpired in the CLIL language.

Irene: Not too good.

Maire: How come?

Irene: Well, someone, Igor, I mean someone, well, Igor shot me.

Igor: You're such a baby.

Maire: What happened?

Igor had pointed his pellet gun in Irene's direction and hit her with a dried pea. After a lively discussion, the class overwhelming decided that guns weren't safe toys. However, Igor wasn't ready to accept the opinion of his classmates.

Igor: My mother bought me that gun. Are you calling her stupid?

Much of the ensuing lesson was spent discussing the topic of toy guns, safety and how to concentrate on one issue at a time. Eventually, Igor apologized. The class congratulated him for being big enough to admit to his mistake. Irene accepted the apology.

This is an example where the students learnt about right and wrong, consequences, responsibility and how to stop someone from skirting around the real issue at hand. They passionately discussed something of importance to them in the CLIL language and learnt lots of new vocabulary. These students were clearly connected with and inspired by the topic and the opportunity to negotiate a meaningful conclusion.

Moreover, this is an opportunity to build relationships, to demonstrate mutual respect. In turn, strong, respectful relationships correlate with student success.

Teacher talk and classroom management

	TIME USE IN CLASSROOMS	
Teachers ...	In teacher-centred classrooms	In student-centred classrooms
ask questions	21%	5%
give instructions	18%	7%
handle discipline	19%	10%
lecture	10%	3%
TOTAL TIME	**68%**	**25%**

(Tribes, 2003)

The results above, produced based on research in North America, offer a useful framework for reflecting on how much class time is actually used for teacher-talk. Even the most seasoned teachers sometimes find it helpful to have an independent observer or a few students time the amount of teacher- and student-talk during a lesson.

At the very start of a primary-level CLIL programme, the teacher speaks more than the students, as there is a need to model the new language. However, students take the lead relatively quickly. After the initial start in primary, and in secondary and vocational CLIL, students usually speak much more than the teacher. Pairwork and groupwork, roleplaying, investigative reporting, as well as contact and communication with CLIL students in other countries, are all strategies that help ensure student participation.

Empowering students to take part in decision making

Taking into account student interests and giving students opportunities to lead conversations is an important first step in connecting learning to learners' lives. Empowering students to join in the decision-making process is the next step. It helps build student–teacher and student–student relationships, increases relevance and further engages students in assuming responsibility for their learning. For students at all levels, involvement in the setting of learning outcomes and, in particular, in discussing the process for achieving these outcomes can be a vehicle for the co-construction of learning.

Increasing self-awareness and the capacity to self-manage are also means for relevance building. Students can be asked to describe in writing which classroom activities help them to learn the best and what makes it difficult for them to learn. This enables both teachers and students to keep learning styles and the learning process on the radar and to adjust learning activities accordingly.

A very powerful tool that helps teachers and students to connect, inspire each other and improve their work has been used under the guidance of CLIL expert Do

Coyle. It involves videotaping a lesson at random. This is usually done by a student. On the following day, students work in groups and review the lesson tape, selecting a short segment (one to three minutes) to show where they felt they were learning a lot, and another short segment where they felt learning was impeded or could be improved. They show their selections and explain their choices, making suggestions for both the students and the teacher. A discussion is held and decisions are made about how to improve learning.

Harnessing emotions: managing the affective side of learning

Learning does not take place without emotions, which inevitably affect the learning process. Emotions touch the core of who we are. They can help or hinder learning. What we feel about something, or someone, defines our perception of reality. It is also said that when emotions struggle with new learning, emotions invariably win and learning loses. Connecting learning with learners' lives involves evoking and managing the emotional dimension – harnessing positive emotions and managing destructive ones.

Language is an emotional vehicle. This vehicle is usually more easily managed when speaking one's first language. Conversations in our first language often follow familiar, comfortable and habitually travelled paths in the mind. In day-to-day discourse these paths, although not separated from emotion, usually help to keep emotions under control as we work to get our point across.

When learning and communicating in a second language, our self-expression (verbal and emotional) is often less sophisticated. We build new paths in the mind, moving in new territories where emotions can surface more quickly and in a less predictable manner. The extra stress of trying to express our thoughts in a second language, of searching for new ways to express ourselves and the associations evoked by the use of a more simplified vocabulary, are all more likely to bring emotions to the surface and into the classroom atmosphere.

Beyond primary school, many teachers shy away from addressing emotions in the classroom, even when teaching in the first language. It is argued that learning in a second language inevitably evokes more intense emotions. These can range from elation and joy to fear and anger – elation at succeeding in getting one's idea across, joy at the wonder of discovery, fear of embarrassment and anger at not being able to get one's point across as clearly as one would like. To manage ourselves and to work more effectively with others, it is advisable to give continuous attention to building what Daniel Goleman has referred to as emotional and social intelligence.

This is done by supporting students to increase their awareness about the role that emotions play in their lives. When CLIL teachers help students to build the self-confidence and skills required to become gatekeepers and managers of their own emotions, language and content learning is improved.

As a first step, be it at the primary, secondary or vocational level, this can involve recognizing students' feelings. No matter what emotion a student or a group is feeling, it deserves to be recognized. To do this, teachers and students need to explore, adopt and use a lexis of emotion. For example:

I see you are very happy (satisfied, pleased) with that result.
You have achieved a good result.
What is it that you are most pleased with?
Is there anything you did in preparing this assignment that you are particularly proud of?

Students would also benefit from a language support sheet listing emotions. These words might be organized under headings such as *positive emotions* and *potentially destructive emotions*, or under headings such as *adjectives, adverbs, verbs*, etc.

This will help students to tap into positive emotions and link positive emotions to learning through CLIL. It will also help the student to better understand his or her own investment in an assignment. Also, it is an act of recognition of student effort.

An emotional lexis is a valuable tool in helping individuals to manage both their positive and negative emotions within a group dynamic. For example, the mental process of trying to label negative or destructive emotions can help students to calm down. Pursuing a discussion to understand the source of the emotion and exploring possible solutions will often defuse an emotionally charged situation. It can help solve issues that could otherwise start to fester and adversely affect learning. A sample of needed language knowledge and process skills follows:

I see you are frustrated.
What are you feeling at the moment?
Are you angry, frustrated, disappointed or ...?
What are you angry about?
What is causing that feeling?
Why might that person have behaved that way?
Can you name a few possible solutions?
What can the two of you agree on?
How can we move forwards?

Both the language of emotions and the knowledge of how to manage them are valuable life skills put to use in our personal and work lives. We need these life skills to manage personal and group frustrations, channel constructive energy and move beyond stressful situations in all walks of life.

A student's existing knowledge base, interests and attitudes are the major gateway to learning. In CLIL we, as teachers, provide opportunities for learners to reflect on and articulate their existing knowledge base, while anchoring learning in student interests. The attitudes which we have, and which we express to others, are a key influence in cultivating relationships and co-constructing meaning. Personal characteristics, emotions and attitudes hinder or enhance this learning process. This is true of any learning, but is particularly important with CLIL because of the use of the additional language as a medium for learning. A confident, aware and connected individual language learner is the springboard for confident, aware and motivated groups of language and content learners in the classroom.

Connecting classrooms to the local community

The classroom is a microcosm of the school and the wider community. Students have much to learn about themselves in interacting with other students and teachers. Yet, remaining strictly within the classroom cocoon will eventually begin to feel artificial and disconnected from the world at large. Connecting the individual students to the community around them will make learning feel more relevant. This is done by creating opportunities for experiencing the power of working with others and for exploring the student's own impact on the community and the community's impact on the student.

Connecting with community members

The local community often has the potential to support CLIL classroom learning. Educators are wise to tap into this resource as no one teacher or group of teachers can provide students with the diverse use of language found in everyday life. Creating opportunities for contact and communication with speakers of the CLIL language helps to provide students with additional language models. Contact with speakers of the CLIL language will not only help students to experience the joy of being able to communicate in the CLIL language, but also to understand how the CLIL language is used outside the classroom. Moreover, through communicating with guests, community members or other speakers of the CLIL language, students experience and learn to cope with different accents and registers of language.

Content, language and learning skills can all be developed by working with community members. Asking community members about their language skills and their willingness to volunteer time to work with CLIL students can yield very positive results. Speakers of the CLIL language can be found by contacting:

- community papers and asking them to publish a call for native and non-native speakers of the CLIL language to support the school;
- local cultural organizations;
- employers who work with clients who speak the CLIL language;
- local and national government officials;
- consulates and embassies;
- people in any profession that speak the CLIL language;
- parents and grandparents that speak the CLIL language;
- travel agencies;
- art galleries and museums that may have bilingual or multilingual staff;
- other schools that offer CLIL programmes;
- senior students;
- university students;
- junior chambers of commerce and other organizations that do youth work;
- sports trainers;
- politicians;
- libraries.

Relevance building through community-centred projects

The Journal of Mathematics and Culture (2006) describes how some teachers in a bilingual community have worked to make mathematics relevant to their students. It reports on teachers who had their students create and/or answer maths questions about their own lives, their school and community. For example, students measured favourite parts of their own school. This required learning how to measure a room that is irregular in shape.

Furthermore, students visited a police station to find out about crime statistics. These statistics were analysed. Students surveyed local residents and calculated fractions and percentages of people who held various beliefs and attitudes. In turn, members of immigrant groups were considered. As many immigrants came into the country in question illegally across a desert, students calculated distances walked and the amount of water required per day when walking in the hot sun. Among other factors, the weight and volume of the water could also be incorporated into the equation.

Building on these ideas, students can measure percentages of space devoted to various functions within a school or other community buildings. They can calculate heating and lighting costs and even the costs of eliminating graffiti. Water usage can be quantified and analysed and proposals made for reducing consumption. A city official can be asked to speak to students about water consumption issues. Vocational students can be involved in refitting plumbing to reduce consumption.

The local community can be mapped. Students can map crime incidents and statistics, dangerous stretches of road, teenage pregnancies, alcohol- and drug-related deaths and their economic cost. Many police departments hire people who can speak foreign languages spoken in the community. If a speaker of the CLIL language is available, that person could be asked to attend a question and answer session with students.

Projects that analyse some aspect of community life can lead to students developing a series of recommendations and suggested measures for their implementation. These can be presented to the appropriate authorities, such as the local government, in oral and written form. Representatives of the authorities would be expected to respond orally on the spot and commit to providing feedback about proposed changes. Once content needs and activities have been established, language-learning outcomes are determined and language support is designed. For example, if no local official can be found that speaks the CLIL language, the dialogue with the local official takes place in the first language, but preparations and debriefing take place in the CLIL language. Vocabulary and discourse patterns are provided in two languages. As an outcome, students can be expected to formulate their recommendations in two languages.

Interviewing senior citizens can be a fine vehicle for learning in history, citizenship and/or mathematics, as well as for building language and learning skills. The interviews can be conducted in the CLIL language, or if that is not possible, the student's first language can be used. The survey is written up in the CLIL language.

The interviewing project can be based on a seven-step process:

- discussing and setting the learning outcomes (eg, the student describes life 50 years ago from different perspectives such as economic, childhood and lifestyle);
- determining processes and language required for setting up an interview;
- pitfalls of interviewing;
- conducting and recording interviews;
- interpreting data;
- writing conclusions;
- presenting results.

Agreeing on how to start an interview may involve saying hello, identifying oneself, asking if the person has time to speak, explaining the goal of the survey, giving the person an opportunity to ask questions and thanking the person in advance and afterwards. The following is a sample protocol that can be given to students to reinforce processes and provide needed language.

> *Hello, my name is ... and I am a student at ...*
>
> *Is this Mr, Miss, Mrs, Ms ...?*
>
> *Do you have a few moments to speak to me?*
>
> *I am doing a school project about ... It involves interviewing people about life in the 1930s.*
>
> *We hope to learn about what life was like in the 1930s in various countries.*
>
> *Would you be willing to answer some questions in person or over the phone? Your answers will be combined with other people's answers and no one else will be able to know exactly what you said.*
>
> *The interview could take 30 to 60 minutes.*
>
> *When could we meet?*
>
> *During the days I go to school, I am free on Monday and Tuesday evenings and at the weekend.*
>
> *Can we meet in the library?*
>
> *The library is located at ...*
>
> *Shall we meet in the foyer?*
>
> *My mobile phone number is ...*
>
> *Do you have a mobile phone?*
>
> *Thank you for taking the time to speak to me. I look forward to seeing you.*

During an interview, the student fills in a chart that leaves sufficient space for writing and that may include some of the following points:

Background information	
country born in	
country grew up in	
city, town or region where they lived at age 16 (an age that is close to the student's age)	
number of brothers	
number of sisters	
number of people living in home	
number of rooms in home	
number of people who slept in an average bedroom	
Personal perspective	
toys played with in childhood	
favourite foods	
typical Saturday night	
biggest worries of parents	
daily or weekly chores	
one lesson learnt in life	
School	
favourite school subjects	
a typical class in school	
upsetting moment at school	
knowledge and skills developed at school that were most useful in life/at work	
what the person wished he/she had learnt more about in school	
number of years of schooling before going to work	
Economics	
number of adults working outside home	
types of jobs held by each person	
electrical appliances in home	
costs of one litre of milk, one loaf of bread, chocolate bar	
number of cars in the family	
did he/she have a bicycle and does he/she remember how much it cost?	
number of pairs of trousers or dresses	
what clothes were made at home	
cost of a city bus ticket	
cost of going to the cinema	
was money tight*/was there just enough/was there plenty? (* was there a shortage of money)	

Data from the senior citizens survey can be discussed by students working in groups of five to draw conclusions about family size, lifestyle, lessons learnt, education, standard of living, values and, among others, gender roles. Students can compare and contrast their lives as sixteen year olds with those of the older people interviewed. They can draw up tables and pie charts. Needed language patterns are provided (eg, *over 50 per cent of respondents reported ...*, *most people interviewed did not have a family car*). Interviewees are invited to the school for a presentation of the research results and a follow-up discussion.

Job shadowing

A particularly valuable tool in vocational education is job shadowing. This can be done for as little as one day. If possible, it is preferable to find a workplace where the CLIL language is used. Students can write a report in the CLIL language about the experience, which will be the measurable outcome. The report might contain some of the following sub-headings: *introduction, educational requirements, three things I learnt today, language use, prevalent attitudes, needed skills, benefits of the job, downsides of the job, problems in the workplace, people hired, things I can do now to prepare for the job I want to do in the future* and *conclusions*.

Another option for vocational students is to interview people in a profession of interest to them. The students can be encouraged to develop their own questionnaire by using what is commonly referred to as think-pair-share. Students first develop some questions on their own, then further develop them in pairs and later in a group. Finally, the whole class can work to develop a common list. The teacher can help raise questions that they may have missed. Interviews are conducted in pairs. Questions may include:

What do you like best about your job?
What was the most difficult skill to learn?
What makes a good ... (eg, *electrician, baker, mechanic* or *computer programmer*)?
Can you describe a crisis you have faced and how you solved it?
What do you do to get on with co-workers?
How do you handle a difficult co-worker?
How do you handle a difficult client?
How do you ...?

Nature as a member of the community

Nature is a major force in any community. We can be affected by nature and we can affect it ourselves. Nature is also a source for learning. For example, CLIL educator Tuula Asikainen had her eleven to twelve year olds who were studying trees and plants in biology class go into the school playground. She aimed to have students consolidate learning by situating it in the immediate environment. The final outcome was a map indicating trees found in the playground, observation notes, a written report and an oral presentation. The exercise develops skills from across the curriculum, such as map reading, groupwork, estimating, measuring, comparing, surveying and reporting skills. It reinforces language involved with reading and interpreting instructions, describing natural phenomena or the environment, describing places, comparing and contrasting. It uses several registers of language for reporting, making notes, dialogue and presentation.

The students are equipped with a map of the school playground (with buildings marked), tape measures, pencils, string, notebooks and sticks. Their first task is to conduct a tree survey. This involves:

- walking around the playground to count all the trees (*How many are there? Where?*);
- identifying the trees (*What different kinds are there?*);
- plotting each tree on the map and naming the tree type;
- estimating which tree is the tallest, the shortest, the thickest and the thinnest;
- measuring the tallest, the shortest, the thickest and the thinnest trees.

The following explanations and instructions can be given to students to measure the approximate height of trees:

Place a stick that is as long as you are tall in the ground at a distance from the tree that you estimate to be the height of the tree. You lie down on your back with your feet both facing the tree and against the stick. When lying down, the top of the stick needs to align in your field of vision with the top of the tree. You will probably need to move the stick several times. Once you manage to do this, you stand up. The distance from the stick to the base of the tree is the approximate height of the tree.

Girth is measured using a piece of string and measuring the string against a tape measure.

Report writing is supported by providing a framework for the content, including key phrases such as: *We found xxx trees in the playground. Most trees grow in the middle of the playground.* and *The tallest tree is a Scots pine and it's xx m tall.* Two schools can share data, comparing and contrasting results.

The vitality of the community is as relevant to the classroom as the vitality of the classroom is to the community. However, the walls of the classroom can unintentionally block out connections with the community. By consciously connecting with the community we can further create an authentic context for the work we do in the classroom.

Connecting classrooms to the world

> It has been said that arguing against globalization is like arguing against the laws of gravity.
> **Kofi Annan**

Textbooks are often so politically correct that they can seem unreal. They rarely evoke strong emotions. Emotional connections help us personalize information and learn. Moreover, it is difficult for any textbook to compete with the real world in real time, as they quickly become dated.

From the perspective of the average student, a one-year period carries much greater significance than it would for the average adult for whom, mathematically speaking, another year represents a much smaller part of his or her life experience. For many students, an event from ten years ago can seem like ancient history and one that is far removed from their reality.

In the developed world, students tend to operate on 'Internet time' and with a new technologies mindset. For them, it is the here and now that is most relevant. They are connected to world trends in information sharing, fashion, entertainment and technology, all of which are driven by immediacy. Significant parts of their lives are spent in this real-time global media space.

That is why so many authors today work to ensure that textbooks lead students beyond the pages of the book to open new doors and discover new worlds. These new doors can be found on the Internet; but also by working with other media, in libraries, by talking with members of the community, by exploring one's own thoughts and feelings, or by communing with nature. Publishers are now increasingly supporting this process by linking textbooks to the Internet, to other media resources and to the community in which students live. Through an exploration of the language and content of the here and now, one can connect with oneself, the past and the future.

In the here and now, our capacity to grow and be happy is influenced by our own ability to manage our emotions and learning. It is influenced by our own capability to understand and make the most of the communities in which we live. More and more, our personal and local actions are linked to global processes, and global processes in turn are linked to the local community and our own lives. We benefit from international communication, mobility, perspectives and discoveries.

Yet, we also suffer the impact of complicated, cross-boundary issues that have high-stakes consequences – HIV, pollution, wars and forced migration, to name a few.

Thus, the imperative to connect learning to the world at large is driven by the realities of our interconnected planet and by virtue of the fact that many of our students live in a connected media world where yesterday's events may already be old news. Students, who use these tools on a daily basis for expanding their knowledge base and for communicating with others, expect to use these same instruments in structured learning as well. Subject and language teachers have always understood the value of connecting learning to the real world. As educators, the interconnected world offers endless new opportunities for facilitating learning.

Avoiding the technology trap

Technology is seductive. It seems relevant in and of itself, by virtue of the fact that it is integrated into so many leading-edge developments. Yet it is above all a tool that supports learning. Good pedagogy still drives education, not technology.

For new technologies to be truly relevant in the educational context, they need to be used to support young people in taking their thinking another step forward. It is by using these technologies in new ways, by accessing new information, by connecting with others and by building something new that is connected to the students' lives, their community and the world at large that new technologies become effective, relevant educational tools.

Some of the ways of connecting students with others in the world, and which can also support learning through CLIL, are:

Ways of learning about how to connect	Sample activities/projects
TWINNING	
In today's multicultural world students or parents may have links to a school abroad. http://www.bbc.co.uk/worldclass/ helps you find a twin and provides guidance on how to organize and run an exchange. http://www.etwinning.net/ww/en/pub/etwinning/index2006.htm/ This EU organization helps schools find a twin, provides toolkits for projects, provides rewards for excellence in twinning and facilitates dialogue among teachers. http://www.globalgateway.org.uk/ British Council database for finding partners in other countries, and providing guidance. http://www.iearn.org/ An NGO working in 115 countries facilitating some one million students in joint projects, and providing guidance. http://www.rafi.ki/This site, which is run by a charity, enables you to put your school on its website, to find partners, to work on co-operation projects and to participate in moderated chats. http://www.factworld.info/ This site is for teachers and its network is used by teachers seeking partners for co-operation projects. Embassies and consulates can also tell you whether their countries are involved with international twinning programmes for schools.	The European Union's e-twinning project provides several kits on exchanges. One is on entrepreneurship education. It suggests that teachers first agree on goals and other project parameters. In CLIL, this would include language goals. Students decide on a name for the companies they are creating. They create a logo and by-laws. Students then get to know their prospective customers and suppliers. This may involve requesting information, making presentations, doing market research, creating catalogues and placing orders. Students process orders, receive and sell their products and finally dissolve their companies. To finish the project, they write a financial report, analyse their performance, create photo albums and celebrate success.
E-PALS	
http://www.epals.com/ This site connects more than seven million students and educators in over 190 countries. The site helps create links for classroom-to-classroom project sharing, practising language and literacy skills and teacher-supervised communication between pen pals across the globe. The site can be accessed in English, French, German, Spanish, Portuguese, Arabic, Chinese and Japanese.	War-Affected Children – this e-pals project helps students understand the complexity and impact of war. Students look at issues such as wars that target children, child soldiers, media and communications, and war prevention.
SPONSOR A SCHOOL OR A CHILD	
There are many websites offering this service. Some may not have sufficiently transparent financing or the experience that helps demonstrate proof of success. Some have hidden agendas. The following have stood the test of time. http://www.plan-international.org/ Founded in 1937 and originally named 'Foster Parents Plan for Children in Spain', this organization now sponsors children throughout the world. It has sister organizations in over 20 countries that manage and channel aid. If your CLIL language is Japanese, you can sponsor a child through the Japanese plan office. This will ensure communication in Japanese and bring you letters from the sponsored child in Japanese. http://www.sos-childrensvillages.org/ Founded in 1949, this organization has offices in many countries throughout the world. It allows you to sponsor a child or support a special project. One can easily work through a regional office using the CLIL language. Embassies of countries where the CLIL language is spoken as a native tongue or studied as a state language can be contacted for information about agencies that facilitate these types of partnerships in their country.	See Chapter 1 page 16.

Ways of learning about how to connect	Sample activities/projects
GIS	
Geographic Information Systems are available through various sites including Apple interchange. (http://edcommunity.apple.com/ali/story.php?itemID=786/) These sites enable students to work with geographically referenced materials by which they can explore regions of the world in relation to many different features, including time. This not only enables integration of content and language, but also development of critical thinking, mathematical, spatial and interpersonal skills.	The Apple site hosts a number of projects, one of which involves students analysing changes in the regions in which they live over a period of some 100 years. This is done using maps from different decades. Students can analyse land usage, population density, environmental improvement or degradation, transport infrastructure and air pollution, amongst other themes.
GLOBE	
The GLOBE programme is a hands-on international environmental education project active in over 100 countries worldwide. GLOBE students measure their local environment using standardized techniques and report their findings over the Internet. The students' data is then used to provide visualizations of the state of the planet, with online maps and graphs. GLOBE aims: • to enhance environmental awareness worldwide. • to increase scientific understanding of the Earth. • to provide practical opportunities for students to increase skills in science, geography, citizenship, maths and I.C.T. The programme covers four main areas: weather, water, soils and land cover. All resources are freely available from the website (http://www.globe.gov/).	Students (ages five to eighteen) undertake environmental measurements using rigorous scientific standards. Students investigate soil, the atmosphere, land cover, GPS and the Earth as a system. The student data is submitted to a central data processing facility via the Internet. In return, students receive vivid images based on their data and on that of other schools working through GLOBE. Students co-operate with peers from other schools and with scientists. Scientists actually use the data collected by students to improve their understanding of the global environment. Students receive feedback from scientists about how valuable their submitted data was.
FORUMS	
When students have a tough assignment, they often enter forums to ask for advice about where to get information or find someone to explain a concept they do not understand. By typing the word *forum* and a topic from history into an Internet search engine, or the words, *geography*, *plumbing*, *climate change*, *globalization* and so forth, one can easily find a forum. Students can go into a forum and have a live discussion with their classmates and people in other countries. They then simply print out the debate as their homework assignment. http://www.plbg.com/ This site allows people to ask practical questions and get answers about plumbing. Similar sites are available in several languages by typing *plumbing* and *forum* in a given language into any Internet search engine. http://www.simaqianstudio.com/forum/index.php?act=home/ is a site that enables students to discuss and debate many historical topics. Much supportive historical information can be found here, for example, by clicking on the page number icons next to forum titles. If you have trouble finding them simply ask the students to find them.	When using a forum on plumbing, vocational students can group the first 50 plumbing questions or problems raised on the site according to which problems can be handled by an amateur and which need a professional. They can work to improve the clarity of two answers given on the site. In a history forum, students could print out a discussion about a given topic and analyse it. They could prepare for and hold their own debate. They could print out their own debate and it could be analysed in class for precision of self-expression, accuracy of facts and use of logic.

Ways of learning about how to connect	Sample activities/projects
FACEBOOK™	
http://www.facebook.com/This site allows the user to record basic information about him/herself, post photos and leave and receive messages. Facebook is about communicating a global image of yourself. By supporting students in presenting themselves in the second language, they rethink how to present themselves and can be guided in making a sensible choice when communicating through new technologies. This can be a first step in building understanding about how to present oneself in a public space.	Students can set up their own Facebook profiles. Secondly, students can analyse how their entry might be perceived by an employer. This may be used as a jumping off point for getting ready to learn about writing CVs.

One result of a twinning project can be an exchange visit. Exchange visits are an excellent opportunity for both students and teachers to put language and content knowledge to use. They can do a great deal to motivate students, build student–teacher understanding and launch friendships that may last for decades.

It is a fallacy to assume that the best language learning experience will come from running an exchange with a school in a country where the CLIL language is a national language or otherwise spoken as a native tongue. Many successful exchanges are run between countries where the CLIL language is not a native tongue for either school group. For example, Swedish and Slovakian students who are studying in French can very successfully use that language as their medium of communication. When both sides communicate through their second language, it creates a more level playing field.

However, running face-to-face exchange programmes is time-consuming and costly. Without proper preparation and structure, exchange visits can resemble excursions, as opposed to being educational, partnership-building exercises. Partnerships require taking the time to learn about each other and working to create something new together. If this time is not taken, exchanges can even reinforce negative stereotyping, as opposed to deepening understanding. Some suggestions for managing exchanges are listed on the following page.

Managing an exchange

DOs	DON'Ts
• agree on goals with your partner school • agree on selection criteria for students • have students fill out an application form with contact numbers for their family, details of allergies and other pertinent medical information, dietary restrictions, interests and values • work with the students to get to know the community they will be visiting (exchanging letters and videos) • talk about how students might expect a guest to behave in their home, clothing and the negative side-effects of taking too many nice clothes and how to deal with unexpected foods and customs • agree with students on a code of behaviour and have all students sign it (the teacher signs it too) • have parents sign a permission waiver, meet with parents to discuss plans and concerns, let parents express their concerns, outline the responsibilities of the chaperones and make it clear that they cannot keep an eye on 30 students 24 hours a day, ask parents not to send a child on an exchange who is likely to use illegal substances (With young adults it is important to talk through the substance abuse issue. Roleplaying or talking through various scenarios and solutions can be helpful.) • ensure your host gives you a list with all of the students' home and, if possible, mobile telephone numbers • stress that you are going as a group and that you expect the students to be supportive of one another • let your exchange partner know that you want to have an hour a day alone with your own students (During this time, sit in a circle and have each person relate what is going well and have students raise any concerns. If there are common group concerns, they are discussed and possible solutions are proposed.) • organize on-site activities that require co-operation and that support the two groups of students in jointly creating something • work through the goals/learning outcomes with the students • agree with your partner and your students which language will be used where	• assume your partner has the same goals, commitment and values (Dialogue and thorough planning are key.) • twin boys with girls (Exchanges can be challenging enough without turning the whole process into a blind date.) • forget to raise your students' awareness of language issues, such as slowing down speech and avoiding slang • try to outdo your partner in offering a much richer programme in your community than was or could be offered to your group in their own • forget to understand the economic circumstances of your partner community and the need for some teachers to teach their full load • be more focused on language acquisition than relationships • forget to give your students some of the day-to-day language, including slang, that they are likely to encounter

International projects do not have to be large in scope or highly time-consuming for teachers or students. Even if limited in scope, these projects can have a major payoff. For example, students from two countries could compare ten aspects of their communities and lives. As a first step, students work in groups of five to fill in a chart about their partner community. Each student in the group assumes responsibility for learning about two aspects of the other community, such as education and energy. Topics under study can include economy, food, transport, clothing, vegetation, climate, homes, health, traditions, languages, architecture, gender, social life and religion. As a next step, students from both countries exchange these charts. Many forms of subject-specific analysis and debate can be carried out. At the simplest level, each side details for the other what they felt their partner did well and describes what they learnt about their own community. Points of disagreement can be raised and discussed.

When both sides have finalized the charts, they can both look at a third community. For example, they can take a virtual tour of a village in another country, such as

India, to compare their communities with another village (http://virtualvillage. wesleyan.edu/). This site was found by typing *virtual village India* into an Internet search engine.

Categories	My community	Partner community	Indian community
Economy			
Foods			
Architecture			
...			

A topic that has taken the world by storm can be used in class to extend learning about content, different perspectives, language, critical thinking, bias and/or logic. Rarely does a day pass without some major news story hitting the headlines across the globe. In 2007, Russian scientists placed their country's flag on the floor of the Arctic Ocean. This was the first time anyone had reached the Arctic seabed. It was a major achievement. However, as this symbolic act was interpreted by many nations as Russia claiming much of the Arctic as its own territory, this caused considerable controversy. In this case, students working through English could have looked at articles in several newspapers such as the *China Daily*, Russia's *Moscow Times*, Canada's *Globe and Mail*, America's *New York Times*, Chile's *Santiago Times*, or *The Australian*. Many newspapers provide free online access for a given day's paper. If CLIL students are working through Russian, French, Chinese or a host of other languages, there are newspapers published in many parts of the world in these languages.

As a warm-up exercise, students can be provided with a series of headlines from newspapers in the CLIL language. The list could include two headlines from local newspapers in the first language. (The occasional mixing of languages helps build the habit of using more than one language to source information.) Students can rank these headlines according to those that are the most emotional or factual through to the least emotional or factual. As a next step, they can analyse the articles. Students either access these articles themselves or copies are provided. The following graphic organizer focuses on language and content. The exercise is suitable for groups of four to five students.

INFORMATION FOR ANALYSIS						
Newspapers	Print size and tone of headline	Five to ten adjectives used	Five to ten other words that set the tone	List of opinions expressed	List of facts presented	Includes multiple views? Yes/No
The Australian						
China Daily						
Globe and Mail						
Moscow Times						
Santiago Times						

DRAWING CONCLUSIONS			
Newspapers	Factual? Yes/No	What else does the reader need to know?	Whose interests are being served?
The Australian			
China Daily			
Globe and Mail			
Moscow Times			
Santiago Times			

Links can be drawn to work done in geography on Russia, the Arctic, the Antarctic or the climate. Links can be made to history and national expansionism. This can be followed up by analysing long-term potential consequences of this Russian move on international relations, the environment or international organizations. This type of exercise may also suit a language class where students are developing media literacy. Here students can analyse who is the gatekeeper of the information. An article about a rock concert could be rewritten by changing the gatekeepers of the information from a local business organization to owners of a music magazine, to a local residents' organization or to a police department. In turn, these can be analysed and the dangers of unbalanced reporting discussed.

In mathematics, connections can be tied to a host of current national and international statistics. For example, students can chart the spread of tuberculosis and other contagious diseases. Another option is to use the following formula to determine the portion of a country's inhabitants that are of working age and who therefore contribute to supporting younger and older members of society. It is called the dependency ratio.

$$\text{Dependency ratio} = \frac{(\% \text{ under 15}) + (\% \text{ over 65}) \times 100}{\% \text{ between 15 and 64}}$$

The age breakdown of any country is easily found by typing *world factbook* (https://www.cia.gov/library/publications/the-world-factbook/) into an Internet search engine and viewing country-specific demographics. In 2007, 34 per cent of the population in Cambodia was estimated to be 14 years of age or under and 3.6 per cent was 65 or older. Thus the dependency ratio for Cambodia is estimated to be:

$$\frac{34 + 3.6}{62.4} \times 100 = 39.7\%$$

Furthermore, students can determine and analyse their own country's dependency ratio. The ratio for neighbouring countries and regions that are considered major economic competitors can also be determined and analysed. Long-range projections can be made and possible consequences analysed.

In history class, numerous historical sites can be toured virtually. These are easily found by typing *virtual tour historical site* or more specific information such as *virtual tour ancient Egypt* into a search engine. For example, historical sites in China and Egypt can be toured online, with students looking at slides accompanied by short texts and videos. The texts often give basic factual information in plain language, and as such, are ideal for CLIL students. Students can simply search these sites at home and bring interesting visual links to class, or send an email to you with facts about life in Egypt in 200 BC under topics such as government, economy, religion and family life.

The options are endless. Mastering these technologies is not as important as creating opportunities for students to use them and to connect with the world at large. Increasing awareness of global interconnectedness, creating opportunities for contact and communication with people abroad and doing this using the technologies familar to students can make learning more relevant, effective and enjoyable.

Making meanings matter

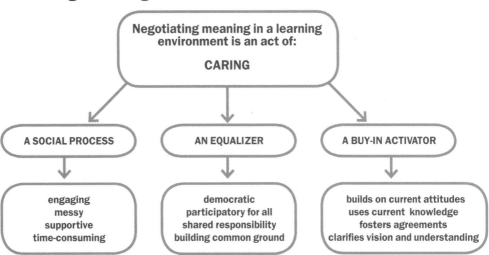

Meaning-making is a social process: we co-construct meaning through interaction. It is only when we have discussed and used information in co-operation with others that it takes on a collective meaning for individuals and groups. Anthropologist Lawrence Rosen refers to this process as 'bargaining for reality'.

In education, the term 'negotiation of meaning' refers to a process where students and teachers work to pass on information, thoughts and opinions to one another in a manner that leads them to a common understanding of what is being communicated. This is often done by one person restating in his or her own words what the other person has communicated, by clarifying differences and by confirming facts, opinions, thoughts and so forth.

Negotiation nullifiers
- feeling/showing irritation when someone asks for clarification
- being threatened by having to revise one's own views
- asking questions that require a 'yes' or 'no' answer

In content classes, using the content takes precedence over having the students speak in full sentences. Short phrases are often more effective tools in negotiating meaning.

This applies both to the teacher and the student. Phrases that are linked to immediate action, such as an instruction followed by an act of doing, are more easily retained than lengthy statements. Once the content is mastered with the basic elements of language, the language and the content can be expanded.

Strategies for negotiating meaning operate on two levels. Firstly, they are directed at achieving a common understanding. Secondly, at taking that understanding another step further. These strategies include:

- asking for summaries of key points;
- encouraging students to ask for clarification;
- inviting personal interpretations;
- using free association to bring out personal opinions/understanding;
- appreciating risk-taking;
- providing definitions;
- using synonyms;
- paraphrasing;
- writing key words on the board;
- using gestures and mime;
- slowing down speech;
- using pictures, realia and demonstrations;
- having students perform actions in direct relation to words;
- presenting one instruction at a time and ensuring it has been followed before presenting the next one;
- taking an experiment or project one step further;
- having students draw schemes or pictures to summarize points;
- analysing student drawings and schemes;
- looking at a topic from different perspectives.

Negotiating meaning in pairs

Student A has a drawing and student B has a blank sheet of paper. Student A describes to B, using words only, what is in his or her drawing. Student B draws a picture according to A's instructions. Finally, conclusions are drawn about how to improve communication. Students A and B switch roles. As a variation, two students can start with the same drawing and each make seven changes without discussing or showing them to one another. Student A describes his or her changes to student B, who tries to draw them, and vice versa.

Maths: The drawing consists of various mathematical shapes such as rectangles with three circles on top, etc. Precise measurements can be included like area, circumference, length, width and depth.

Art or psychology: A student in one country describes via email a nationally renowned painting to a student in another country and vice versa. Results are scanned or digitally photographed and exchanged. Students give more instructions to try to improve the final result. Finally, pictures of the original paintings are exchanged. Students can proceed to analyse moods and relationships as reflected in the paintings.

Science or biology: One student looks at a specimen through a microscope and describes it to the other.

Negotiating meaning does not always mean simplifying language. While it is wise to start talking about a concept in science in everyday language, this is only the beginning of a longer process. Students need the language of specialists to explain things and understand texts that are intended for a higher level of thinking and for communication used in the workplace or in scientific literature. They need opportunities to restate content using the appropriate level of language.

Negotiating tip

Information exchange provides more opportunities for negotiating meaning than general discussion. Why? Because passing on information requires a greater level of precision.

Students can support each other in negotiating meaning by first writing down some of their own thoughts about a topic. They then work in groups to pool ideas and align understanding. The teacher intervenes in groupwork only to help keep students on task, or when they are having serious difficulty or requesting help with language. Afterwards, groups share information with the class as they all try to create one common understanding.

Collaborative projects such as creating advertisements, blogs, demonstrations, graphic organizers, labelled diagrams and pictures, mobiles, murals, posters, science experiments and timelines that summarize learning will all help the teacher and the students arrive at the essence of the content. Also, the assignments help develop the language skills required to clearly express and discuss the content with others.

Students can also analyse recordings of their own pairwork where they themselves have been involved in negotiating meaning. For example, two students work with slightly different pictures that they do not show each other. They try to identify where the pictures differ, only by speaking. Afterwards, they listen to the recording and identify the points where they faced difficulties in exchanging information. Students state what they would do next time to improve their communication. The exercise is then repeated with new pairs and afterwards, using the audio recording, students analyse their progress.

This is an opportunity for highly individualized reflection on the learning process students have just experienced. Also, this exercise could be adapted so it can be conducted via email or text-speak in trans-national class projects.

Negotiating the meaning of content can, on an emotional level, be both exciting and threatening. Learning influences our view of the world. As our views change, we change as people. Thus, negotiating meaning is strongly tied to attitudinal change.

Negotiating meaning involves regularly assessing whether students have understood a given point and how they are feeling about a task. Yet getting feedback from students is not always easy. The widespread tactic in classrooms of simply asking if everyone understands is usually not an effective strategy.

Partway through a lesson you can ask students to anonymously write on a piece of paper a number from one to five. The number one indicates that a student understands the topic at hand, while a number five shows that he or she is completely lost. A number in-between indicates various degrees of understanding. A student can quickly tabulate the results. Another option is 'splitting the atom', which is particularly useful in assessing attitudes. This technique is described on page 83 in Chapter 3.

Negotiation of meaning helps confront the illusion that that we can move forwards with new material and that the students are with us when they are not. In a student-centred classroom, it is the ability of students to clarify, restate and use new language and content in a meaningful context that attests to whether they have understood and can apply new learning. Once assimilated, the habit of negotiating meaning supports students in taking responsibility for their learning. Students will be more likely to use the teacher and other students as a resource and less likely to accept feeling lost. They learn to take charge of their own learning and insist on clarity so they can stay on track.

Helping learners help themselves

The development of learning skills is the last core feature of the CLIL method to be discussed separately in this book. Learning skills are tools used to enhance our ability to learn. On the one hand, learning skills development is simply good educational practice. On the other hand, it plays a very significant role in CLIL.

As a case in point, a CLIL programme in Montreal allowed students to set their own learning objectives, choose activities of interest to them and proceed at their own pace. These students assumed greater responsibility for their learning than would be the case in a teacher-centred class.

Learning how to manage one's own learning is itself a learning skill. When comparing second-language acquisition in the student-centred CLIL programme in Montreal, where 40 per cent of instruction was delivered through a second language, and a teacher-centred programme in the same city where 80 per cent of the instructional time was delivered in the second language, student results were almost equal. Despite receiving half the amount of instruction through the medium of the second language, students in the student-centred programme scored equally well on speaking and listening tests and almost as well on reading and writing tests (Genesee, 2005 referring to Stevens, 1983).

Yet how does one convince students of the need to develop learning skills? How does one inspire students to take control of their learning? Many of the strategies discussed in the previous sections of this book support students in assuming this responsibility. However, sometimes, for a complex package of strategies to work, a single and simple catalyst is needed. One possibility is to have students analyze what type of mindset they have. Do they have what Carol Dweck (Stanford University) refers to as a 'growth mindset', or do they have a 'fixed mindset'? Do they see their intelligence level as fixed or do they consider it more like a muscle to be exercised and improved?

This can be done by having students search the Internet for information on this concept, distilling the key elements onto one page and analysing their own mindset. Another option is to ask them to answer the following questions and to compare examples from their lives where they have reacted with a fixed mindset or a growth mindset:

How do you feel and what do you do:

- *when you are faced with a problem or obstacle?*
- *when you are criticized?*
- *when you are faced with a challenge?*
- *when you are asked to expend a lot of effort?*
- *when you see someone else succeed?*

The assignment can be done in writing and through a group debrief. Students can discuss related situations from their lives. Consequences of their actions can be analysed and conclusions drawn. Students are more likely to respond well to this philosophy if you too do some self-analysis and share your own journey of personal growth. Over the coming days and weeks, when a situation arises that could benefit from being viewed from a different perspective, you can ask how someone with a growth mindset and someone with a fixed mindset might deal with this given situation.

Learning skills are tools for coping with and moving beyond obstacles, problems, criticism, challenges and envy. The following list of tips summarizes learning skills related to managing one's feelings, reading, writing and studying. They can be adapted depending on a student's grade level. The content is suitable for primary, secondary and vocational levels. Improving learning skills and becoming more attuned to and being better capable of managing feelings are topical issues at every stage in life.

These learning skills tips can be distributed to students one set at a time. To help students internalize these tips, they are asked to verbalize examples of situations in their lives when they applied some of these skills or should have applied these skills. This can be done in pairs, in groups or as a whole class. By returning to the growth mindset versus fixed mindset descriptions they can draw conclusions about the choices they have made and intend to make in the future.

Ten tips for students: Managing feelings in CLIL

Don't make fun of other people's language mistakes. Others will probably treat you the way you treat them. If someone forgets the rule and makes fun of you, remind them of the agreement. You cannot learn without making mistakes.

Accept some confusion and frustration. This is a natural part of learning. You don't have to understand everything.

Be your own best friend. Don't let that voice in your head trap you in a vicious circle of self-criticism for not progressing fast enough. Review your goals to make sure they are attainable, take some time to study and then reward yourself for making progress. Then give yourself a break. Shift your focus from learning through CLIL to something else like exercising, speaking with friends or reading.

Keep a journal to increase your self-awareness and self-reflection. Write about what you are feeling during class and while studying. Analyse what triggers those feelings. What are some possible solutions for raising your comfort level, for creating a better learning climate?

Build a personal dictionary of words and phrases to talk about and analyse feelings. This will help to equip you with the tools for talking and writing about what you are feeling. It will help you better manage and learn from your emotions, as well as take control of your learning in general.

Observe yourself. List classroom activities and types of interaction that make you tense, or that help you feel confident and calm. Identify learning styles that work for you. Let your teacher know what types of activity make it harder or easier for you to learn.

When discussing a problem in class, **start your sentence with '*I feel ...*'**. Starting with the word 'you' can sound like an accusation. Instead of saying *you are wrong* say *I feel differently*.

Ask for more than one point of view. Listen carefully to those points of view that are different from yours.

Trust your feelings. If deep inside you feel something is not right, you are probably right. If someone keeps pressuring you and you cannot come up with a logical argument for saying *no*, you can always say *I am not feeling comfortable with this*.

Take some quiet time (without TV, music, the Internet) each day. In other words, stop the bombardment of new information for a few minutes. This helps stop the noise in your head. This also means taking a break from the CLIL language.

Journal ideas

I admire … (name of a person). In tough situations this person …

I feel most comfortable in class when …

I learn better when …

I get stressed in class when …

When I study, a fly on the wall would see and hear …

If I am upset about something I think about …/I talk to …/I try to …/I look for …/ I move on by …

When I can't find the word in the CLIL language, I …

I reward myself for progress in language learning by …

I reward myself for progress in content learning by …

Writing is different from speaking as it creates a more permanent product. Although some types of writing, such as text messaging and emailing, are very close to spoken language, most forms of writing are more demanding and require higher level skills. Many students fear writing. CLIL students sometimes become obsessed with not making mistakes when writing in the second language. In this case, they avoid taking risks and experimenting with language and content. They tend to stay within their comfort zone, only using familiar discourse patterns. The fear of making language errors can override their willingness to express higher order thinking about content. Writer's block is not just something famous authors experience. Many children are fearful of setting words down on paper. To build confidence and develop the tools needed to write, students must become aware of the writing process and related techniques. They also require language support.

Writing is not part of instinctive language use. It is a learnt process in the first language, which requires considerable guidance over a child's whole educational career path. The same is the case as they develop their second language. Moreover, as each language has its own writing conventions and discourse structures and markers, CLIL students will benefit from all teachers creating opportunities for and providing guidance in writing.

The following tips can be shared and discussed with students to raise their understanding of the fact that writing is a skill that can be learnt and developed.

Tips for students: Writing in the CLIL language

The title to a work of writing is like a house's front porch ...
It should invite you to come on in.
Angela Giles Klocke

Read, read, read. Read everything – trash, classics, good and bad,
and see how they do it.
William Faulkner

When I write, I read everything out loud to get the right rhythm.
Fran Lebowitz

Omit needless words. Vigorous writing is concise. A sentence should
contain no unnecessary words, a paragraph no unnecessary sentences,
for the same reason that a drawing should have no unnecessary lines
and a machine no unnecessary parts.
William Strunk, Jr

Understanding the purpose

Know your reader. Who is the text being written for and what background information does this reader need?

Read evaluation criteria. Look at how marks are allocated.

Getting started

Do a little brainstorming by yourself. Jot down every idea that comes to mind before you start analysing or criticizing what you have written.

Look at examples of similar texts. If you are writing a formal letter, a story or an essay, read what others have done. Decide what makes the writing easy to understand and what makes it difficult to follow.

Brainstorm useful words and phrases for the writing task in a group.

Structuring a text

Write a short outline. Jot down an idea or two for the introduction, each of the sections or paragraphs and the conclusion.

Write an introductory paragraph. This usually states the primary focus of the text and shows how the remainder of the text is organized.

Write a topic sentence for each paragraph. This sentence expresses the main idea of the paragraph.

Follow the topic sentence with supporting details.

Write a conclusion. This summarizes the ideas expressed in the text.

Writing style

Keep sentences and paragraphs short.

Use a standard subject, verb and object order.

Reduce the number of synonyms.

Use clear discourse markers including connectors, eg, *first, second, third, at the beginning, at the end, however, moreover.*

The cyclical process

Several drafts are required. Even the most experienced writers re-draft their work.

Drafts are not expected to be perfect. They are part of the search for the right path. Don't waste time putting yourself down. Concentrate on improving your work.

Read each other's drafts. Even the most experienced writers work with editors. You and your classmates can act as a team of editors.

Set each draft aside for a while and come back to it with a fresh perspective. Sleeping on it can be helpful.

Edit for special purposes:
- re-read the evaluation criteria to ensure that your work closely fits what is required.
- anticipate how the reader will understand the text. Writing is about interpretation, so when you write, you need to put yourself into the head of the reader.
- check for structure. Make sure the introductory paragraph follows the standard sample format, and so forth.
- check for logical flow of ideas.
- check for spelling and grammar.

Tips for reading

Attitude

Take control. Some students dread reading. That feeling usually comes from being overwhelmed by certain types of text. The overwhelmed reader is usually a passive reader. Passive readers do not have a special purpose for reading, they just read. They do not first review headings and diagrams to see how the text is organized. They do not first read the questions and look for the answers.

Face reality. Texts often need to be read more than once. We shouldn't assume that everything can be understood on the first read.

Speed

Read two to three words at once, not one word at a time.

For example, / try to grasp / two to three / words at once, / not one word / at a time.

Practise reading faster. Speeding up can help improve concentration. If you want to work on this skill yourself, there are lots of speed-reading books and courses available.

Build concentration skills. If you have trouble concentrating on reading, break the task into smaller parts. Read one page, half a page or even one paragraph at a time and take a short break before continuing.

Preparation
First survey the text:
- How long is it?
- Is there a table of contents?
- Are there any subheadings?
- Are there any diagrams?
- Is there a conclusion?
- Are there any unfamiliar words that are repeated a lot?

Look up in a dictionary any unfamiliar words that are used a lot.

Read headings, conclusions and diagrams.

Find the right place to read. Even if feels comfortable, lying down is not recommended for serious reading.

Purpose
Decide on why you are reading the text. If you are looking for someone's name and address in a list, or a birth date, you can skim the materials looking for numbers. You do not need to read the text.

Process
After reading a paragraph, try to summarize the main idea in your head.
If there are no subheadings, create your own.
If you have to answer questions, first read the questions, then the text.
If there are no questions about the text, make up some of your own.
Make some bullet point notes as you proceed through the text.
Summarize the main message.
If you are reading a non-fiction book, first read the introduction and the final chapter.
If you are reading a chapter, read the conclusion first.
Make a mind map or another graphic organizer to summarize information.

As with other learning skills, study skills need to be discussed and developed in class. Students can brainstorm what distracts them from studying, as well as ways of improving concentration. They can share their studying strategies. During class, students can practise and analyse how to review a topic in a study group. They practise managing their own study groups, which includes analysing how to improve their group's effectiveness.

Tips for students: Studying

Planning and concentration

Identify what usually distracts you from studying and decide how to avoid those traps.

Pick a place to study. Some places are full of distractions, which make effective learning difficult or impossible. Don't set yourself up for failure. Look for a place with minimal distractions and where you have maximum control over the situation. Lying down is not advised.

Divide the work you have to do into a number of tasks. This helps to prevent you from being overwhelmed. With each task, understanding and recalling content is essential. You also need to make certain you have the language needed to properly express the content.

Plan in advance how you will approach the task. This will help you to stop wasting time on worrying, which gets you nowhere. Will you first study by yourself and then get together with friends to summarize your learning and to test each other? Will you write questions for yourself before you start? Will you summarize each paragraph after you have read it? After you are finished, will you practise using last year's exam questions?

Plan to do as much studying during daylight hours as possible. Research shows that studying during daylight hours is 50 per cent more efficient. Of course, that doesn't mean one should not study after the sun goes down. Evening study sessions can also be helpful, but you need to be aware of when to stop.

If you have trouble staying on task, start with short study sessions. If, even after proper planning, you are having trouble concentrating for more than a few minutes at a time, study in short spurts. If ten minutes is your limit for concentration, break up your studying into ten-minute spurts. Set a goal to build up to fifteen-minute sessions.

Improving memory

Organize content information into groups or categories (eg, eating habits, habitat, life cycle, appearance).

Group words (eg, adjectives, nouns, phrases, verbs, language needed for various topics in science or geography).

Make personal dictionaries.

Create your own content and word wall at home. Leave it up for a few days and then test yourself. Take down those words and bits of content information that you can recall.

Work actively with a text as you read it. Otherwise, you may realize you have just finished reading a page and recall nothing. As you are reading, summarize each paragraph. Use textbook questions, or write your own questions, before you re-read the text and look for the answers.

Try to associate new words and information with pictures in your mind. Visualization helps improve recall.

Use it or lose it. Practise talking and writing about new concepts.

Compare topics looking for similarities and differences.

Divide information according to fact and opinion.

Using study groups (two to five people)

Someone should always chair the session. This person's main role is to keep everyone on task. Each group member takes a turn chairing a whole session.

Agree on what you are going to accomplish. Setting goals and agreeing on tasks will help you to do this.

At the end of each session, analyse whether you accomplished what you set out to do. This will help to increase the effectiveness of your team. Be prepared to temporarily exclude people who continually undermine the group goals.

Agree on who will prepare what for the next study session. People should come prepared to these sessions. For example, each person may have a responsibility for working through one aspect of the study topic and being the expert in the field that will help others to understand the topic.

7 Cruising with CLIL

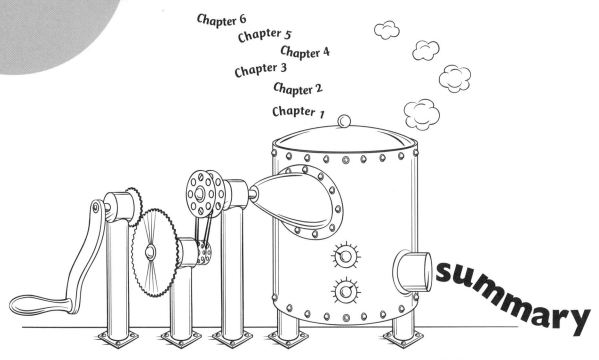

Chapter 6
Chapter 5
Chapter 4
Chapter 3
Chapter 2
Chapter 1

summary

We have now come full circle in our journey to uncover CLIL. It's time to step back and take a look at the big picture.

Painting the big CLIL picture with broad brush strokes requires fusion – fusion of CLIL core features and guiding principles. Four verbs that fuse much of the methodology and give a feel for the essence of CLIL are:

| Connect | Inspire | Deliver | Advance |

You can use these verbs at various points during a lesson to quietly assess your own progress in applying best practice in CLIL. These verbs can also be used to get a quick sense of how the whole CLIL initiative/programme is progressing. It is all a matter of degree, getting a feel for the extent to which the methodology is being realized in practice. After reading this book and practising the implementation tips contained therein, we hope you will be able to answer these questions with a confident *yes*.

Are my students connecting? (with each other, with me, with the material, with their past learning and interests)

Are my students and I inspired? (inspiring each other and themselves to learn and create through the content and language)

Are my students and I delivering on the content, language and learning skills outcomes? (talking the talk and walking the walk)

Are we advancing? (summarizing learning, deciding how to move forwards, demonstrating growth)

These four verbs and the relational links shown below can help not only to monitor, but to energize CLIL practice.

Connect

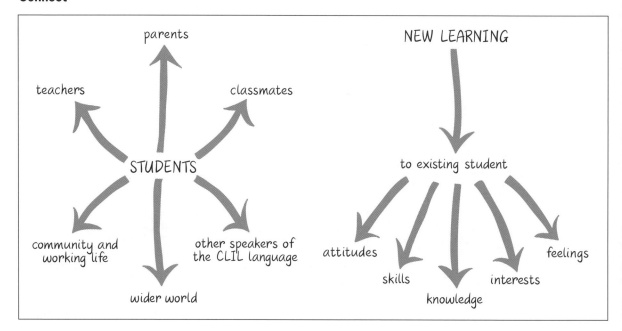

Inspire

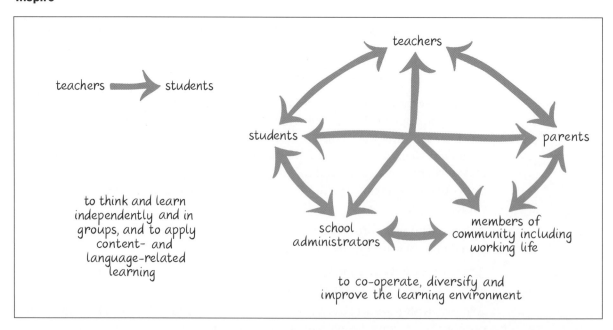

Deliver

- on content, language and learning skills outcomes, commitments and plans;
- on development and personal growth.

Advance

- on previous learning;
- through demonstrating growth by assessing progress made in achieving learning outcomes;
- by making decisions about how to move forwards;
- by creating something new.

Clearly, a good teacher who is not familiar with CLIL is well on the way to becoming a good CLIL teacher. Yet, teaching through another language brings with it special challenges. Agreeing on the commonalities in good practice, and the features unique to CLIL, is an ongoing process of meaning-making. This helps build a common, coherent and integrated educational approach in schools offering CLIL.

The co-construction of meaning also enables each school to take into account its own particular needs. For each group of students, it will take time to find the right balance in applying the various elements of CLIL methodology. Moreover, each teacher will always bring to the CLIL classroom his or her own experience and style. Thus, despite certain commonalities that are always reflected in good CLIL practice, CLIL remains a flexible approach by taking into account local circumstances and needs.

The key is finding the right balance between connecting, inspiring, delivering and advancing within the ever-changing classroom, community and world context. In the long run, the journey down the CLIL road can deliver big results and provide a firm foundation for successful lifelong learning in the interconnected global society.

8 More tools

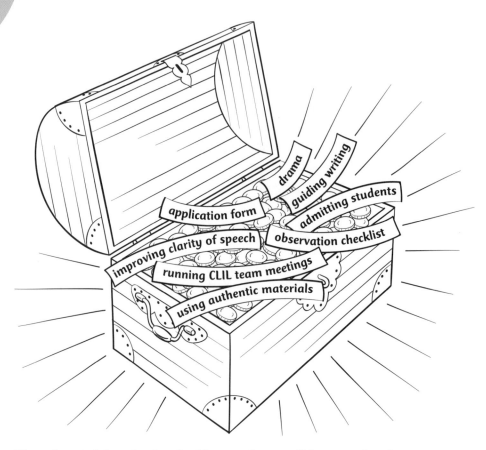

application form
drama
guiding writing
admitting students
improving clarity of speech
observation checklist
running CLIL team meetings
using authentic materials

How to guide students through a writing project: A step-by-step guide

Writing as a process

Laying the foundation
- Plan with fellow language and subject area teachers for possible integrated topics and agreement of skills to be emphasized for the writing project.
- Look for opportunities to let the writing grow out of reading, drama, history, current school or community events, special days or traditions, etc.
- Determine what students already know (ie, vocabulary, subject matter).
- Determine the language and information they still need to complete the project.

Pre-writing

NB: This information should be recorded electronically, on the board or on chart paper for reference.

- Determine the goal and audience for the writing project – this will dictate the content and type of language to be used.
- Agree on the type and elements of the language to be used according to the selected text form.
- Agree on the structure of the text as dictated by the selected text form.
- Brainstorm the necessary language (eg, list, web) depending on the selected topic and text form.
- If required, plan how to access further information on the selected topic (eg, people, resource materials).
- Present and explain the evaluation criteria or achievement scale.

Drafting

- Students brainstorm their ideas working either alone, in pairs or in small groups.
- Students put their ideas on paper in draft form, working either alone or in pairs, whilst respecting loosely the elements of the selected text form.

NB: The emphasis is on getting the student's message in print. Students are praised for getting something down and no criticism of their work is made. Organization, accuracy and quality of content and spelling will be examined later.

Conferencing

Ongoing teacher–student conferences during the writing workshop provide the opportunity to:

- assist students in selecting appropriate topics for their writing;
- discuss content and language separately;
- work with students to refine writing and help clarify ideas;
- refine a particular area of a student's writing;
- review language conventions and vocabulary use.

NB: These conferences may be of two types: roving or scheduled. Conferencing also takes place during the editing stage.

Revision

Students work individually or in pairs with the aim of:

- improving the organization of the text (ie, structure, logical linkage and development of ideas);
- verifying that the format respects the selected text form;
- refining thoughts (ie, making certain the intended message is clearly expressed);
- improving word choice (ie, avoiding repetition, using accurate words);
- reviewing the goals and writing from the target audience's perspective;
- reviewing the evaluation criteria to ensure that all the necessary elements have been taken into account.

Editing

- With the aid of reference materials, students proofread their writing to eliminate inaccuracies and errors in content and language.
- Teachers provide a checklist (generic or individualized) to assist students in focusing on certain elements (eg, punctuation, particular verb tense).

Sharing

A daily or regular period that provides:

- students with the opportunity to share their work in progress or completed texts with others (students in pairs, small groups or the whole class);
- teachers with the opportunity to model evaluation of writing.

Publishing

- Before the final copy is prepared for publication all errors or inaccuracies in language and content are corrected.
- Students produce (hand-write or type) a clean final copy of their revised and edited text for display, presentation or inclusion in their portfolios.
- Students self-assess and the teacher evaluates the completed piece against the agreed-upon criteria.

High-octane feedback

Conferencing and peer evaluation can fuel learning and save time. Feedback on language and content given before the completion of an assignment is more likely to be assimilated and put to future use than feedback provided after the completion of an assignment.

Processes for selecting and admitting students

Student admissions: Options and consequences

In addition to using the options for selecting students described below, some primary schools invite parents interested in the CLIL programme to a briefing session, and sometimes, an interview. In secondary and vocational schools, students are also invited to an interview. The goal of the interview is to ensure that parents and students have realistic expectations and understand the consequences of their decision. For example, with CLIL programmes beginning in secondary school, students may initially need to do more homework.

Option 1: First come, first served

Criteria/Process	Benefits	Risks
• applications are accepted beginning on a specific date for two weeks • completed and signed applications are stamped and marked with the time and date received • for CLIL classes/programmes beginning after year one, a student should be deemed average or above average in achievement. Senior students are sometimes asked to attach a copy of the report card.	• can help avoid elitism, as students with a broad range of abilities can gain entry into the programme • the criteria are usually easily understood and accepted • this option has been successfully used in many regions • parents can influence results by being among the first to submit an application	• some parents will try to circumvent the procedure • some very weak students may gain entrance to the programme

Option 2: Lottery

Criteria/Process	Benefits	Risks
• applications are accepted during a specific period and checked by a school official to ensure they are properly completed and signed • applications are registered, dated and signed by a school official • the names of students whose applications have been received are placed into a padlocked box • the lottery is carried out in public, in a transparent way	• can help avoid elitism, as students with a broad range of abilities can gain entry into the programme • it gives everyone an equal chance • the criteria are understood by all • this option has been successfully used in many regions	• is likely to leave some parents disgruntled, as it is based purely on chance with no means for influence

Option 2: Lottery (continued)

Criteria/Process	Benefits	Risks
• all names in the box are drawn and registered in the order they were chosen • if anyone does not wish to exercise his or her right or a child's right to enrol in the programme, the next person whose name is pulled out of the box is chosen		

Option 3: Testing

Criteria/Process	Benefits	Risks
• students are given standard or purpose-designed tests or other tests that are marked by the school • students may also undergo oral testing in the national and/or CLIL language • students may be tested for CLIL language knowledge or the ability to repeat phrases in the CLIL language • senior students may be admitted according to report card results	• classes generally will be made up of academically strong students • if a school is trying to be elitist this programme combined with strict selection criteria can bring in a larger than average number of bright students	• the criteria are less transparent than the above options and are often treated with suspicion • the programme may become elitist and create resentment amongst non-CLIL students, teachers and parents • elitist programmes are at risk of attracting negative political attention • this option may exclude students who could benefit greatly (the brightest children are more likely to succeed anyway) • elitist programmes may foster in students elitist habits of mind and perspectives • if the programme becomes a magnet for high achievers, it may undermine other schools in the area

How using drama can extend your teaching repertoire

What is drama?

In drama, roleplaying is the main strategy used by teachers and students. It involves engaging the students and deepening their understanding of content, while developing their language skills. Drama does not require either the teacher or the students to possess acting skills.

Roleplaying requires students to understand context, explore thinking or subtext and to form text. More specifically, in drama, students:

- explore and understand the circumstances and situations surrounding the role they are playing (context);
- think like someone else: the main character in a story, the police officer in a newspaper article, an animal in a television show or the person in the photograph on the desk in the corner (subtext);
- communicate through words and body language as if produced by that person/animal/object (text).

What drama is not

Drama is not theatre. Both are intimately related, but they are not one and the same. Theatre is a performance-focused art form. Drama is more focused on a personal journey in a given context. In theatre, the memorization of words created by others, no matter how passionately spoken, is different from the drama technique of spontaneously finding the words to communicate an important idea during a moment of significance. In theatre, in order to have students perform for an outside audience, teachers must carefully support the development of acting skills – projection, believability, use of gesture, body language and much more. In drama, students share their work with others. The primary focus is on their message rather than on theatrical form.

What are some of the benefits of using drama in CLIL?

Content acquisition is enhanced through drama. Drama requires students to use their imagination and to visualize situations, processes and options. Imagination and visualization build bridges from one's current state of knowledge to a new level of knowledge and understanding. For example, by having a student roleplay a contagious tuberculosis virus and by talking through the virus's journey with the support of a teacher, the science content will become much better encoded into the student's memory. A student's current knowledge base is tested and expanded.

Language acquisition is also enhanced through roleplaying. In a role, students find and use language appropriate to a wide variety of circumstances. They communicate the words and thoughts of many different people to a wide range of 'others'. Their vocabulary, tone, expression, level of formality, speed of communication and ability to listen change and adapt to the drama being developed. As students engage emotionally, they find words deep within themselves because the need to communicate is both immediate and compelling. In these situations, CLIL students may use some words in their first language, but when these are mirrored back by the teacher in the CLIL language, they are quickly incorporated into the dialogue. Moreover, as the new vocabulary and discourse patterns are being used in a highly meaningful context they are more likely to become embedded in long-term memory.

Roleplaying creates a certain distance from self, and is thus a safe space for students. While roleplaying, students are speaking as someone or something else – separate from themselves – expressing the thoughts, feelings and emotions of that someone else. They are doing this along with their peers rather than for an audience. Also, they are not trying to 'become' that someone else in terms of external appearance and physical characteristics. Rather, they are focused on finding the words and the emotions, the decisions and the consequences of those decisions for the characters they are assuming. As they do this, they are becoming aware of their own feelings and reactions and how those might be different from or the same as those in the drama.

What are some common drama strategies?

Some universally recognized drama-in-education strategies that can be used in language, history, science, geography and other subjects follow:

Tableau(x)

Students create still-life images or frozen moments with their bodies. Tableau is a useful device for introducing students to drama and roleplaying. It is less risky for students to begin roleplaying without words. Words can be brought in as a second step as you help students move through a variety of stages that eventually lead to full roleplays. Tableau is also very useful with students who have a limited level of language knowledge.

For example, primary students studying the life cycle of the butterfly could be divided into small groups. Instruct each group to choose one stage in the life cycle of the butterfly and to create a tableau with their bodies showing that stage. Give the students a few moments to plan their tableau. Planning talk takes place in the second language. To ensure that all groups are ready to share their tableaux, count out loud: *one, two, three, freeze!* and have the students freeze into their images. Count ten seconds for them while they hold their positions in silence and then instruct them to unfreeze. Have each group show their tableau to the others, who guess which stage of the life cycle is being shown.

After all the tableaux have been viewed, discuss some of the different approaches used to show the same stage in the life cycle. Language and content support can be provided by placing a series of words on the board, which have been grouped according to approaches used in presentation and in the butterfly life cycle. For example, words to describe the different approaches might include *posture, gestures, expressions, symbols* and words referring to the life cycle might include *metamorphosis, egg, larva, caterpillar, pupa, chrysalis* and *adult.*

If a particular stage in the life cycle was not selected by any group, the class can then create a whole-class tableau showing that stage.

'Statues' refers to a tableaux activity in which each student is responsible for creating a shape unrelated to anyone else's shape. You can use spontaneous statues for clarification purposes. For example, to conclude the exercise, you can ask all students to spread out and to think about which stage of the cycle is the most dangerous for the insect. Then have the students show that stage with their bodies in a statue when you call out *one, two, three, freeze!* The statues would then be discussed.

This last statue activity can be expanded upon. For example, all of the students who chose to become caterpillars could gather together, as could all those who became eggs or butterflies. These small groups would brainstorm all of the dangers to the insect at that stage of development. If you wish to have the groups share these dangers using drama instead of telling each other what they decided, each group could then create a series of tableaux, one showing each of the dangers. These tableaux could be shared with the others. You can journey further into roleplaying by tapping one of the frozen students and having him or her speak a few words. For example, a predator could say, *I am going to eat that caterpillar.* Another idea is for each group to be divided into two, with one half of the group making the tableau and the other half narrating the events being displayed.

Tableaux with teenagers can be a powerful tool for exploring difficult emotions, as well as a basic tool for synthesizing information. For example, students examining World War II could be assigned to select the key causes of the war and to show each one in a tableau. Each group quickly decides on the three most important causes and creates three tableaux, all within fifteen minutes. They can narrate the tableaux scenes. The ensuing discussion about choices made by different groups would be the focus of the work.

Music can be a useful tool. It helps to inspire, to allow students to concentrate and to build mood. It can be played during the sharing of tableaux, the volume turned down low if people are narrating and raised during transitions.

Movement/Word work

Movement can be created instead of tableaux when there is sufficient space for the students and when they are comfortable doing so. Movement can be a potent way for students to depict an emotional situation. For example, vocational students can work in small groups to develop a movement story with no words, showing people being injured as a result of a particular violation of a safety rule. They can show these stories with the safety law/rule projected high on the wall behind the students, who are moving through the drama in silence or accompanied by appropriate music. Movement work, as an initial stage in roleplaying, can be further developed. For example, each group can create a roleplay showing the parents of the injured person hearing about the accident. Writing in role can then follow, with the students writing as the victim to their best friend, or from the grave to other workers.

Writing in role

Writing done in role demands a high level of language competence from students. When you write in role, you need to adapt to the context and language of the character you are exploring. During the writing stage, as students ask for language support, you write the requested vocabulary and discourse patterns on the board. The writing is much more effective if it is set up by a previous drama activity which first engages the student in the role. It is the reflection and emotional engagement of the previous drama work that provides the student with the sense that he or she has something important to say in the writing. Just saying to students *imagine yourself in a situation* is nowhere near as powerful as having students first do a tableau or a more sophisticated form of roleplay.

Role on the wall

This strategy allows students to explore their understanding of a character in a story or of a role they are creating themselves. A simple outline of a human being is drawn on a large piece of paper and posted on the wall. Students are asked to do this activity in silence. Music can be played softly to assist the students with maintaining concentration. Students are then instructed to stand up and go to the human figure posted on the wall and write an adjective that describes this person physically, on the outside of the shape. The students are also asked to write this character's personality traits on the inside of the shape. Alternatively, students could also be asked to describe the character's actions on the outside of the shape and their emotions on the inside of the shape.

Once all ideas have been exhausted, the music can be turned off. You lead a discussion that aims to agree on whether all the written text will be accepted as part of the character. Conclusions are drawn about this character. If two different characters are handled this way, comparisons can be drawn. This strategy can serve as a springboard for tableau work and more developed roleplaying.

Talking walls

Talking walls can help build a personal connection with literature and history. Powerful feelings underlying a story or a significant historical event can be explored using this technique. For example, if the independence of India from British colonial rule and the life of Mahatma Gandhi were being studied, students could use this technique to consolidate learning. Students could be arranged in a rectangle as if they were the walls of Gandhi's prison, or the office of the British viceroy of India. Each student is instructed to think of a small group of words or a very short sentence that characterize(s) what the various Indian residents would have thought about the independence movement or what they might have said to Gandhi or the viceroy.

You enter the room in character as the viceroy or Gandhi. All of the students begin whispering their selected words or phrases quietly. As you walk near to a student, that student speaks in a louder voice until you pass by.

A debrief is done where students talk about what they felt as they participated in the roleplay. The words or phrases used while they were in role can be analysed for their relationship to historical events. For example, when discussing a famous strike from history, what sort of vocabulary did those students roleplaying strikers, policemen, politicians or factory owners use to convey their concerns? The class can brainstorm vocabulary that could be useful for additional roleplays where students further explore multiple perspectives within each of these groups. As various members of society may have different levels of knowledge, no student's statement is considered right or wrong. Each is placed in the larger historical context and analysed according to generally accepted facts.

Questioning in role

Whatever roleplaying strategies are used, you can deepen the work by questioning the students in role. You may or may not be in role as a character, depending on the circumstances of the drama, but the students are always in role when this technique is used. In primary school, for example, the students can imagine that they are historical figures they have studied. The students sit in a circle. You thank them all for coming to the meeting and then proceed to ask them questions, all of which the students answer as their character. With small children or children with limited CLIL language proficiency, all of the students can be playing the same character simultaneously. When you ask the questions, any student can answer in role as that character. Students can ask you questions. At the simplest level, the students can be reporters questioning the character you are playing. In a more complex roleplay, you could be Galileo Galilei arguing that the sun is at the centre of the universe, giving proof and justification for your argument. The students could be the members of the Inquisition, defending the theory that the Earth is at the centre of the universe.

Drama for a science unit

In a science unit on floods, drama could be used in the following ways:

Inform the students that they will be playing a role along with you. They are to imagine that they are members of a fishing village in the Ganges delta in Bangladesh. Bangladesh is a low-lying country that suffers from frequent flooding. Tell the students that there was particularly serious flooding two years ago. At the time, many villagers died and much property was lost. The highlands are far away and the villagers need to live near the water, as it is their main source of food and employment. It is now two years since the big flood. They have rebuilt their lives close to their old village, but the floods are bound to come again.

Have the students take five minutes to decide who they are in the village, their age and what they contribute to village life. Tell them to do this independently and not to worry about what other students are deciding at this point in the drama.

Ask the students to stand up and to make statues with their bodies that will reveal what kind of work they do in village life.

Walk around and stop in front of a particular student. Question him or her in role about the work. For example: *I see that you are making rice cakes. Is it easy to produce enough rice for this village?* Ask five or six students questions about their lives as villagers.

Have the students return to their seats and move on to writing in role. Ask the students to write a short paragraph beginning with: *It has been two years since I escaped death in the big flood. Much has changed in my life, and much has not. I …*

Have the students arrange themselves as if seated around a village fire in the early evening, relaxing after a hard day's work. Tell them that you will be entering the village in role and that you will begin a drama with them. Leave the 'village' area and then return to it in role, as a tired traveller. Greet the students and ask for permission to sit by their fire. Engage in conversation with them. Introduce yourself as someone from a nearby village who also escaped the flood but who chose to rebuild his or her life in Dhaka, the crowded capital of Bangladesh. The textile factory where you are working is hiring more people. You will get money for every new worker you find, but you are willing to give this to anyone who comes to work with you. You are here to find out if any of the villagers are willing to move. Engage the students in debate, seeing how many of them you can convince to come with you. Use arguments that will require students to use their knowledge about floods and about how to cope with them, as well as to raise awareness of the pros and cons of urban life in developing countries. Do not be afraid to twist the facts in such a way as to entice students to correct you with more accurate knowledge.

If you want the roleplay to extend into another lesson, you may find a dramatic way to pause the drama work. For example, the students may be divided about whether or not to stay in the village or to take up factory work in Dhaka. You can suggest that a group of villagers be selected to travel to the city and bring back their knowledge about city life and factory work to the rest of the village. The other group can work to provide all of the reasons why it would be wisest to stay in the village, explaining how they can further adapt to flooding. Content direction can be taken from the subject under study, be it geography, biology or health.

Alternative drama ideas

Choose a contemporary or very recent incident from the news in which widespread flooding took place. Have the students roleplay aliens from outer space landing near this site 24 hours before the flood. You can have them send reports back to their planet, attempt to convince citizens to leave, attempt to intervene scientifically to prevent the flooding, etc.

Have the students write or discuss in role as world leaders why people insist on living in high-risk areas, how they could be encouraged to move, where they could be relocated, or how to reduce risks for those people who continue to live in those areas.

Conclusion

Drama offers a multidimensional approach to learning. It helps tap into a variety of student learning styles, making it easier for them to visualize and personalize content. The students' use of language deepens and their vocabulary expands as they work to communicate from a wide variety of perspectives and in diverse situations. Roleplaying facilitates learning through communication and interaction about content in a set context. Partners in these roleplays actively engage in a meaning-making process where new realities are negotiated. Co-constructing meaning with students is a key characteristic of CLIL. Drama offers another path for realizing standard language, content and learning skills goals.

The above section was written by drama educator Jane Deluzio, in co-operation with the authors of the book.

How to improve clarity of speech

All languages of the world have one thing in common – most of the loudness of speech derives from the lower pitched vowels and most of the clarity or intelligibility derives from the higher pitched consonants. There are subtle differences between languages but, in general, this is true of all languages.

There are some fundamental differences between how lower pitched vowels and higher pitched consonants travel through the air to the students' ears. Lower pitched sounds tend to travel quite well through air, and indeed, through walls. In contrast, higher pitched consonants (because of their shorter wavelengths, for those who like physics) bump into air molecules and other larger obstructions like walls, desks and even students. Subsequently, the vowels have no trouble being heard, but the higher pitched consonants are usually heard at a much quieter level than that which they were uttered at. Shouting will only further increase the loudness of the vowels, but will do little for the important clarity-carrying consonants. One can yell the word *father* and, while the 'a' is louder, the 'f' is still quite quiet. It is therefore interesting, and rather counterproductive, that people tend to speak louder to a person whose native language is not that of the speaker's.

Improvements in the intelligibility or clarity of speech can be brought about by four main methods: 1) being closer to the listener, 2) speaking more slowly, 3) minimizing reverberation and 4) minimizing background noise.

Being closer to the listener has clear benefits. These include maintaining the balance between the lower pitched vowels and the higher pitched consonants, such that speech is both comfortably loud and optimally clear. One can be 'close' in two different ways. One can be physically closer, or one can use an assistive listening device such as an FM sound field system. As the name suggests, an FM sound field system uses the same technology as a radio, and is really just a low-powered personalized radio station. The speaker uses a (lapel) microphone and, through an invisible FM radio signal, the speaker's voice is routed to a series of loudspeakers arranged throughout the classroom. Students at the back of the room can hear as well and as clearly as students who are seated only three feet from the teacher. Such inexpensive systems have been in use for over 20 years and have been shown to be beneficial for students with a wide range of learning problems, ranging from attention disorders to hearing loss.

Speaking more slowly not only increases the speaking life of the teacher by minimizing vocal strain, but also maintains the balance of speech between the lower pitched vowels and the higher pitched consonants. As long as the higher pitched consonants are at an adequately loud level (eg, in a quiet room), then speech understanding will be optimized. It is actually not so much an issue of speaking more slowly as it is of not speaking more quickly. When we increase our rate of speech, for ease of articulation, we tend to leave out (or significantly shorten) the consonant sounds. This understandably can degrade speech intelligibility.

Reverberation sounds like an amorphous word, but it actually has a well defined physical interpretation. Reverberation is the amount of reflection of sounds off walls, ceilings, floors and other structures in a room. And (again because of the shorter wavelengths of the higher pitched consonants), it is the higher pitched consonants that reflect and echo around a room. That is, the higher pitched consonants see the walls and floors as obstructions and reflect off of them just as if they were mirrors. The listener not only hears the sound of the speech, but unfortunately also hears the reflected consonant sounds a moment later. This has the effect of compromising speech intelligibility. Wall coverings (eg, curtains and artwork) absorb some of this unwanted echo, thereby making speech sound clearer.

Minimizing background noise is both intuitive and has scientific theory to back it up as a useful classroom practice. Because of the way that human (and indeed all mammalian) ears are constructed, lower pitched sounds such as background noise tend to cover up the more important higher pitched consonants. Masking is an important part of how we hear and in part accounts for why music sounds so beautiful. However, too much masking, for example being at a noisy party or near a noisy street, can cover up and degrade the important consonant sounds that are required for optimal intelligibility.

The above was contributed by Marshall Chasin, a renowned expert in hearing health.

How to create CLIL teaching materials from authentic texts

Additions to the article are indicated by underlining; subtractions by crossing out text★.

Children risk permanent cognitive impairment (brain damage) from lead poisoning

Children living near (close to) the former Splash paint factory in Manburton appear to be suffering from lead poisoning.

Children living in the neighbourhood of the former Splash paint factory have higher than permissible (allowed) levels of lead in their blood. These children all play in Downwater Park. which The park used to be a dump site (waste products collection site) for the now defunct (closed) Splash paint factory.

Soil samples from the park contain very high levels of lead. Trident University researchers warn in an independent medical journal named the Trident Review that this will likely (probably) have severe consequences for children and adults living in the neighbourhood.

Facilitating comprehension

- removing part of the text

- inserting synonyms in brackets

- having students analyse context to guess the meaning of a word like 'impairment' (Do you think poisoning will improve brain functioning?)

- highlighting key terms, words, ideas and facts

- using different colours of highlighter for different issues, aspects or categories

- using graphic organizers such as:

I know	I want to know	I learnt

The lead is most likely entering the children's bloodstream through the breathing in of lead-laden dust. The children may be tracking home mud (taking home mud stuck to shoes) from the park, which dries and turns to dust. The children are also exposing members of their family to this dust. Young children who often play with earth may be ingesting (swallowing) the poisoned soil as well. Dirt gets under fingernails. Fingers are often placed in the mouth.

Widespread impairment

Experts have known for a long time that even low levels of exposure to lead can lead to decreased intelligence, poor school performance and impairment in reaction time and visual-motor function, among several other problems. The lead poisoning will most likely trigger (set off) numerous problems among these children.

Expert opinions

Dr Mary Ferugia from the City Health Department stated that lead accumulates in various organs in the body. It can damage the liver, the brain and the immune system. It can also damage muscles. It can affect the capacity of both sexes to have children.

According to Dr Germaine Harmin, who is a professor of immunopharmacology at Trident University, all city dwellers will have been exposed to very low levels of lead. Leaded petrol is often the culprit. However, the children in the study were found to have been overexposed. Dr Harmin points out that the National Centre for Health states that 10 micrograms per decilitre of blood is seen as the level of contamination where problems will begin to become visible. However, Dr Harmin also adds that the National Centre for Health warns that recent research seems to be pointing to the fact that even half that much exposure can lead to serious health problems.

Fostering critical thinking

Organizing information under headings

- impact on health
- other impacts
- reactions/opinions
- solutions

Using diagrams

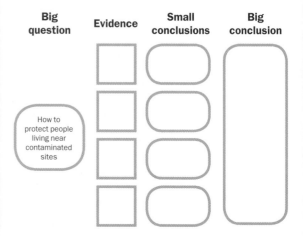

Analysing different perspectives

- residents living next to the park
- the mayor
- the minister of health
- the minister of the environment
- the former owners of the factory

Comparing pollution statistics

- your community
- another community
- a highly industrialised area
- a remote rural area

Learning outcomes

Students:
- determine and articulate key issues regarding industrial pollution
- articulate concerns from different perspectives
- present arguments clearly and convincingly
- choose the appropriate language for writing to government officials
- propose realistic solutions

Parent reactions

Parents want the park closed and the contaminated (polluted) soil removed. At last night's community association meeting, parents discussed ~~the option of~~ starting a class action suit against (taking to court) the city and the former owners of the Splash paint factory.

Government reaction

When asked this morning what the city would do, Mayor Door said the situation should be studied further.

After the parent association meeting, which took place later in the day, a spokesperson for the mayor's office said the city government would work hard to solve the issue. The issue will be discussed at the next city council meeting. The removal of the contaminated soil will be complicated and is likely to constitute a health hazard in and of itself. In the meantime (until then), parents are advised not to allow their children to play in the park.

The national minister for health was not available for comment. It is not known how many other sites could be similarly contaminated throughout the country.

*This article was written expressly for the purposes of this book.

What the teacher does

- discusses the learning outcomes with students
- explains evaluation criteria
- has students brainstorm what they know about industrial pollution
- helps students categorize brainstorming outcomes
- guides students in separating fact from opinion
- models agreement and disagreement statements (including reasoning)
- supports students in analysing the reasoning behind their agreement and disagreement statements
- facilitates groupwork
- guides self-analysis of letters to be sent to government officials

What the students do

- read the article in groups
- organize the information in the article using one or several of the graphic organizers presented above
- analyse the problem from various perspectives
- find and analyse pollution statistics in order to compare communities
- present in writing their group's findings re: facts, opinions, perspectives, possible solutions
- respond to another group's presentation with agreement and disagreement statements (using evidence)
- develop a plan for identifying and dealing with contaminated sites
- identify and analyse models of letters intended for government officials
- write a letter to a government official
- seek outside opinions on the letter
- analyse learning process and outcomes, and draw conclusions

Year VI – Late CLIL programme sample application form

important for maintaining gender balance

Student's first name (please print)

Student's date of birth (day/month/year)

Parent or guardian's first and last name (please print)

Sex (please tick)   Male ☐   Female ☐

My child is currently in year five at: _____ **(name of school)**

I have read the school's CLIL programme information materials and am aware of the application process and admission criteria. I understand that if my child is accepted into the programme, it is recommended that he or she continue in the CLIL programme until the end of school. Also, I am aware that a key factor contributing to student success is the quality of the partnership that develops between the home and school. I am prepared to attend home and school meetings, enter into dialogue with my child's tutor and attend CLIL programme events.

Parent or guardian's signature: _____   date: _____

Please provide the following contact information. Please also circle your preference for how you wish to be informed about the results of your child's application.

Address: _____   Telephone: _____

_____   Email: _____

How did you become aware of this CLIL programme?

_____

_____

Student's statement

I wish to study in the CLIL programme. I understand that I will begin to study the following subjects in … (name of the CLIL language) … I also understand that initially this will require an extra effort on my part. I am aware that it is recommended that I remain in CLIL until the end of the programme. I have read the school's CLIL brochure.

Student's signature: _____   date: _____

Applications can be submitted to the school secretary in the school's main office from 5–20 June, from 09:00–16:00 on weekdays. The school is located at _____ **(address).**
For additional information, please call 666-6666 on weekdays from 09:00–16:00.

For official use only by secretary

Date and exact time of application _____ at _____   Application complete and signed ☐

Copy of report card attached ☐   Signature and seal _____

Sample agenda for a weekly CLIL team meeting

Time: 60 minutes

Participants: Ideally, all CLIL teachers in a given grade.

Even having some people at the meeting is better than not holding it. Also, in an ideal world, teachers teaching CLIL students subjects in the students' first language are on occasion included. This allows for the creation of cross-curricular themes. It supports the acquisition of terminology in both languages. In particular, the mother tongue language teacher is included to make sure his or her concerns are addressed. This teacher is a key player in ensuring long-term success of the CLIL initiative, as he or she can choose to either support or undermine the work being done.

Agenda points:

1) Sharing classroom problems

All teachers face problems in their work, especially in today's ever-changing world. These need to be brought out in the open. A work culture that legitimizes the discussion of problems avoids personal criticism or blame. It focuses on jointly talking through possible solutions. This helps build a sense of team, de-stress staff and deal with problems more quickly and effectively than by working alone.

2) Agreeing on a common language goal/outcome for the week

Goals may be driven by newly visible problems, such as verb tense errors, a lack of discourse patterns for a given topic or errors that are becoming engrained.

3) Looking for integration opportunities

This may involve agreeing on a cross-curricular theme, or simply finding a way of including vocabulary or concepts from one subject in another. Ideally, one student assignment would be of a cross-curricular nature, marked by at least two teachers.

4) Sharing resources

This is the moment to say: *I'm teaching about the extinction of dinosaurs. Does anybody have any materials or ideas?* It is human nature to reciprocate. If you share with others, then others are likely to share with you.

5) Celebrating success

Teachers live such busy lives that they often focus too much on their daily work and problems that inevitably emerge. They rarely find time to celebrate their own successes. Opportunities are often missed to re-energize individuals and teams through recognition and celebration of successes large and small.

Planning and observation checklist

for professional dialogue between CLIL educators*

Grade level: _____ Number of students: _____ Date: _____ Lesson planned/observed: _____

The following seven category labels and their descriptors identify key pedagogical goals in CLIL settings. The subsequent indicators illustrate possible observable features of goals achievement. All features would not be observable in any one class.

THE CLIL TEACHER AIMS TO:	INDICATORS:
1 Integrate content and language	
1.1 Specifies the planned content outcomes and the content-obligatory language outcomes for each lesson.	Planned outcomes are on the board or stated and recognizable as driving all activities.
1.2 Uses authentic texts, artefacts and materials to teach content and language.	Some of the listed elements are present.
1.3 Focuses corrective responses on pre-determined content and language outcomes based on the lesson, and the developmental level of the learners.	Students successfully follow instructions and complete assignments. Language that is too difficult is avoided and future topics are not addressed at length.
1.4 Has a well balanced lesson.	Warm-up, teaching/learning, analysis and reflection are present.
2 Create a rich learning environment	
2.1 Creates a friendly and safe learning environment.	Teacher uses routine activities. The classroom seems stress free. Students support one another and participate actively. They experiment freely with language. Rules created with students are posted and observed. Students respect the rules.
2.2 Surrounds learners with rich subject content and extensive oral and written language input.	Content is challenging, linked to a relevant context and previous learning, and is successfully applied by students during a task requiring higher order thinking. Synonym and antonym work is done. Language is displayed. A reading corner, learning centres and/or electronic media are available.
2.3 Creates numerous opportunities for students to speak and write.	Students speak more than the teacher. (First weeks of programme are an exception.) Peer co-operative work encourages equal participation. Students express own understanding in writing.
2.4 Organizes classroom so it promotes learning.	Teacher displays student work, language is displayed, supplies are in logical places and seating configurations promote co-operation.
3 Make input comprehensible	
3.1 Uses body language, visuals, realia and manipulatives to communicate meaning.	eg, facial and hand gestures, pictures, actual objects.
3.2 Elicits and draws upon prior knowledge, experiences and current attitudes vis-à-vis new topics.	Students are encouraged to link new learning to previously taught topics. Attitudes towards new topic are determined and discussed.
3.3 Uses a variety of pre-reading and pre-writing activities to make content and language more accessible.	eg advanced organizers, concept and word charts or maps.

+ observed / – not observed / 0 NA

+ / – / 0	COMMENTS:

THE CLIL TEACHER AIMS TO:		INDICATORS:
3.4	Breaks complex information and processes into component parts.	The theme/information is organized into sub-units or sub-themes. Teacher scaffolds both content and language input by chunking information, breaking instructions or assignments into manageable pieces.
3.5	Makes frequent use of comprehension checks that require learners to demonstrate their understanding.	Students can articulate what they have learnt and can apply it through an assignment or activity.
3.6	Selects and adapts instructional material for learners' developmental level.	Texts may be shortened, sub-headings inserted and language support sheets created. Students cope with the assignments and participate actively.
4	**Use 'teacher-talk' effectively**	
4.1	Uses normal level of volume, articulates and enunciates clearly.	Does not raise volume above normal levels to achieve comprehension. Students can follow most instructions and use teacher recasts. Teacher speech habits are reflected in the quality of student output.
4.2	Slows down and simplifies language when developmentally appropriate.	Messages are repeated in different ways without excessive volume. Students are interested in what is going on.
4.3	Avoids 'teacher-speak'.	Students, at times, take the lead in conversations. Non-classroom situations are roleplayed.
4.4	Models accurate use of language.	Syntax and grammar are accurate. Parasitic words or expressions such as *You know!* are avoided. Intonation is natural. The teacher's accent does not impede comprehension.
5	**Promote extended student output**	
5.1	Plans for and employs questioning techniques that encourage extended discourse and foster higher order thinking.	Students participate in discussions. Elements of critical and creative thinking are present. Follow-up questions take thinking a step further.
5.2	Structures and facilitates high-interest, student-centred activities.	eg, roleplaying, plays, debates, presentations, peer co-operative work, peer and group teaching.
5.3	Provides all students with the opportunity to participate and speak.	The teacher uses grouping techniques such as dyads, think-pair-share, small groups, etc, and output-orientated activities such as roleplays, simulations, drama, debates, presentations, etc.
5.4	Promotes learning from and with peers.	eg, peer editing, peer tutoring, student study groups.
5.5	Communicates and consistently reinforces clear expectations about learning goals/outcomes related to content, language and learning skills.	The teacher verbalizes his/her expectations and is consistent in reinforcing students who meet expectations and applies related rules with consistency.
6	**Attend to diverse learner needs**	
6.1	Takes into account different learning strategies and helps students develop learning skills.	All students are motivated. Teacher uses co-operative learning strategies and mixed ability grouping. Visual, tactile, auditory and kinesthetic approaches are visible. Teacher invites students to share different problem-solving approaches and learning strategies.
6.2	Surveys and takes into account student interests, opinions and wishes.	Students pick topics, decide on order of activities and bring into the lesson elements that they clearly cherish.

+ observed / − not observed / 0 NA

+ / − / 0	COMMENTS:

THE CLIL TEACHER AIMS TO:	INDICATORS:
6.3 Makes use of a wide variety of activities through learning centres where students can work at a level that is appropriate for them.	Students are given a choice in activities. Easier tasks are at the top of activity lists. There is a variety of activities suiting visual, aural, kinesthetic, and reading and writing learning styles.
7 Attend to continuous growth and improvement in accuracy	
7.1 Creates an opportunity for evaluation of content and language learning (including learning process) during each lesson.	Either self-evaluation by the student, peer evaluation or teacher-directed evaluation takes place during the lesson.
7.2 Uses a variety of effective feedback techniques.	For encouraging growth in understanding and using content, the teacher details what is correct, indicates points requiring further reflection, provides clues, creates relational links and asks probing questions. In supporting language growth, the teacher uses among others the following techniques: elicitation, clarification requests, repetition, recasting, explicit correction, as well as body language and other non-verbal cues.
7.3 Attends to errors in both oral and written language.	Teacher models the right answer. Teacher encourages self- and peer-repair.
7.4 Differentiates between feedback on form versus meaning.	Students receive verbal reinforcement or marks for content, eg, the teacher says: *I like that idea. How might you say it more precisely? How might you expand on that idea? What would an opponent say?*

* This checklist is adapted from the Immersion Teaching Strategies Observation Checklist *by Tara Fortune and is printed with permission from the Center for Advanced Research on Language Acquisition (CARLA) at the University of Minnesota. See www.carla.umn.edu/immersion/acie/vol4/Nov2000.pdf/. This adaptation was produced by the Estonian Language Immersion Centre in discussion with its partners in education, and further modified by the authors of this book.*

+ observed / – not observed / 0 NA

+ / – / 0	COMMENTS:

Index